D0982945

Nightmares and Human Conflict

NIGHTMARES AND HUMAN CONFLICT

John E. Mack, M.D.

Associate Clinical Professor of Psychiatry
Harvard Medical School, Boston

Little, Brown and Company, Boston

Nightmares and Human Conflict

Copyright © 1970 by John E. Mack

Library of Congress catalog card No. 74–112010

First Edition

Published in Great Britain by J. & A. Churchill, London
British Standard Book No. 7000 0188 3

Printed in the United States of America

To Danny, Kenny, and Tony who showed me
how important nightmares can be

Preface

Of the experiences that terrify mankind and invite our humility, nightmares are perhaps the most widespread and characteristic, for human beings are the only creatures so fully aware of the precariousness of their existence. It is precisely this sense of vulnerability that is the most essential feature of these dreams. The nightmare is the prototype of man's terror. The common feature of helplessness in a confrontation with forces that threaten to be overwhelming has led to the application of the word *nightmare* to any psychological horror or external catastrophe over which the persons involved have little or no control and which makes them feel gravely imperiled. No group of human beings seems to escape at least the sporadic occurrence of these terrifying dreams. Very small children and adults of all ages, emotionally ill and relatively healthy persons, primitive peoples as well as members of the most highly civilized societies —all may have nightmares. Any theory that attempts to offer a general explanation of this type of dream must take into account this universality.

In this book the feature of helplessness is considered the starting point, and its significance and implications in nightmares are explored as they occur under a wide variety of circumstances. The emphasis here therefore differs from that in Ernest Jones's well-known work [1] on the subject written almost sixty years ago. In his classic study Jones stressed the libidinal aspect, the underlying incestuous impulses that seem to be present in persons suffering from nightmares. As I have tried to show in this book, however, these dreams may be concerned with other conflicts, especially those with which the subject feels powerless to cope.

The various psychological and biological determinants of nightmares are thus approached with regard to how they contribute to the ego state of helplessness and to the quality of being overwhelmed that exists in these dreams. The mechanisms of ego functioning are considered both within the dreams and in the individual's efforts to deal with the anxiety of the nightmare experience in the thought and behavior that accompany the dream.

Nightmares and Human Conflict has several purposes. One of them naturally is to provide a general survey of the subject, to try to understand why these particularly disturbing dreams occur, and to set forth the various determinants of the overwhelming anxiety experienced in them. Since the nightmare is the principal condition in which dreaming and severe anxiety occur simultaneously, it affords an excellent opportunity to study the relationship between these two universal human phenomena. Finally, consideration is given to the relationship that nightmares may have to certain forms of creativity and to various pathological states, especially acute psychoses.

This book is based primarily on my own clinical experiences, and actual case examples from child and adult patients in psychoanalysis and psychotherapy form the principal documentation. Other appropriate material from experimental research, literature, biography, and the psychopathology of daily experience of nonpatients has also been drawn upon. The first and second chapters provide a general survey of the subject of nightmares and night terrors in children and adults, and document the various determinants of their clinical occurrence. These are followed by chapters on the relationship of nightmares to creativity, aggression, and psychosis. A later chapter deals with the contributions made by recent work on the physiology of dreaming to our understanding of nightmares and night terrors. In the final chapter, the theoretical implications of the preceding material are discussed, and the place of nightmares in relation to a broader view of dreaming is considered.

The similarity of the nightmares of children and adults provides one of our most convincing pieces of evidence that the archaic fears, conflicts, and mental structures of early childhood may be preserved throughout the course of a person's life. The nameless terror, the sense of helplessness, the violence, the persecution by monstrous forces, the carry-over of the affective and even of the perceptual experience into waking—all may occur in the child and adult alike. Thus, although I have of necessity treated the nightmares of adults and children separately at certain points, the features that terrifying dreams of all ages have in common provide a unifying theme. My approach throughout the book has been to consider these dreams—which may, of course, occur under pathological conditions or as symptoms of emotional disorder—as reflecting the individual's struggle to resolve conflict rather than as pathological entities per se. In small children the sporadic occurrence of nightmares at times of stress is a commonplace; in adults nightmares may follow such traumatic events as the sudden loss of a loved person without other symptoms or evidence of significant emotional disturbance.

JOHN E. MACK

Reference

1. Jones, E.   *On the Nightmare*. London: Hogarth Press, 1931.

Acknowledgments

It is easier to specify the concrete ways in which one's teachers and colleagues have contributed to a piece of work than to assess the many intangible ways in which each of these and other individuals have played a part in one's professional development through inspiration and personal example. For this reason the brief acknowledgments of indebtedness which follow here are incomplete.

Elvin Semrad has taught me many things, but perhaps has conveyed nothing so relevant to the present study as the awareness that real life is much more than raw material for the next night's dream. The continuous exchange of ideas with Gregory Rochlin over many years has fostered in me a tendency to evaluate critically every half-formed thought and, when possible, to follow each one through to completion. During the writing of this book Jack Ewalt has provided the steady support and encouragement needed to see it through. Among those who have given their time generously in reading and commenting upon the manuscript, I wish to thank especially Charles Fisher, Lee Macht, Samuel Kaplan, Alan Hobson, Melvin Stern, and my father, Edward Mack.

Some relatives, friends, and colleagues have shared not only their dreams but their nightmares as well, and will, I hope, be tolerant on finding excerpts from their mental life captured in the pages that follow. I wish also to thank Edward Khantzian,

Dennis McCrory, Raymond Yerkes, Ben and Adele Shambaugh, Victoria Levi, John Mackenzie, William Kates, Edward Sachar, Peter and Sigrid Tishler, Gary and Sharon Turndorf, Ben Gurian, and John Robey for providing useful clinical illustrations or other relevant observations.

Patricia Carr, my secretary, deserves special appreciation for enduring so patiently the many drafts of these chapters. I am also grateful to Rosanne Kumins for her help in preparing the manuscript. Susan Payne, librarian at the Massachusetts Mental Health Center, has given invaluable assistance in tracking down many difficult-to-find references. Finally, I thank my wife Sally for listening and reading, for knowing when to comment and when to be silent.

J. E. M.

Contents

Nightmares and Human Conflict

I

The Characteristics of Nightmares

But yester-night I prayed aloud
In anguish and in agony,
Up-starting from the fiendish crowd
Of shapes and thoughts that tortured me:
A lurid light, a trampling throng,
Sense of intolerable wrong,
And whom I scorned, those only strong!
Thirst of revenge, the powerless will
Still baffled, and yet burning still!
Desire with loathing strangely mixed
On wild or hateful objects fixed.
Fantastic passions! maddening brawl!
And shame and terror over all!
Deeds to be hid which were not hid,
Which all confused I could not know
Whether I suffered, or I did:
For all seemed guilt, remorse or woe,
My own or others' still the same
Life stifling fear, soul-stifling shame.
—COLERIDGE [1]

Definition

Since the term is used so variously, my preference in defining *nightmare* is toward inclusiveness. Fisher et al., for example, although restricting their use of "nightmare" to an explosive or catastrophic type of reaction, acknowledge that only six of their thirty-seven subjects had such dreams, while the other thirty-one

1

nevertheless called their severe anxiety dreams "nightmares" [2, 3]. Liddon has noted the shift in meaning of the term *nightmare* that has occurred over the past hundred years [4]. Originally the word referred to the "night-fiend" that was thought to be the cause of such nighttime terror experiences (see discussion, page 3). With the increasing awareness of the intrapsychic origin of dream experiences, especially in this century, nightmare has come to stand for the dream itself. The earlier meaning, based essentially on a mythology, will not be used here.

In the classic description of the nightmare or "incubus" written by Ernest Jones in 1910 and 1911, intense dread, paralysis of movement, and a sensation of crushing upon the chest interfering with respiration were regarded as essential features [5]. In a description by Bellamy as early as 1915, however, paralysis was not included [6], and in more contemporary accounts such as Verteuil's [7], the emotional qualities of dread or horror are stressed, and the sensations of suffocation or paralysis are not considered necessary accompaniments. None of Fisher, Byrne, and Edwards' subjects reported feelings of paralysis. Hadfield includes bodily sensations such as palpitation, sweating, and suffocation, but regards these simply as the natural accompaniments of intense fear. He regards the distinction between an anxiety dream and a nightmare as one of degree rather than of kind and recognizes "all degrees in between the anxiety dream and the nightmare" [8]. The common feature of all descriptions of nightmare is the terror of overwhelming intensity that accompanies the dream images.

In order to keep pace with the shifting meaning of an essentially nontechnical term, it seems advisable to stay close to popular usage. With this in mind, I would define the nightmare as an anxiety dream in which fear is of such intense degree as to be experienced as overwhelming by the dreamer and to force at least partial awakening. Fisher and Trosman have observed that nightmares occurring in the dream laboratory situation are rare [9, 10], but this is not surprising, since nightmares are naturally occurring events that take place infrequently in normal subjects, often as a result of specific preceding circumstances [11]. The dream reports obtained in the laboratory, on the other hand, tend to be those that result from forced awakenings.

Etymology

The etymology of the word *nightmare*, studied extensively by Jones, is quite complex. However, the theme of an oppressing, powerful force or creature that threatens to overwhelm or destroy the sleeper seems to be common to all of the possible origins and definitions. The Anglo-Saxon *mare* was a demon, deriving from the Sanskrit *mara*, or destroyer, which, in turn, may come from *mar*, to crush [12]. Similarly, the French word for nightmare, *cauchemar*, is compounded from this root together with *caucher*, to tread upon [13]. Later, possibly in the latter part of the Middle Ages, the root *mara* became assimilated with the English word *mare* or female horse. Shakespeare, for example, in *King Lear*, refers to "the Night-Mare, and her nine-fold" [14]. This meaning of the word is linked with the highly sexual significance of some nightmares, the horse being a ready symbol for a powerful, active sort of sexuality. The attribution of the nightmare to an incubus, a mythical male demon that seeks to lie with women, or to a female succubus that lies similarly with men, also suggests a sexual significance. The Latin *incubare*, to lie on, from which comes the English incubate, to lie on and hatch eggs, also has a sexual meaning. However, if we demonstrate the sexual significance of a nightmare in any given instance, we are still faced with the more fundamental task of explaining why such sexuality should be overwhelming, terrifying, and associated with violence, crushing, and destruction. It is probably no more correct to attribute all the violence of nightmares to sexual impulses than it is to explain all violence in waking life on the basis of sexuality.

In a recent study of the Baleh Iban tribe of North Borneo, Freeman has described the curious mixture of sexuality and aggression that is attributed to the incubus or *autu buyu* by these primitive people. "The incubus," Freeman says, "though essentially a figment of the dream, is fully accepted by the Iban as a

part of present reality, an evil and threatening force from which
only their *Manang* [shaman] can protect them, a deadly being
which only a master Shaman is able to overcome" [15]. The
incubus appears characteristically to the woman in the dreams as
a handsome, alluring man. Not only can he have sexual intercourse with the women, but he is thought to have the power to
conceive children. Furthermore, when a woman loses her child,
the incubus is held responsible. Although he seems to come
upon a sexual mission, he is really a monkey or some other malevolent creature in disguise who employs seduction in order to
pursue a fundamentally destructive purpose. Like the Utes'
ghosts (see page 11), an incubus among the Iban can be removed only by the skills of a powerful master shaman who is
capable of killing them in a thoroughly convincing ritual performed before a not unskeptical audience.

Historical Accounts of Nightmares

Nightmares were observed by the ancient Greeks, notably by
Hippocrates [16]. In a discussion of epilepsy, he suggested that a
warming of the brain may take place when excessive amounts of
blood pass through its vessels. This occurs, he asserted, "in great
quantity when a man is having a nightmare and is in a state of
terror." Hippocrates was well aware that certain dreams reflected
serious mental disturbance and that nightmares in particular
could reveal conflict over criminal impulses. In the nightmare,
Hippocrates wrote, the dreamer "reacts in sleep in the same way
that he would if he were awake; his face burns, his eyes are
bloodshot as they are when scared or when the mind is intent
upon the commission of a crime. All this ceases as soon as the
man wakes and the blood is dispensed again into the blood vessels."

Some of the earliest accounts of terrifying dreams are found in
the first pediatric writings in the fifteenth and sixteenth centuries. A gastrointestinal disruption was usually held to be
responsible. The Belgian physician Cornelius Roelans (1450–
1525) listed "dreams terrifying them" or nightmares as ninth
in a list of fifty-two diseases afflicting children [17]. The first

English pediatrician, Thomas Phaer, in *The Boke of Chyldren* (1545) noted, "oftentimes it happeneth that the chyld is afraid in ye slepe & somtymes waketh sodainly, & sterteth, somtyme shriketh and trembleth, whiche effect commeth of the arysing of stynkyng vapours out of ye stomake into the fantasye" [18]. This tendency in early accounts to attribute nightmares to gastrointestinal disturbances persisted and was nicely captured by Robert Louis Stevenson when he referred to "the raw-head-and-bloody-bones nightmare, rumoured to be the child of toasted cheese" [19]. Jones has provided numerous other accounts from seventeenth-, eighteenth-, and nineteenth-century writers [5].

We are fortunate in being provided with some of our most vivid descriptions of nightmares by great writers who suffered from them. Coleridge, especially, it would seem, in the year 1803, suffered from frequent nightmares, influenced perhaps by opium [20], which he described in letters and poems. To Thomas Wedgwood he wrote: "While I am awake, by patience, employment, effort of mind, and walking I can keep the fiend at Arm's length; but the Night is my Hell, Sleep my tormenting Angel. Three nights out of four I fall asleep, struggling to lie awake—and my frequent Night-Screams have almost made me a nuisance in my own House. Dreams with me are no Shadows, but the very Substances and foot-thick Calamities of my life" [21]. Concluding this same letter, he offered to "write as a Post-script an Epitaph, which I composed in my sleep for myself, while dreaming that I was dying:

> Epitaph.
> Here sleeps at length poor Col. and
>   without Screaming,
> Who died as he had always liv'd,
>   a dreaming·
> Shot dead, while sleeping, by the Gout
>   within,
> Alone, and all unknown, at E'nbro'
>   in an Inn."

Still alive, he wrote in the same words two weeks later to his brother of the continuing struggle to "keep the Fiend at arm's length" and said that he "sometimes derived comfort from the notion, that possibly these horrid Dreams with all their mockery of Crimes and Remorse and Shame and terror might have been sent upon me to arouse me out of that proud and stoical apathy, into which I had fallen" [21].

Another famous opium eater, Thomas De Quincey, with pitiable and relentless insight has shown how terrifying dreams may carry back into the unfortunate dreamer's awareness the full impact of painful events seemingly buried in the obscurity of early childhood [22]. Such dreams demonstrate dramatically that the vivid perceptions and powerful emotions that once accompanied such tragic events as death and loss may remain fully alive in the individual's mind. After describing the deaths, occurring when he was respectively eighteen months and six years of age, of two of his older sisters, Jane and Elizabeth, whose room he had shared and to whom he was deeply attached, De Quincey relates a dream from the time he was eighteen in which these two events, now condensed in his mind, are relived.

His sister Jane's death, although of causes not clearly disclosed, was associated in his mind with her brutal treatment at the hands of a female servant. He states that the episode filled him with horror and confronted him with the fact of mortality, the possibility that a person could disappear or cease to exist. In a passage extraordinary for its disclosure of the depth that childhood anguish can reach, De Quincey takes us movingly through his shattering grief and desolation at the death of his beloved sister Elizabeth when he was six and she nine. This loss haunted him thereafter. Following this, in a section of his work titled "Dream-Echoes of these Infant Experiences," De Quincey observed that the "psychological experiences of deep suffering or joy first attain their entire fullness of expression when they are reverberated from dreams." He recalled a frightening dream at age eighteen in which, as is characteristic of nightmares, the victim became, not the lost loved one, but the dreamer himself. "Once again, after twelve years' interval," he wrote, "the nursery of my childhood expanded before me: my sister was moaning in bed; and I was beginning to be restless with fears not intelligible to myself. Once again the elder nurse, but now dilated to colossal proportions, stood as upon some Grecian stage with her uplifted hand, and, like the superb Medea towering amongst her children in the nursery at Corinth, smote me senseless to the ground. Again, I am in the chamber with my sister's corpse, again the pomps of life rise up in silence, the glory of summer, the Syrian Sunlights, the frost of death. Dream forms itself mysteriously within dream; within these Oxford dreams remoulds itself continually the trance in my sister's chamber. . . ." [23].

Lafacadio Hearn has described with equal vividness the nightmares he experienced when he was locked in a room as a five-year-old child. Assurances that he had nothing to fear failed utterly to protect him from the haunters that besieged him once he fell asleep. "They were not," he insisted, "like any people that I had ever known. They were shadowy dark-robed figures, capable of atrocious self-distortion,—capable, for instance, of growing up to the ceiling, and then across it, and then lengthening themselves, head downwards, along the opposite wall. Only their faces were distinct, and I tried not to look at their faces. I tried also in my dreams—or thought that I tried—to awaken myself from the sight of them by pulling at my eyelids with my fingers; but the eyelids would remain closed, as if sealed" [24]. Hearn continued with the description of the nightmare's features, the numbing of will, the powerlessness, the struggle to escape, the terrifying muffled sound of the haunter's step and, above all, the utter horror and "abominable electricity" of its touch. How similar is the description of the nightmare of Hearn at age five to that of Coleridge at thirty-one.

Charles Lamb described similar early childhood night terrors. From his fourth to his seventh or eighth years, he wrote, "I never laid my head on my pillow . . . without an assurance, which realized its own prophecy, of seeing some frightful spectre." Parents, he warned, "do not know what they do when they leave tender babes alone to go to sleep in the dark" [25]. As an adult, Lamb confided, he still had occasional nightmares, "but I no longer keep a study of them." Fisher et al. have demonstrated more scientifically the antidotal value of light suggested by Lamb in preventing nightmares. One of their experimental subjects, a young man who had frequent severe nightmares, had considerably fewer such dreams when he slept with the lights on [2].

At the age of twenty, Helen Keller wrote an account of her dreams, observing that she dreamt "oftenest of the unpleasant and horrible" [26]. Before her teacher came to her when she was seven, and even for a brief time thereafter, fear was the only emotion she experienced in dreams. Locked into a sightless, soundless world, she nevertheless often dreamed as a little child "that I ran into a small, dark room, and that, while I stood there, I felt something fall heavily without any noise, causing the floor to shake up and down violently; and each time I woke up with a jump. As I learned more and more about the objects around me, this strange dream ceased to haunt me; but I was in a high state of excitement and received impressions very easily. It is not strange then that I dreamed at that time of a wolf, which seemed to rush towards me and put his cruel teeth into my body! I could not speak (the fact was, I could only spell with my fingers), and I tried to scream; but no sound escaped from my lips" [26]. The basic features of these nightmares experienced by this child, who had lacked sight, hearing, or voice from the age of nineteen months, differ little from the previous accounts. It would appear that the basic features of the nightmare are not dependent on the intactness of any particular peripheral sense receptors. As a young adult, Helen Keller continued to have terrifying dreams, particularly in response to disturbing reading that recurred in distorted form in the dreams. After reading of a massacre in India, she dreamt that she was in a small prison. "At first," she reported, "I noticed only a skeleton hanging up on one of the walls; then I felt a strange, awful sound, like heavy iron being cast down, and the most heartrending cries ensued. I was informed that twenty men were being put to death with the utmost cruelty. I rushed madly from one room to another, and, as each ruffian came out, I locked the door behind him, in the hope that some of the victims might thereby be saved. All my efforts were futile, and I awoke with a sickening horror weighing down on my heart" [26]. The compelling power of the experiences revealed in these and countless similar accounts perhaps justifies Cason's view that "the nightmare dream is the most important psychological process that occurs in sleep" [27].

Cultural Considerations

Returning to Ernest Jones' monumental survey of the nightmare from the perspective gained by the lapse of nearly sixty
years, one is struck now, not so much by the varied nature of the
demons that cause oppression in these dreams or by the symbols
of sexuality that can be found in them, as by the objective reality
people of earlier centuries attributed to these visions [5]. Jones
points out that, from the earliest period of Christianity, church
and society lent support to the belief that oppression in nightmares by devils, werewolves, or witches represented actual visits
by such creatures. In the sixteenth century, for example, the
church took very seriously the attitude of the dreamer toward his
visitor, taking note of whether he submitted to the incubus, in
order to assess actual guilt. In the case of this type of dream, in
which reality-testing tends for the individual to be most difficult
under any circumstances, the society and its authorities were
confirming the actuality of the fantasy. Thus, a kind of mutual
validation persisted through the centuries between certain
dreams, which have such vivid reality for the individual, and the
reinforcing influence of the myths and attitudes of the society
that supported the belief in this reality.

Coleridge, even in the nineteenth century, speaks of "the
fiend" as if it were an actuality and of his oppression as a real
persecution. In Chapter 5 I will discuss the close relationship
that seems to exist psychologically between the persecutory experience in the nightmare and in certain acute psychoses in which
similar oppression is perceived with a greater loss of reality grasp.
The deepest anxieties of the nightmare relate to a time in early
childhood when the ability to differentiate between what is inside and what is outside is a fragile or developing capacity, easily
upset under the conditions of sleep. It is the time before age
five when dream experiences are accepted as real and when the
malevolent agents the small child confronts in the nightmare
cannot be put aside by his own corrective powers. The parents
must intervene; if they cannot convince the child of a different
version of reality, they must do battle with the demons them-

selves, especially in the case of children under three or four years of age (see the example of Sam in Chapter 4).

The activity of the parents in combating magically the monsters or other creatures that threaten their children in nightmares seems similar to the role of the shaman in relation to dream characters that threaten members of primitive tribes. Stewart, for example, has described how the shaman of the Negritos of Luzon in the Philippines sets out to introduce authorities who become allies and servants of the dreamer and help him to destroy and conquer his dream enemies [28]. (See descriptions on pages 3 and 11 of the similar roles of medicine men in relation to attacking figures in dreams among the Baleh Iban of North Borneo and the Utes of Colorado.)

Even when the most compassionate parental support has been provided during the night, the small child—and some adults as well—may still be confronted the next day by the memory of the nightmare as if it were an alien experience that must be assimilated bit by bit. In most instances, with the reestablishment of waking ego defenses and activities and through the support provided by persons close to the child, the dread and frightening images of the nightmare will recede during the day. However, in some instances (as will be discussed in Chapter 5 and elsewhere in this book) the dream's disturbing aftereffects may linger on in the form of frightening fantasies or, in extreme instances, as a hallucination or daymare.

It seems likely that the development of the above capacities for reality-testing and appraisal for each individual are affected profoundly by how the society, particularly as transmitted through the parents in early childhood, regards the validity of the dream perception reported by the child. Lewis Mumford has suggested that the dream may be the earliest vehicle of man's transformation from an animal ruled largely by instinct to a socialized being [29]. From the dream, he points out, follow myth, ritual, dance, and religion. However, still another step in the evolution of a society toward a rationalistic world view would occur when the content of dreams was no longer regarded as having an external or prophetic validity. An important step would then be taken from a society imbued with magic, in which the fantasy products of dream mentation and activity are granted a status equivalent to the phenomena of the external world, toward a culture in which the outside and inside worlds can be perceived and mastered separately by the means most appropriate to each task. Only in the past century, and especially since the work of Freud and Jones, has it been possible to approach nightmares and other dreams as having primarily a psychological or physiological reality or as reflecting man's struggle to integrate internal and external realities, rather than as possessing objective validity in the surrounding environment.

Although many writers have studied the dreams of primitive cultures, the nightmare in these societies does not appear to have been extensively examined [30]. According to Lincoln, nightmares and severe anxiety dreams are very common among primitives. "Most of them [the nightmares]," he found, "show violent conflicts with spirits or dead relatives who come and pursue the dreamer" [31]. Spencer also noted that nightmares occur among primitive peoples and that oppressors that come in the night are treated as real and the dream itself as an actual experience [32].

Margolin, in his studies of the Utes of Colorado, has described how seriously these Indians regard their dreams [33]. A person who appears to a Ute in his dream is considered as real a visitor as if he were encountered during waking life, and the visit must be dealt with appropriately. If a person known to be dead appears in the dream, then it is believed that his ghost has come. The illness of one Ute man began when he saw his sister-in-law in a dream. As she was dead, the appearance of her ghost meant that she had a claim on him. The dream continued for three to four nights, after which his three-year-old son began to have nightmares, which meant that the sister-in-law's ghost was entering into the little boy. In order to get rid of her or get her out of the boy, he went to a medicine man, who had the man and his son sit in a special little house for three days without food or drink, coated with mud and ashes, in order to fool the ghost and convince her that they, too, had died. For the next two or three weeks the man slept perfectly, and the boy had no nightmares.

Fundamental Characteristics

If nightmares may occur in children and adults, in ancient societies and modern ones, in healthy persons and in mentally ill individuals, we need then to ask what are the features that these dreams have in common whenever and wherever they may occur. There are actually very few essential features. Most particularly, these are the intense anxiety of overwhelming proportions, the sense of danger and helplessness, and the occurrence or threat of violent attack, directed especially at the dreamer. It is important to keep these basic features in mind, because any theory that may be applied to nightmares must account for them.

Feldman and Hyman have recently done an analysis of the content of protocols describing the last remembered nightmare of twenty-one male and forty-nine female college students [34]. They found that the dreamer characteristically found himself to be the victim of an animal or human aggressor or an "impersonal object" and felt helpless in the face of this danger. In 75 percent of the reports, the dreamer was himself the victim and suffered the consequences of the danger situation in the form of death, physical injury, social humiliation, or failure. Frozen or passive inaction was a common stance in the dream for both men and women, while flight was a more frequent response for the women. Feldman and Hyman observed that "danger and helplessness may be keynotes of nightmare dreams."

The agonizing quality of this intense helplessness was well captured in the following tape-recorded statements of a twenty-four-year-old man who suffered from severe nightmares in which he was persecuted above all by a terrible noise. "I'm trying to scream, trying to move, anything," he complained, but "it becomes so terrifying, being so helpless, being so defenseless against it. You know, like you kind of lose yourself after a while . . . no one ever heard me [scream]. I tried, but, but it never . . . y'know, that's the worst part. Jesus, that's the worst part. Not being able to do *anything*. Just being paralyzed. Like you're just struggling, like a madman, to move. Y'know, to protect yourself. You're just tryin' to move, and you just can't move fast enough." He then described the "potential violence and the potential threat to myself" in the nightmares. Although this patient described an intense feeling of paralysis, and paralysis has been said to be among the cardinal symptoms of nightmares, none of the subjects with nightmares described by Fisher et al. [2] reported having feelings of paralysis.

The physical features or properties of the persecutors in nightmares may vary according to the age of the individual, the heroes, or villains that are contemporaneous in a given culture, and the institutional and technological characteristics of that culture. Nevertheless, their relation to the helpless victim varies little. Whether the dreamer is threatened by an ancient demon, a vampire, a lobster, a fairy story monster, a robot, or an atomic ray, his experience is in each instance like that of a helpless child confronted by powerful forces with which he is unable to deal effectively. A vivid illustration of this experience is provided by the following account of his nightmare that a six-year-old boy related to his grandmother. "I have terrible dreams," he told her spontaneously one morning. "They're about a robot. There was one 'specially terrible one. He almost killed me. He was in a house, and he chased me all around. There were lots of people all around. And then he caught me, and it was terrible. There was a lot of banging and it got to be dark. And when it got black, that was the end of the dream—see, I woke up. Gosh, it was like a movie where there's a ship that gets dynamited, and everybody falls overboard, and all the lights go out, and when it's all dark that's the end of the movie, of course [gesticulates with a sweep to indicate the end]. But this one was really double price."

Physiological Types of Nightmares

The time may not be far off when we shall be able to distinguish both psychologically and physiologically two types of nightmare: (1) the non-REM (nonrapid eye movement) nightmare occurring in the period of slow-wave sleep, from which dream recall is less frequent; and (2) the REM (rapid eye movement) nightmare, or severe anxiety dream, occurring in the period of fast or paradoxical sleep that is thought to be more usually associated with dreaming. According to the recent observa-

tions of Fisher et al., [2, 3], non-REM nightmares can be distinguished in the laboratory from severe REM anxiety dreams by
violent onset; by a more abrupt and catastrophic breakthrough of
severe anxiety accompanied by screaming, bodily motility, and
autonomic discharge; and by a dream report of shorter duration.
Although these features of the two types of sleep experience
strikingly parallel the clinical differentiation that has been emphasized in pediatric accounts between night terror (*pavor nocturnus*) and nightmares (see Table 1), it is not always possible
at present clinically to separate non-REM and REM anxiety
dreams. For example, the severe nightmares that precede or accompany delirium tremens in alcoholics have been shown to
occur almost entirely in the REM state [35, 36]. In several instances, Fisher found that nightmares with screaming and terror
occurred during a REM period [37]. It is likely that some of the
clinical examples that follow have occurred in non-REM sleep
and some in the REM period.

Although the nightmare has been traditionally regarded as a
type of severe anxiety dream, Gastaut and Broughton have questioned whether nightmares really are dreams [38]. These authors regard as of primary significance the physiological arousal
or awakening phenomena they have shown to occur in association with nightmares; they see the psychological content, when it
does occur, as a rationalization of the anxiety that is associated
with the physiological changes the subject experiences. This conviction is based on the finding that the majority of nightmares
they studied in the laboratory in children and adults occurred—
as may also be the case with enuresis and somnambulism—during arousal from slow-wave (non-REM) sleep rather than from
REM sleep, during which dreaming has more frequently been
demonstrated. Broughton classes the nightmare, together with
enuresis and somnambulism, as a confusional sleep disorder because of the poorly coordinated behavior, slurred speech, mental
confusion, and poor dream recall that regularly accompany abrupt arousal or awakening from slow-wave sleep [39]. Fisher et
al. have suggested recently that "it is perhaps best to consider
that the Stage 4 nightmare is not a dream at all in the ordinary
sense, but a symptom, a pathological formation of NREM

sleep brought about by a rift in the ego's capacity to control anxiety" [3].

As the above workers have demonstrated, even if we appreciate that in most instances physiological changes associated with abrupt arousal occur with nightmares and may make the individual more susceptible to intense anxiety, we are still left with unanswered fundamental questions. We do not know, for example, why the nightmare victim is aroused by overwhelming anxiety while the enuretic child is awakened instead by an intense need to urinate or the somnambulist by an urge to walk; neither do we know what type of stimulus, psychological or physiological, initiated the arousal. Broughton acknowledges that some type of psychic conflict or activity may initiate the arousal, but it has not been possible to demonstrate in the laboratory what this could be. In short, we know that a severe nightmare forces waking, but we do not know what provoked the nightmare at that particular moment of the night. The clinical examples that will be cited give ample evidence that intensifying psychological conflict preceded the nightmare attacks; here, too, there is no way to prove that mental activity related to such conflicts immediately preceded the nightmare during sleep. As numerous workers have shown, however, mental activity occurs during all the sleep periods and may be recalled after the subject awakens from slow-wave sleep in a certain percentage of instances [40–42].

Regarding the question of dream content in nightmares, positions vary, depending to some degree on definition. However, even if we limit the term nightmare to the explosive type of episode associated with overwhelming anxiety, content that is recovered may nevertheless be quite vivid and terrifying. This was found, for example, by Fisher et al., who also observed that the psychic content associated with the non-REM nightmare is coherent, psychodynamically organized, and related to the subject's preexisting conflicts and traumatic experiences and to the REM dreams of the same night [2, 3]. Although the content may continue to be elaborated after waking, this is a complex psychological process and is not simply rationalization, as has been suggested by Gastaut and Broughton [38]. Furthermore, as Fisher et al. have shown, non-REM nightmares and REM dreams of the same night may deal with the same themes, usually of an oral-destructive nature in their examples, suggesting a relationship between the anxieties experienced throughout the sleep cycle and ongoing psychological conflicts. The work of these and other authors who have dealt with the physiological aspects of the nightmare problem will be discussed further in Chapter 6.

Central Conflicts in Nightmares

Nightmares are concerned with life-and-death matters. The attempts to apply Freud's wish-fulfillment theory to anxiety dreams have frequently led to unproductive theorizing and have perhaps delayed a more comprehensive view of these important dreams. Similarly, Jones' emphasis on the incestuous sexual content of nightmares and his insistence that "this always relates to the normal sexual act" provide too narrow a view [5]. Jones acknowledged this himself toward the end of his work on the subject, observing that "here and there one catches glimpses of material older than that derived from either the phallic phase of sexual development or even the excrementitial one . . . namely from the primordial penis-womb phantasies of infancy" [43]. Although most students of child psychology no longer credit infants with such fully formed fantasies, we must agree that nightmares do involve the very earliest and most powerful anxieties of childhood. As I will try to show, the analysis of nightmares regularly leads us to the earliest, most profound, and inescapable anxieties and conflicts to which human beings are subject: those involving destructive aggression, castration, separation and abandonment, devouring and being devoured, and fear regarding loss of identity and fusion with the mother.

Rivers, in a most interesting discussion that has been largely neglected, points to the close association between nightmares and issues of survival, matters that, in psychoanalytic theory, would be the province of the ego or self-preservative instincts (see further discussion in Chapters 2 and 7) [44, 45]. Rivers pointed out the helplessness of all animals, including human beings, during sleep. He suggested that the creature would derive protection from danger by "some kind of mechanism by which the animal began to adapt its behavior to danger while still asleep. If this mechanism also helped to awaken, it would still further increase its helpfulness to the sleeping animal" [44]. Rivers suggested that the primary function of the dream, and especially the nightmare, might be to awaken the organism and thus adapt it to danger, even if the awakening reaction were out of proportion to the actual external threat. A similar theory of the function of dreaming was suggested by Snyder over forty years later; Broughton's recent work on the occurrence of nightmares in the sleep cycle has shown that they do occur in relation to arousal from sleep [39, 46]. One of the principal objectives of this book will be to show, not only that nightmares are based on the internal conflicts that have generated anxiety in the course of psychosexual development, but also that these internal struggles are intimately associated with external danger situations that threaten the individual currently or have done so in the past. The ego in the nightmare reacts with a kind of anxiety consistent with the perception of intense actual danger threatening survival, that is, as if the threat to the dreamer were absolutely real. It is this quality of vivid and actual threat that perhaps most sharply characterizes nightmares and for which we must try to account.

Nightmare and Night Terror

The distinction between nightmares and night terrors [47–49] has received considerable attention in the literature on this subject. According to the well-known child psychiatrist, Leo Kanner [50], for example, in children night terror attacks differ from nightmares in several respects, as summarized in Table 1. In the night terror attack, in contrast to the nightmare, the child moves about, is more likely to scream loudly, has a more severe degree of terror, is more difficult to calm, does not recognize objects, continues to hallucinate, perspires heavily, and has amnesia for the episode. I have not always found it possible to apply these distinctions sharply in clinical practice. It is extremely difficult, for example, for a parent to determine the degree to which a child is awake when the parent has just been aroused to tend the child and often remains in a half-asleep state. The duration of

Table 1. Differences Between Nightmares and Night Terror Attacks in Children Compared with Differences Between Severe REM Anxiety Dreams and Non-REM Nightmares in Adults

	Children [50]		Adults [2]	
	Nightmare	Night Terror	Severe REM Anxiety Dream	Non-REM Nightmare
Time of occurrence	During sleep	During sleep or in a somnolent twilight state	Emerges out of a long dream	Occurs spontaneously, usually during first Non-REM period of the night
Motility and activity	Slight movements only	Child sits up in bed, jumps to the floor, runs about, cries out	Muscle tone and motility not regained; vocalization may occur, but screaming rare	Muscle tone and motility regained with violent body movement; subject may sit up in bed or get up and move about the room; screams
Mental content	Persecutory, violent, and elaborate	Severely persecutory, vivid and less elaborate	Threatened destruction, more elaborate and disguised	Violently persecutory, oral-aggressive content
Affect	Fear	Severe terror and overwhelming	Intense anxiety	Disorganizing terror and panic
Mental state following arousal	Can be calmed, coherent, oriented, not hallucinating	Incoherent, cannot be calmed, does not recognize objects, continues to hallucinate	Subjects lucid; Broughton [39] refers to REM dreams in general	Disoriented, confused, unresponsive to the environment and often hallucinating
Physiological changes	No perspiration	Perspires heavily	Not observed	Massive autonomic discharge
Recollection of the episode	Incident recalled; content remembered more or less clearly	Complete amnesia for the content and the occurrence of the episode	Dream activity generally recalled; see Broughton [39]	Generally an amnesia for the episode

episodes of either type has not to my knowledge been measured; neither has the child's ability to recall the episode been carefully correlated with any particular features of the attack. In a study of hallucinations in children, Schur distinguishes night terror from nightmare by the greater degree of panic in the former state and the fact that the child does not really wake up [51]. In nightmares, according to Schur, the dreamer experiences helplessness and immobility, while in night terror motility is restored. This finding is consistent with Kanner's differentiation of the two conditions and also with Fisher's observation that, in the non-REM nightmares of adults, motility is restored, whereas in severe REM anxiety dreams the subjects remain immobile. (See discussion of REM and non-REM nightmares on page 13.) Although more common in children, particularly below the age of five, night terror attacks *do* occur in adults. Dement, for example, has offered a vivid description of such an episode in a study subject [52], and Fisher has recently provided several detailed examples [37].

In some accounts, night terror is distinguished as lacking identifiable hallucinatory content. In children, however, whether such content is discovered may depend upon whether they are old enough to be capable of communicating their dream experiences and upon the effort expended by the parent or the doctor in inquiring as to what is disturbing the child. I have not infrequently heard parents report that they had no idea what their child had been hallucinating when he woke up screaming in terror, but have myself then obtained a vivid dream report from the child. I have become increasingly doubtful whether night terror attacks without some form of hallucinatory dream content actually occur. This impression is supported by Fisher's recent observations [37]. I recently had the opportunity to interview a young schizophrenic woman who was deeply disturbed by frequent night terror attacks for which she communicated no dream experience, denying that she recalled any content. With repeated interviews, however, she revealed a typical nightmare sequence in which a threatening man resembling her stepfather had come to strangle her, and she had wakened in great fear.

Hallucinosis, Nightmare, and Daymare

In recent years, there has been considerable interest in the hallucinatory experiences of children [53–55]. Many of the clinical examples supplied in articles on this subject are clearly features of nightmares that have persisted into the daytime. In each of the five cases that Esman discusses in his paper [53], the episode has begun with a nightmare in which the hallucinatory experience, frightening in each instance, has "progressed" into the waking day. Esman stresses the importance of external threats or traumata in precipitating hallucinatory episodes but, as will be discussed in Chapter 2, this is true of nightmares in general. Schur has also found that hallucinations in childhood are often preceded by night terror attacks or nightmares [51].

Careful comparison of the examples provided by contemporary writers on visual hallucinosis in children with the observations of earlier authors on "daymares" or "day terrors" reveals that the phenomena under consideration are very similar [56, 57]. As Eisenberg has discussed in his review [54], and Wilking and Paoli's [55] series confirms, hallucinations occur more frequently in children who are not thought to be psychotic or schizophrenic than in those who are. Conversely, hallucinations appear to be less prominent in the psychopathology of psychosis in the child than in the adult [54]. However, if hallucinations occur in childhood most frequently as an "extension," "continuation," "progression," or "intrusion" of a nightmare into the waking hours, we are left with the unsolved problem of assessing and understanding the significance of such persistence of the dream phenomenon. From the psychological standpoint, this needs to be approached in terms of the immaturity of the ego and the incomplete development of the psychic apparatus. From the physiological side, the relationship of these hallucinations of childhood to the various sleep phases, to delirium tremens, or to other deliria that emerge from nightmares or seem intimately associated with them requires further study [35, 58–59].

Children's Nightmares

The night Max wore his wolf suit and made mischief of one kind and another his mother called him "WILD THING!" and Max said "I'LL EAT YOU UP!" so he was sent to bed without eating anything. That very night in Max's room a forest grew and grew and grew until his ceiling hung with vines and the walls became the world all around and an ocean tumbled by with a private boat for Max and he sailed off through night and day and in and out of weeks and almost over a year to where the wild things are. And when he came to the place where the wild things are they roared their terrible teeth and rolled their terrible eyes and showed their terrible claws until Max said "BE STILL!" and tamed them with the magic trick of staring into all their yellow eyes without blinking once and they were frightened and called him the most wild thing of all and made him king of all wild things [60].*

Sleep disturbances are one of the most sensitive indicators of emotional distress in childhood and one of the earliest types of symptomatic expression to be recognized by parents, pediatricians, and child psychiatrists. Nagera has recently provided a comprehensive review of this subject, noting, as have other child psychiatrists and analysts, that nightmares, *pavor nocturnus*, and severe anxiety dreams may be observed from the end of the first year of life and are the most frequent and most easily recognized of the sleep disorders [49, 61–63]. Indeed, in a study of the emotional sequelae of surgery in small children, Levy found that night terrors were the *characteristic* form of disturbance of one- and two-year-old children, present when other troubled reactions were not [64]. Nightmares may occur at any time from infancy to the end of life; a number of analysts have treated adult patients who have had repetitive nightmares without respite since early childhood [37, 65]. It was the observation of their severe nightmares that led Macnish [66], an early writer on the subject of troubled sleep, to become one of the first to question the view of childhood as a time of innocence and peace. "Many of the dreams experienced at this early period," he wrote, "leave an indelible impression on the mind. They are remembered in after-years with feelings of pain, and, blending with the more delightful reminiscences of childhood, demonstrate that this era, which we are apt to consider one varied scene of sunshine and happiness, had, as well as future life, its shadows of melancholy, and was not untinged with hues of sorrow and care. The sleep of infancy, therefore, is far from being that ideal state of felicity which is commonly supposed. It is haunted with its own terrors, even more than of adults; and, if many of the visions which people it are equally delightful, there can be little doubt that it is also tortured by dreams of a more painful character than often fall to the share of after-life" [66]. The occurrence of nightmares in a three-year-old child convinced Waelder of the powerful instinctual forces that produce inner conflict and made him argue against more philosophical explanations of human emotional disturbances [67].

There has often been a curious vagueness, a tendency toward broad inclusiveness and generality in certain descriptions and explanations of nightmares in children. James Goodhart, a pediatrician of the last century, regarded nightmare and night terror as "sleep disorders where cerebral under-currents seethe below a placid surface. . . . It is a mallady [sic] of little detriment in itself; but, as an indication of a nervous organization, it is most valuable. It is the 'slacken speed' to the engine-driver which must never pass unheeded" [68]. Leo Kanner has more recently written similarly of nightmare and night terror as "more or less drastic indications that something is wrong with the child and that it is his personality that is in need of investigation and adjustment" [69]. Such generalities may prove to be more apropos than we recognize, for these dreams are indeed highly sensitive expressions of intense psychological distress, of imbalance, or of disturbed integration of the personality. They may occur in the regression of sleep during which defensive barriers are lowered, while the child's behavior in the waking state may give no comparable indication that something is wrong. It is for this reason that nightmares seem to be so frequent at times of developmental progress or situational change that disrupt the balance of forces within the personality when there may be no indication of gross psychopathology. It is also largely for this reason that I have tended to approach these dreams from the standpoint of normal development and the forces impelling the child toward conflict resolution, mastery, and personality integration, rather than to look upon them as psychopathological entities per se.

As Klein makes clear in her early papers, attacks of *pavor nocturnus* may be the first expression of fundamental anxieties with which the individual may be forced to contend throughout his life. According to Klein, later symptoms or other pathological manifestations may be repeated expressions in only slightly altered form of the original *pavor nocturnus* attacks of early childhood. She asserts that "in several cases in which I analyzed anxiety attacks in quite little children, these attacks proved to be the repetition of a *pavor nocturnus* which had occurred in the second half of the child's second year and at the beginning of its third year" [70]. Klein expresses the hope that "if it were possible to undertake an analysis of the child at the time of the *pavor nocturnus* or soon after it, and to resolve this anxiety, the ground would be cut away from under the neurosis and possibilities of sublimation would be opened out" [71].

There have been several studies of the incidence of various types of children's dreams [72–75]. These studies vary so markedly in the criteria for dreaming, methods of dream collection, reasons for assigning labels to different kinds of dreams, the age ranges included, and the kinds of data recorded that one must be cautious in drawing any conclusions. Despert, for example, in a study of 190 dreams of forty-three preschool children, obtained quite extensive data from individual play sessions, daily behavior notes, and reports from home [72]. She found that the dreams reported were predominantly anxiety dreams or nightmares; the predominant themes were the danger of the child's being bitten, devoured, and chased. Foster and Anderson specifically sought evidence of "unpleasant dreams" in groups of children age one to four, five to eight, and nine to twelve through parental reporting of moans in the night, coming to adults, and reporting bad dreams in the morning [73]. By this method they found an incidence of 93 percent of "bad dreaming" in the forty children age one to four, which reduced to 71 and 39 percent, respectively, in the five-to-eight and nine-to-twelve groups. Kimmins in his study of the dreams of 5,900 children age five to sixteen is less specific about how the dream data were collected. In the five- to seven-year-olds, he found an incidence of only 25 percent and of 17 to 18 percent in the eight-to-fourteen group [74]. Jersild et al., in a report of 400 children age five to twelve, reported only that the children were "questioned" [75]. The results are reported in a confusing manner, but the authors conclude that fewer children failed to report "bad" dreams than "good" ones. It is difficult to draw any conclusions from this literature. It would appear that, in the preschool group, nightmares or other unpleasant dreams predominate, but this becomes less the case for children of six years and above. Although simple wish-fulfillment dreams may occur, especially in very young children, the bulk of evidence tends to refute Freud's contention that children's dreams are usually direct, undisguised fulfillments of a wish.

In his writings, Freud never dealt with children's nightmares as such, although he reported dreams of this sort in *The Interpretation of Dreams* and in two of his most famous case histories [76, 77]. Little Hans had an anxiety dream that preceded by a few days the outbreak of his phobic state. We are not told much about it except that he had awoken in fear, having dreamt "to the effect that" his mother had gone away and that now he had no mother to "coax" with. Although Freud calls this a punishment and repression dream, attributing the anxiety to Hans's fear of punishment for his forbidden oedipal wishes, we see, in the fragment of manifest content provided, the evocation of an earlier form of anxiety, fear of loss of the mother.

Similarly, the Wolfman's famous dream of the wolves sitting on the walnut tree was a typical nightmare of a four-year-old child. Although Freud traced the dream's anxiety ultimately to a profound fear of castration, he discussed also the anal-homosexual fixations underlying the dream and the pregenital fears aroused in it, especially the fear of being eaten. These preoedipal conflicts contained in the Wolfman's nightmare receive considerable attention in the writings of others [48, 78–83]; the reader who is interested in exploring this subject further may consult these sources.

On the one occasion when he did discuss the *pavor nocturnus* of children, Freud called it a type of anxiety attack, a form of hysteria [84]. Freud continued to regard anxiety in dreams of both adults and children as a problem of neurosis rather than of dreaming. In 1925, for example, he stated that the explanation of anxiety dreams would not be found in the theory of dreams but that these instances of anxiety were a problem of neurosis [85].

Freud accepted with reluctance the possibility that the anxiety dream could represent an exception to his theory that all dreams represent an attempt at fulfillment of an unconscious wish. Since the dream was the product of conflict, he asserted in his last writing on the subject, "something that is a satisfaction for the unconscious id may for that very reason be a cause of anxiety for the ego" [86]. Late in his career, however, in a discussion of the traumatic neuroses, one of the cardinal symptoms of which is recurrent nightmares, Freud suggested another possibility [87]. Here, he allowed, the laws peculiar to dreaming might come into "collision with other forces." In these disorders a "traumatic fixation" has occurred and, with the relaxation of repression at night, becomes active once again. The dream-work fails to "transform the memory traces of the traumatic event into the fulfillment of a wish." We are dealing now with the memory of an external event that has itself become traumatic. The ego reacts in the dream once again as if its existence were threatened, as if it were once more confronting the reality and helpless before it. Inasmuch as children, particularly in infancy and early childhood, are in fact repeatedly encountering an environment which they perceive as threatening and before which they feel especially helpless, the regular occurrence of nightmares in association with such danger situations has important theoretical implications for our understanding of the traumatic neuroses of adults; furthermore, it draws our attention to the similar mechanisms that are operative in the two situations. Children's nightmares, as well as the repetitive nightmares that characterize the traumatic neuroses, draw to our attention the fact that it is not only the inner desires and unconscious wishes whose power may threaten the ego [88] or whose fulfillment may place the individual in danger by virtue of the prohibited and dangerous nature of such wishes. We must look carefully also at what events in the outside world have occurred to threaten the ego or to confirm the individual in his fears.

In a previous publication dealing exclusively with nightmares in children [48], I employed a developmental approach to the study of these dreams. In each instance the dream was found to give expression to those acute anxieties and conflicts that were current in the child's life, while at the same time, under the regressive conditions of sleep, anxieties relating to earlier developmental phases were revived. A girl of eight or nine, for example, as in the case of the child, Carol, described in Chapter 4 (page 139), might experience severe anxiety in a nightmare precipitated by her wish to eliminate her mother as a rival for her father's love. Her intolerant conscience, whose influence, once asleep, she could no longer ward off, demands her death as just retribution, and a nightmare is precipitated. However, under the conditions of sleep, regression of various ego functions occurs, with impairment of reality-testing, failure of recently acquired defense functions, abandonment of object ties, and return to earlier, more symbolic and concrete forms of thought. In the face of this ego regression and relative helplessness, earlier conflicts and anxiety situations are aroused; typically, these are wishes and fears related to eating and being eaten or the earliest kind of terror over the loss of the mother's love.

The orality reflected in dream states and dream content has been stressed by many writers [89–91]. Spitz described this process of regression to orality in sleep eloquently, if rather romantically, in these words: "When, however, the body relaxes diurnally in the passivity of sleep, the activity of the mind will retrace its way toward the primal process, and the primal cavity then becomes the cavernous home of the dreams" [91].

An aggressive, devouring orality is prominent in children's nightmares. Being eaten or eaten up, and equivalent forms of devouring, such as being ground up inside large machines, occur with particular frequency in the nightmares of children under five. It is striking, however, that often such themes of the nursery years may reappear in the nightmares of older children and even of adults. Anxieties derived from the child's early mode of expressing affection by devouring, incorporating, and thus retaining the other person "inside," * or venting aggression by biting or

* A five-year-old expressed the warm feelings that can be associated with this wish to devour in these words, as he kissed his father affectionately, "I'm going to eat you up, Daddy, and then your bones will be in here (pointing to the abdomen) in my fireplace."

eating someone, readily find their way into nightmares. There seems to be a particular tendency for conflicts stimulated in later developmental phases to be expressed in nightmares in oral destructive terms. Furthermore, in the nightmare the frightening conflicts concerning devouring and being devoured that characterize the period under four are regressively revived.

Developing genital interests and fears may become linked in children's nightmares with older anxieties about being devoured or separated from the parents.

Rachel, a girl of three and a half, was referred for treatment because of nightmares and fears of sleeping alone. After frequent previous absences from the household, the father had separated from the family when she was two and a half. This occurred after violent arguments in which the child saw the father grab, punch, and choke the mother; later, she would frequently remind the mother of what she had seen. For three months before the separation, the child slept in the same room with the parents where she would have had the opportunity to observe their sexual activity. For several weeks prior to coming to the clinic, after having observed the mother's pregnant sister, Rachel had expressed the wish that her mother produce a baby brother for her. After the separation, Rachel and her mother moved to the grandparents' house and then to an apartment alone about one month before she was seen in the clinic.

The mother sometimes responded to Rachel's childish stubbornness and provocations by losing her temper and spanking the child. Although Rachel had always been a restless sleeper, awakening at night, screaming had begun at the time her parents separated. At bedtime each night she insisted on sleeping in her mother's bed instead of sleeping alone. Even when the mother gave in to this wish, which she was doing less and less, Rachel nevertheless awoke during the night from fearful dreams, requiring that the mother hold and comfort her.

In her initial play interviews, after a brief shyness Rachel revealed her aggression by shooting several toy animals, saving an extra "big one" (shot) for a large elephant. Then she noticed a small block with a glove painted on it and proceeded to tell about "grabby monsters" that came into her room after she was asleep at night. They tried to take her away, but she stayed in her bed and screamed for her mother. Sometimes the monsters went into her Nanna's (grandmother's) room to take her away. When her mother came to her bedside, Rachel said she sometimes spanked her for making such a disturbance, but she also spanked the monsters and drove them away. At other times a monster made growling noises and grabbed her and others with its mouth and teeth and threatened to eat them all up. Rachel seemed to feel that the monsters came because of her naughtiness, such as breaking mother's glasses.

The monsters were not always scary. Sometimes they were friendly, and even the "eating up" had an element of pleasure about it in some of Rachel's accounts. She continued to fear the monsters during the day, sometimes confusing them with characters she had seen on television monster movies, but as it became darker she became increasingly anxious as she anticipated their return in force after she had gone to sleep. Rachel's monsters had characteristics that were a mixture of various animals and a man. One of them had a huge "grabby" head, three legs, and a beard. Others were specifically associated with her father. On one occasion she drew a picture of an airplane that had taken her father away into the sky, after which she saw him no more. She feared he would be hurt. She made a drawing of her father and attached a long rolled-up piece of clay in his genital region, calling it a snake. She became concerned when the snake continually fell off or broke and insisted that the doctor attach it firmly. Then she said that this same snake was "grabby" and "growly" and was one of the monsters that came at night to grab and eat her.

When first seen, Rachel was entering a period of increasing interest in the body's anatomy and in the processes of pregnancy and the production of children. She had also been subjected to frequent absences from her father, ending in his separation from the family, and a more recent separation from her grandmother and grandfather. In addition, she had been a witness to her father's frequent violent assaults upon her mother and possibly to her parents' sexual intercourse, which she may have perceived in similar violent terms. In her nightmares the anxieties related to her genital interests and fears were revealed in association with earlier and perhaps deeper fears of separation, abandonment, annihilation, and being devoured. In her dreams the grabby monsters threaten to take her away from those she loves and upon whom she is vitally dependent or to take them away from her. They threaten to eat her up, in part, it would seem, as a punishment for her own aggressive wishes and impulses toward those same persons. These monsters have characteristics that demonstrate their association with her father, whom she has witnessed grabbing and choking her mother, with whom she is identified. Her concern that the snake-penis must stay attached to the father's body is most likely related to her hostile wishes toward him, at the same time reflecting her concern about the absence of a penis on her own body. However, the snake, which is on the one hand part of the man's body, is itself one of the devouring monsters, thus revealing the link between her phallic interests and fears and her earlier, more profound anxieties about eating and being eaten.

Rachel continued to have to deal with her nightmare monsters during the day and even confused them with creatures from television shows. So vivid were their images to her, and so intense was her anxiety about them, that she could not help regarding them as real despite her other achievements in differentiating memory, fantasy, and current reality. Because of this regression of ego functions with which they were associated, Rachel's nightmares, which reflected her struggles to resolve the conflicts described above, upset her developing mastery of the differentiations between inner and outer realities.

Through various clinical illustrations in this book I will try to show that this aspect of ego regression, together with the revival in the dream of earlier conflicts that have never been completely resolved, accounts for the tendency of nightmares to resemble one another in fundamental ways throughout life, including old age. This developmental approach may thus be applied to the nightmares of adults in whom these conflicts may be seen to persist.

Children's Dreams and the Development of Ego Functioning

Dreaming affords an opportunity to study the development of reality-testing and other ego functions in childhood. Szalita-Pemow regards the dream process as "the very laboratory in which thought is produced" [92]. In her view, emotions stimulate the formation of new combinations from stored perceptions, "their segregation, the selection of the suitable, the elimination of the unsuitable, their preliminary classification," a process that starts with feelings and desires and ends with logical, organized thoughts. In sleep, the individual is directed away from reality, but in dreaming the perceptions are formed into new combinations through primary-process thinking, and thought is redirected toward reality.

At a very early age, children develop psychic or behavioral defenses in order to avoid or escape the terror and feeling of helplessness they experience in nightmares. Small children may avoid sleep, pack their beds with protective animals, or insist upon the performance of bedtime rituals whose function is to offset by magic the threats that may be encountered in sleep for which their own inner resources or protective powers are inadequate. During the period from ages six to eight, the child first begins to be able to separate or "free up" a portion of his ego that is not absorbed in the dream process. He learns to tell himself within the dream that he is only dreaming and even to force himself to awaken by sheer will. At this age the child is not as dependent upon the parents for direct comforting following the dream. From a strict theoretical standpoint, it might be argued that these defenses are directed, not against the dream or even its anxiety, but only against the unacceptable unconscious impulses or latent wishes that gave rise to it. This would not really be accurate, however, for the nightmare and its antagonists may have an influence of their own that can powerfully affect the individual even after waking and that require measures aimed at counteracting their threats.

In older children and adults I have seen instances in which, either as a result of developmental gains or an increased ability to deal with aggressive impulses, the attitude of helplessness or victimization in relation to the attacker gave way to one in which the dreamer became the aggressor and turned the tables on the would-be assailant. An example of such a situation, such "identification with the aggressor," occurred in the life of a twelve-year-old girl who had suffered from nightmares since the age of five. She could trace three periods in her experience with these dreams. In the first, witches and vicious animals had cut off her fingers. In the second, beginning about age six, "bad guys" killed her. In the third period, which began at age ten, she developed the ability to offset the fears, both within and without the dreams. Typically, these were of vampires who appeared as dark men in black capes. They tried to sink their fangs into her neck, suck her blood, and kill her. They never succeeded because, before one of them could get to her neck, "I would stick a pitchfork through his heart and kill him." The vampire then screamed, "I wouldn't really hurt a flea," but it was she herself who was screaming as she awoke. Other measures she took in the dreams to ensure her safety were to fill in the graves from which the vampires might have emerged, so they could not possibly return, or to shrink them down to the size of a bat or make them disappear altogether.

Her treatment of the vampire at certain times left little doubt that it was her own aggressive and sadistic impulses with which she was struggling in these dreams. She would decisively overpower and "stick" the vampire, victimizing him in a manner that filled her with mixed pleasure and horror. In other dreams she beat up and killed bad guys like those that had attacked her during the second period of her nightmares. So pervasive were such dreams in this child's mental life that she had to struggle during the daytime in order not to believe that vampires really existed. Although she "knew they weren't real," she would nevertheless question friends to find out if they might be vampires. One girl in particular, whose father had died, seemed "suspicious" to her because of the appearance of her eyes.

How the child regards the dream experience; what status in reality he gives the dream's feelings and percepts; his capacity to assess after waking the claims to validity of the dream scenes, and the ability in latency to know even while a dream is going on that it is a dream—all of these capacities bear on the development of reality-testing. Piaget [93] and Werner [94] have observed the small child's tendency to treat the dream experiences after waking as if they had really occurred and to regard the dream as emanating from external sources and as caused by outside agencies. Piaget has outlined three stages spanning the period from five to ten in which the child gradually comes to understand that the dream is the product of thought and takes place inside himself [93]. He notes how the child may confuse dream and reality, particularly in nightmares. "Everyone knows," Piaget observes, "how hard it can be to calm a child who has just woken from a nightmare, and how impossible it is to convince him that the objects he dreamt of did not really exist" [95]. A mother recently told me how she had tried to comfort her six-year-old boy who had come into her room announcing that he was in terrible danger from a huge bunny. "But I can't get it out of my mind," he wailed. "It scares me. It looks so real." Despite his struggles, nothing but the warm physical presence of his mother could comfort him. Just how practical children are in recognizing that their perceptual powers need all the assistance they can obtain in dealing with frightening dreams is well illustrated by an anecdote reported at the turn of the century by Guthrie. A small child who suffered from nightmares was told that she need not fear the dark because "God would be with her." She is said to have replied, "I wish you'd take God away, and leave the candle" [96].

The ego's capacity to maintain dream-reality distinctions in the face of intense conflict and anxiety is a hard-won strength and is subject to regression and disruption throughout childhood and adult life. The capacity for this discrimination, fully achieved only in the latency years, is particularly fragile in the child; we saw, for example, how the three-year-old Rachel continued to deal with her nightmare monsters throughout the day as if they were real. For this reason, the carry-over of the nightmare experience into waking in day terrors or childhood hallucinosis, or in febrile and toxic deliria, need not be accompanied by severe regression of other ego functions. Therefore, it is probably not in itself indicative of a psychosis-prone personality. Similarly in adults, under special circumstances such as febrile, toxic, or drug-withdrawal states, the carry-over of frightening dream perceptions into waking, with loss of the capacity for reality-testing, may not necessarily be accompanied by lasting regression of other ego functions. In acute psychoses, disturbances of ego functioning, especially of reality-testing, in relation to nightmares and other dreams may dominate the clinical picture. Such functions, perhaps in part because they are acquired relatively late in childhood, are particularly susceptible to regression in these psychoses, although in schizophrenic states they are accompanied by the regression of other ego functions, as well. Perhaps considerations such as these led Snyder to call the night terror of children "an intermediate condition between dreaming during sleep and psychotic hallucination while awake" [97]. Possible relationships between children's nightmares or night terrors and acute psychoses will be discussed further in Chapter 5.

References and Notes

1. Coleridge, S. T.   The Pains of Sleep. In Coleridge, E. H. (Ed.), *The Poems of Samuel Taylor Coleridge*. London: Oxford University Press, 1912. Pp. 389–390.
2. Fisher, C., Byrne, J., and Edwards, A.   REM and NREM Nightmares and Their Inter-Relationship. Lecture delivered to the Department of Psychiatry, The Mt. Sinai Hospital, New York, April 10, 1968.
3. Fisher, C., Byrne, J., Edwards, A., and Kahn, E.   A Psychophysiological Study of Nightmares. Freud Anniversary Lecture, April 8, 1969.
4. Liddon, S. C.   Sleep paralysis and hypnagogic hallucinations: Their relationship to the nightmare. *Arch. Gen. Psychiat.* (Chicago) 17:88–96, 1967.
5. Jones, E.   *On the Nightmare*. London: Hogarth Press, 1931.
6. Bellamy, R.   The analysis of a nightmare. *J. Abnorm. Psychol.* 10: 11–18, 1915.
7. Verteuil, R. L.   A psychiatric approach to the study of the nightmare. *Canad. Psychiat. Ass. J.* 7:151–158, 1962.
8. Hadfield, J. A.   *Dreams and Nightmares*. Baltimore, Md.: Penguin Books, 1954. P. 178.
9. Fisher, C.   Psychoanalytic implications of recent research on sleep and dreaming. *J. Amer. Psychoanal. Ass.* 13:197–303, 1965.
10. Trosman, H.   Dream research and the psychoanalytic theory of dreams. *Arch. Gen. Psychiat.* (Chicago) 9:9–18, 1963.
11. One psychiatrist engaged in laboratory research told me of a rather striking exception to this statement. I had asked him if he had encountered instances of nightmares or anxiety dreams in the laboratory. The only example he could think of had occurred in his own case in the course of investigations of penile erections in relation to the sleep cycle. He had allowed himself to be a study subject one night and had put on a penometer, a device for measuring changes in penile size. He awoke during the night in great fear from a dream whose content reflected obvious castration anxiety.
12. Shipley, J.   *Dictionary of Word Origins*. New York: Philosophical Library, 1945.
13. Onions, C. J.   *The Oxford Dictionary of English Etymology*. Oxford: Oxford University Press, 1966.
14. Shakespeare, W.   *King Lear*, III:4.
15. Freeman, D.   Shaman and Incubus. In Muensterberger, W., and Axelrod, S. (Eds.), *The Psychoanalytic Study of Society*, vol. IV. New York: International Universities Press, 1967. P. 333.
16. Chadwick, J., and Mann, W. N. (Eds.).   *The Medical Works of Hippocrates*. Oxford: Blackwell Scientific Publ., 1950. P. 191.
17. Roelans, C.   On Diseases of Infants (1500?). In Ruhrah, J. (Ed.), *Pediatrics of the Past*. New York: Hoeber Div., Harper & Row, 1925. P. 99.
18. Phaer, T.   *The Boke of Chyldren* (1545). Edinburgh: L. S. Living-

stone, 1955. P. 28. (I am grateful to Dr. Herbert Goldings for calling my attention to this and the previous reference.)

19. Stevenson, R. L. *Across the Plains*. New York: Scribner, 1908. Pp. 216–217.

20. Dr. John Nemiah, who has recently been engaged in a study of Coleridge, has not found evidence that Coleridge's nightmares were significantly related to his taking opium.

21. Coleridge, S. T. Letter to Tom Wedgwood, Sept. 16, 1803. Quoted in Griggs, E. L. (Ed.), *Unpublished Letters of Samuel Taylor Coleridge*, vol. I. London: Constable & Co., Ltd., 1932. Pp. 279–281.

22. Stern, P. V. D. *Selected Writings of Thomas De Quincey*. New York, Random House, 1937.

23. *Ibid*. P. 73.

24. Hearn, L. Nightmare Touch. In *Shadowings*. Boston: Little, Brown, 1900. Pp. 235–246.

25. Lamb, C. Witches and Other Night Fears. In *Essays of Elia* (1823). Boston: Little, Brown, 1892. Pp. 133–143.

26. Jastrow, J. *Fact and Fable in Psychology*. Boston: Houghton, Mifflin, 1900. Pp. 347–358.

27. Cason, H. The nightmare dream. *Psychol. Monogr.* 46:5, 1935.

28. Stewart, K. The dream comes of age. *Ment. Hyg.* 46:230–237, 1962.

29. Mumford, L. *The Myth of the Machine*. New York: Harcourt, Brace & World, 1966.

30. von Grunebaum, G. E., and Caillois, R. *The Dream and Human Societies*. Berkeley: University of California Press, 1966.

31. Lincoln, J. S. *The Dream in Primitive Cultures*. London: Cresset Press, 1935. P. 122.

32. Spencer, H. *The Principles of Sociology*, vol. 1. New York: Appleton, 1896.

33. Margolin, S. Ghosts Versus Superegos (from Studies of Certain American Indians). Talk delivered to Scientific Meeting of Boston Psychoanalytic Society and Institute, Feb. 14, 1966.

34. Feldman, M. J., and Hyman, E. Content Analysis of Nightmare Reports. Presented to the Eighth Annual Meeting of the Association for the Psychophysiological Study of Sleep, Denver, Colo., Mar. 22–24, 1968. Abstracted in *Psychophysiology* 5:221, 1968.

35. Gross, M., Goodenough, D., Tobin, M., Halpert, E., Lepore, D., Perlstein, A., Sirota, M., Dibianco, J., Fuller, R., and Kishner, I. Sleep disturbances and hallucinations in the acute alcoholic psychoses. *J. Nerv. Ment. Dis.* 142:493–514, 1966.

36. Greenberg, R., and Pearlman, C. Delirium tremens and dreaming. *Amer. J. Psychiat.* 124:133–142, 1967.

37. Fisher, C. Letter to the author, Apr. 18, 1968.

38. Gastaut, H., and Broughton, R. A Clinical and Polygraphic Study of Episodic Phenomena During Sleep. In Wortis, J. (Ed.), *Recent Advances in Biological Psychiatry*. New York: Plenum, 1965. Vol. 7, pp. 197–221.

39. Broughton, R. J. Sleep disorders: Disorders of arousal? *Science* 159: 1070–1078, 1968.

40. Rechtschaffen, A., Verdone, P., and Wheaton, J.   Reports of mental activity during sleep. *Canad. Psychiat. Ass. J.* 8:409–414, 1963.
41. Foulkes, W. D.   Dream reports from different stages of sleep. *J. Abnorm. Soc. Psychol.* 65:14–25, 1962.
42. Foulkes, W. D.   Nonrapid eye movement mentation. *Exp. Neurol.*, 1967, Supp. 4. Pp. 28–37.
43. Jones, E.   *On the Nightmare.* London: Hogarth, 1931. P. 289.
44. Rivers, W. H. R.   *Conflict and Dream.* New York: Harcourt, Brace, 1923. Pp. 65–75; 182–185.
45. Freud, S.   Instincts and Their Vicissitudes (1915). In *The Standard Edition of the Complete Psychological Works of Sigmund Freud,* tr. and ed. by J. Strachey with others. London: Hogarth and the Institute of Psycho-Analysis, 1957. Vol. XIV, p. 124.
46. Snyder, F.   Toward an evolutionary theory of dreaming. *Amer. J. Psychiat.* 123:121–142, 1966.
47. Kleitman, N.   *Sleep and Wakefulness* (2d ed.). Chicago: University of Chicago Press, 1963. Pp. 280–281.
48. Mack, J.   Nightmares, conflict and ego development in childhood. *Int. J. Psychoanal.* 46:403–428, 1965.
49. Shackle, J. W.   A note on night terrors. *Lancet* 1:287–288, 1928.
50. Kanner, L.   *Child Psychiatry* (3d ed.). Springfield, Ill.: Thomas, 1957. Pp. 499–503.
51. Schur, H.   Hallucinations in Children. In Kanzer, Mark (Ed.), *The Unconscious Today.* New York: International Universities Press. In press.
52. Dement, W.   An Essay on Dreams. In Newcomb, T. (Ed.), *New Directions in Psychology.* New York: Holt, Rinehart & Winston, 1965. Pp. 135–287.
53. Esman, A. H.   Visual hallucinosis in young children. *Psychoanal. Stud. Child.* 17:334–343, 1962.
54. Eisenberg, L.   Hallucinations in Children. In West, L. J. (Ed.). *Hallucinations.* New York: Grune & Stratton, 1962. Pp. 198–208.
55. Wilking, V., and Paoli, C.   The hallucinatory experience. *J. Amer. Acad. Child Psychiat.* 5:431–440, 1966.
56. Macnish, R.   *The Philosophy of Sleep.* New York: Appleton, 1834.
57. Still, G. F.   Day terrors (*pavor diurnus*) in children. *Lancet* 1:292. Feb. 1900.
58. Gross, M. M., and Goodenough, D. R.   Sleep Disturbances in the Acute Alcoholic Psychoses. Presented at 133rd Annual Meeting of AAAS, Washington, D.C. Dec. 27, 1966.
59. Gross, M. M., and Goodenough, D. R.   Observations and Formulations Regarding REM and Other Disturbances of Sleep in the Acute Alcoholic Psychoses and Related States. Presented at Sleep Research Symposium, 1st. International Psychosomatic Week, Rome, Italy, Sept. 11, 1967.
60. Sendak, M.   *Where the Wild Things Are.* New York: Harper & Row, 1963.
61. Nagera, H.   Sleep and its disturbances approached developmentally. *Psychoanal. Stud. Child.* 21:393–447, 1966.

62. Isaacs, S.   *The Nursery Years.* London: Routledge, 1929.
63. Fraiberg, S.   *The Magic Years.* New York: Scribner, 1959.
64. Levy, D.   Psychic trauma of operations in children and note on combat neurosis. *Amer. J. Dis. Child.* 69:7–25, 1945.
65. Rochlin, G.   Personal communication, 1965.
66. Macnish, R.   *The Philosophy of Sleep.* New York: Appleton, 1834. Pp. 47–48.
67. Waelder, R.   *Basic Theory of Psychoanalysis.* New York: International Universities Press, 1960.
68. Goodhart, J.   *A Guide to the Diseases of Children.* Philadelphia: Blakiston, 1885. Pp. 543–544.
69. Kanner, L.   *Child Psychiatry* (3d ed.). Springfield, Ill.: Thomas, 1957. Pp. 499–500.
70. Klein, M.   Psychological principles of infant analysis. *Int. J. Psychoanal.* 8:25–37, 1927.
71. Klein, M.   Infant analysis. *Int. J. Psychoanal.* 7:31–63, 1926. Footnote, p. 37.
72. Despert, J. L.   Dreams in children of preschool age. *Psychoanal. Stud. Child.* 3, 4:141–181, 1949.
73. Foster, J. C., and Anderson, J. E.   Unpleasant dreams in childhood. *Child Develop.* 7:77–84, 1936.
74. Kimmins, C. W.   *Children's Dreams.* London: Longmans, Green, 1920.
75. Jersild, A. L., Markey, F. V., and Jersild, C. L.   Children's Fears, Dreams, Wishes, Daydreams, Likes, Dislikes, Pleasant and Unpleasant Memories. *Child Development Monographs,* vol. 12. New York: Teachers College, Columbia University, 1933.
76. Freud, S.   Analysis of a Phobia in a Five-Year-Old Boy (1909). *Standard Edition.* 1955. Vol. X, pp. 50–149.
77. Freud, S.   From the History of an Infantile Neurosis (1918 [1914]). *Standard Edition.* 1955. Vol. XVII, pp. 7–122.
78. Brunswick, R. M.   A supplement to Freud's "History of an Infantile Neurosis." *Int. J. Psychoanal.* 9:439–476, 1928.
79. Harnick, J.   Critique of Brunswick's "Supplement to 'Freud's History of an Infantile Neurosis.'" *Int. Z. Psychoanal.* 16:123–127, 1930.
80. Harnick, J.   Response to Brunswick, rebuttal. *Int. Z. Psychoanal.* 17:400, 1931.
81. Lewin, B.   Phobic symptoms and dream interpretation. *Psychoanal. Quart.* 21:295–322, 1952.
82. Weinshel, E. M.   Severe regressive states during analysis. *J. Amer. Psychoanal. Ass.* 14:538–568, 1966.
83. Frosch, J.   A Survey of Psychoanalytic Concepts of the Relationship Between Dreams and Psychosis. Paper read at meeting of American Psychoanalytic Assoc., Boston, Mass., May 10, 1968.
84. Freud, S.   On the Grounds for Detaching a Particular Syndrome from Neurasthenia under the Description "Anxiety Neurosis" (1895 [1894]). *Standard Edition.* 1962. Vol. III, pp. 90–120.

85. Freud, S. Some Additional Notes on Dream-Interpretation as a Whole (1925). *Standard Edition.* 1961. Vol. XIX, p. 135.
86. Freud, S. An Outline of Psychoanalysis (1940 [1938]). *Standard Edition.* 1964. Vol. XXIII, pp. 170–171.
87. Freud, S. New Introductory Lectures on Psychoanalysis (1933 [1932]). *Standard Edition.* 1964. Vol. XXII, p. 29.
88. Freud, A. *The Ego and the Mechanisms of Defense.* New York: International Universities Press, 1946.
89. Eisler, M. J. Pleasure in sleep and disturbed capacity for sleep: a contribution to the study at the oral phase of the development of the libido. *Int. J. Psychoanal.* 3:30–42, 1922.
90. Lewin, B. *The Psychoanalysis of Elation.* New York: Norton, 1950.
91. Spitz, R. The primal cavity: a contribution to the genesis of perception and its role for psychoanalytic theory. *Psychoanal. Stud. Child.* 10:215–240, 1955.
92. Szalita-Pemow, A. B. The "intuitive process" and its relation to work with schizophrenics. *J. Amer. Psychoanal. Ass.* 3:7–18, 1955.
93. Piaget, J. *The Child's Conception of the World.* New York: Humanities Press, Inc., 1929.
94. Werner, H. *Comparative Psychology of Mental Development.* New York: International Universities Press, 1948. P. 91.
95. Piaget, J. *The Child's Conception of the World.* New York: Humanities Press, Inc., 1929.
96. Guthrie, L. On Night Terrors, Symptomatic and Idiopathic, with Associated Disorders of Children. In Albutt, T. C. (Ed.), *A System of Medicine.* New York: Macmillan, 1900. Vol. 8, p. 231.
97. Snyder, F. The new biology of dreaming. *Arch. Gen. Psychiat.* (Chicago) 8:381–391, 1963.

2

The Clinical Occurrence of Nightmares in Children and Adults

So two nights passed: the night's dismay
Saddened and stunned the coming day.
Sleep, the wide blessing, seemed to me
Distemper's worst calamity.
The third night, when my own loud scream
Had waked me from the fiendish dream,
O'ercome with sufferings strange and wild,
I wept as I had been a child;
And having thus by tears subdued
My anguish to a milder mood,
Such punishments, I said, were due
To natures deepliest stained with sin,—
For aye entempesting anew
The unfathomable hell within,
The horror of their deeds to view,
To know and loathe, yet wish and do!
Such griefs with such men will agree,
But wherefore, wherefore fall on me?
To be beloved is all I need,
And whom I love, I love indeed.
— COLERIDGE [1]

The Multiple Determinants of Nightmares

In trying to obtain a thorough understanding of a severe anxiety dream or nightmare, it is necessary to examine several closely interrelated factors, all of which may contribute to the production of the dream. These are:

39

1. External factors, such as environmental events that have threatened the life or body of the dreamer, losses of important persons, changes in the life situation and, especially in the case of children, parental fears or fears of others that are transmitted or communicated to the individual, all of which may become precipitants of the nightmare and be reflected in its content

2. Traumatic memories of events in the recent or distant past

3. Instinctual aspects, or drives arising from within the individual

4. Developmental factors, including the psychosexual level of development and the conflicts that are associated with the effort to master particular developmental tasks

5. The state of the ego, including the ego's capacity for reality-testing

6. The state of the dreamer's relationships with other persons

7. Physiological factors, such as the role of the sleep phases, fever, drugs, alcohol, or recovery from anesthesia

8. Regressive forces, including the regressive aspects of sleep itself, which contribute to the revival of earlier traumatic memories, anxieties, and conflicts.

EXTERNAL FACTORS.   In each example of a nightmare, or *pavor nocturnus* attack, that I have had the opportunity to study intensively, the attack has proved to be the result of the confluence of both environmental and internal factors.

If the external threats to a child's person or body parts are obvious and severe, they may sometimes seem to be responsible in themselves for the attack. Gardner, for example, reports that, among a group of children suffering from night terrors, threats of mutilation preceded the attacks in every instance [2], and Hadfield includes among his types of nightmare those resulting from "objective experiences" [3]. A three-and-a-half-year-old girl, known to the author, began having repetitive nightmares about scary monsters after her older siblings had taken her down to a dark cellar and teased her about monsters that lurked in it. In addition, her uncle had played a game with his hands in which he had pretended to remove her nose. In her nightmares she would sometimes cry out in terror, "Don't take my nose away." The history of several of the patients of Fisher et al. revealed that nightmares had begun following violent traumatic experiences [4]. One young woman began having severe anxiety dreams following a rape, while the nightmares of another began after she had been choked into unconsciousness by her boy friend. A third patient had continuous nightmares since age three or four, when her father threatened to choke her to death.

However, careful exploration of the situation will reveal, as in the cases of Fisher et al., that other factors were also operating. This point is illustrated by a boy nearly five years of age of the author's acquaintance who for three months had awakened almost nightly, screaming with fear for his mother. The only other words she could make out were "Lily [his older sister's name], no." The history revealed that, shortly before the night terrors began, his bitterly jealous sister had threatened him, "Eddie, I'm going to shoot you with a gun, then cut you up with a knife into little pieces and put them in a bag and put them in the water, and then there'll be no more Eddie."

One might think that a threat such as this, which Eddie took most seriously, would be sufficient in itself to precipitate the nightmares. Additional history, however, revealed that a housekeeper to whom he had been devoted had left in anger at about the same time as the sister's threat with the avowal that the children would not see her until her "dying day." Further exploration revealed a desperate concern about when the housekeeper's, his mother's, or his own dying day might come. These anxieties also contributed to the production of the nightmares. Furthermore, the mother and father had recently separated, and Eddie had insisted on taking the father's place in his mother's bed. Fear of punishment for his ostensibly triumphant oedipal wishes, as well as anxiety about the loss of his father, may also have played a part in his night fears.

A nightmare precipitated by an incident similarly perceived as threatening was experienced by a twenty-four-year-old man recovering in the hospital from a drug-induced psychosis. He described to the examiner that in a "vicious dream" he had been trying to escape from a noise that terrified and threatened to destroy him. He was paralyzed, completely frozen, unable to scream, and increasingly terrified as the noise came closer. He felt completely helpless and defenseless, being able in the dream finally to stumble to the door, presumably to escape, and succeeding eventually in waking himself up, whereupon he found himself still in his bed.

When the patient tried to determine what might have precipitated the dream, he recalled that the evening before the nightmare he had watched a boxing match on television with another patient, a former boxer and a stronger and bigger man than himself. The other man was known to the patient as "the one who went beserk and beat up one of the attendants." As they watched the fight, the patient noticed that, whenever one of the boxers "really got hit," the other patient would react to it and play the part of the puncher. As the patient put it, "This is a big guy—he'd already beat the hell out of somebody, and I'm sitting there, and I see him going like this [gesticulates a punch] every time one of them gets wild."

The patient then recalled that he had first begun to have nightmares similar to the one described about four years earlier when his older brother, with whom he had been living at the time, became mentally ill. The brother had developed a violent, uncontrolled temper, and the patient lay awake at night fearing that his brother would go wild and kill him or himself or another member of the family. During this period the patient went to bed at night with a knife under his pillow for protection. It was in this context that the nightmares began. The relationship between the nightmares and the patient's own repressed rage and hostility also soon became evident (see Chapter 4 on the relationship between nightmares and aggression).

It is possible that fear responses to threatening external stimuli may be based in part upon innate releasing mechanisms rather than upon any prior experience of the individual with the particular danger situation in question. Sackett, for example, has shown that monkeys reared in isolation from other monkeys or from human beings will nevertheless show disturbed, fearful behavior when confronted with pictures of another monkey with a menacing expression or posture [5]. This finding suggests that the potentiality for such fear responses is innately present in the organism and requires only the appropriate releasing stimulus to elicit it. The intense fearfulness that occurs in nightmares may be the result of an exaggerated release of such innate fear responses in relation to dream representations of external threat situations whose potential danger cannot be estimated accurately during sleep. Many children under three, for example, seem to develop brief phobic responses or nightmares after having been confronted with a menacing animal, noise, or machine even when they may have had no prior experience that would make them regard the object as dangerous or harmful.

It should be stressed that a child's exposure to violent events or stimuli will not in itself necessarily precipitate nightmares. In a study of the dreams of thirty-two boys of ages six to twelve, Foulkes [6] found no increase in disturbing dreams or dreams with aggressive content following the viewing of a violence-filled film about Indian raiders. If environmental threats are to become traumatic and to play a part in precipitating nightmares, especially in children over 3 years of age, evidently they must be specifically meaningful in relation to the internal fears and conflicts that are current for the individual or that were once active in his life.

Instances in which parental fears or symptoms are transmitted or communicated to children and result in anxiety dreams and other sleep disturbances have frequently been described [7–9]. Hirschberg and Nagera [8, 9] have emphasized the influence of the mother's conflicts, fears, and tensions in producing the child's sleep difficulties. In a previous publication [10] I have described the nightmare of a boy of thirty-four months who awoke in terror, hallucinating that a bird had pecked off the nose of a snowman outside his window. His mother had shown some fear of birds, and several months before the dream she had playfully caught the boy's nose in her fingers at the last line of "Four and Twenty Blackbirds," in which the bird pecks off the maid's nose.

Another example of the influence of parental fears occurred in a nine-year-old girl (see Chapter 4, page 139) who suffered from severe nightmares with violent content based on oedipal anxieties, especially fear of her murderous impulses toward her mother. Interviews with the mother revealed that, several days before the child's dream, she herself had had a nightmare in which she had screamed out in fear while asleep. In this nightmare she had dreamed of the death of her own mother. Also, shortly before the child's nightmare, the mother had cried out in the night during a violent argument with her husband. When the child inquired about the matter, the mother, knowing that the child was aware that she was prone to cry out in her sleep from nightmares, explained that she, too, had had a scary dream. On another similar occasion she explained that she had "hurt" herself. The mother herself had had a terror of the dark as a child; from the time she was four, she had had severe nightmares, which had continued virtually without interruption into adulthood. The mother identified deeply with the fearfulness experienced by the girl in her nightmares and thus could not offer a firm and realistic attitude toward the child's terrifying fantasies. She reacted instead by taking her into the parental bed, which in turn aggravated the child's underlying conflicts.

The psychological processes whereby children incorporate fearful attitudes and even the conflicts of their parents or of other adults are poorly understood. Several mechanisms are involved; the most important appears to be the unconscious confirmation of the validity of the child's fear that is provided by the parents' manifest incapacity to deal with the same object or source of fear as it arises in themselves. In the two examples given above, the playful handling of anxiety in the one instance and the mother's being driven by her own discomfort to inadvertent deceit in the second actually operated as additional threats to the children.

TRAUMATIC MEMORIES.   Disturbing memories may exert a continuing influence, contributing to the production of nightmares long after the occurrence of the events with which they are associated. Nightmares may be a cardinal symptom of the so-called traumatic war neuroses. In these disorders, the subject relives in the nightmare the terror and helplessness he experienced when the traumatic event occurred. The powerful affects associated with this experience are successfully warded off during the daytime but, as repression relaxes during sleep, the traumatic memory forces itself upon the ego, and terror recurs. Often the individual feels that he has betrayed his own ideals or values by not having acted more effectively, for example, to save a friend who was killed. One of the functions of the recurrent nightmare in this situation seems to be to expiate repeatedly the unconscious guilt the dreamer feels. The pain associated with this guilt serves in turn as an additional motive for repression, thus preventing the individual from remembering the experience during the daytime. Sometimes the disorder remains limited to nightmares in which the traumatic memory is circumscribed, while the individual is enabled to function effectively during the daytime. In more severely disabling cases conversion symptoms, including paralyses and psychogenic seizures, can occur. These indicate that the conflicts associated with the traumatic memory have resulted in the inhibition or dysfunction of motor and sensory apparatuses.

The association of severe, repetitive nightmares with a traumatic memory is not, of course, limited to the war neuroses. A traumatic neurosis appears to occur characteristically following severely traumatic events that have occasioned the death or a severe threat to the life of a person close to the individual, with or without serious injury or danger to the individual himself. At the time of the incident, the individual felt helpless and utterly unable to act effectively to protect the victim. Although realistically there may be nothing that the person could have done, a profound feeling of having betrayed one's ego ideal in failing to save or protect the other person may nevertheless occur. The painful guilt and shame associated with the memory of the traumatic event serve as motives for repression and prevent the integration of the incident, which is relived repeatedly in the regressive experience of recurrent nightmares.

A typical example of this type of neurosis was provided by the case of a twenty-seven-year-old mother of two children who was hospitalized because of attacks of overbreathing, associated with difficulty getting air, and paralysis of the right arm of one week's duration. In addition, the patient had also suffered for five years from recurrent nightmares, which occurred about twice each month.

Further history revealed that the nightmares had begun following the death from suffocation of an infant son after a brief respiratory illness. The patient had found the baby in the morning blue and barely breathing. As the nearest hospital was almost an hour distant, the baby was taken by ambulance to the local physician. Despite the administration of oxygen in the ambulance, the baby died on the way to the doctor's office. The patient was visiting her parents in a community some distance from her home and reproached herself through the years with the thought that, had she been at home, a hospital would have been nearby. Because of this feeling of guilt, it became difficult for the patient to think about the loss, to experience fully during the waking hours the pain that accompanied it, or to share feelings of grief with those close to her.

In her nightmares, however, she vividly reexperienced the anguish associated with the traumatic event. She felt intensely frightened; in addition to the details surrounding the child's death, in her dreams she also relived her preparation of the child's clothes for his burial, the funeral and burial, and the ride home from the cemetery. The nightmares recurred more frequently as the anniversary of the child's birth approached. The attacks of suffocation and paralysis that led to her hospitalization occurred as she anticipated the approaching hospitalization of her daughter for a surgical procedure. As she spoke of this to her psychiatrist, she revealed that in her respiratory attacks she was vividly experiencing the suffocation that she imagined her daughter would undergo when she was put under anesthesia.

This difficulty in getting air was also associated with her identification with the suffocation of her infant five years earlier; the daughter's hospitalization had been scheduled for the same date as her dead son's birthday.

The death of her baby was an overwhelmingly traumatic experience for this young mother. She had felt utterly powerless to save the child and had no ego defenses with which she could fully integrate the experience. Her guilt regarding her own contribution to the incident, however unrealistically based, created an additional dimension to her pain and a further motive for repression. During waking hours she was ordinarily able to keep the memory of the traumatic event out of her awareness, but she could not protect herself from reliving the feelings of terror, pain, and helplessness in recurrent nightmares. In her nightmare reenactment of the events surrounding the funeral, the patient revealed her struggle to integrate the traumatic event. When the current stress of her daughter's anticipated hospitalization, surgery, and anesthesia repeated too vividly and literally the traumatic elements of the earlier event, a further failure of repression resulted. The patient was no longer able to limit the reliving of the traumatic event to harmless nightmares alone. She experienced conversion symptoms—hyperventilation attacks, difficulty in breathing, and motor paralysis—that also expressed the essential elements of her conflict. The traumatic neuroses are discussed further in Chapter 7, page 214.

It is less well appreciated that the traumatic memory may be principally of an act or acts committed by the subject himself in which immediate external threat played a relatively minor role. This is strikingly true of adolescents I have known who committed murders. Following the murder, the youth's memory of it and his feeling of responsibility for the act have operated as a severe traumatic element, leading to the production of repetitive nightmares.

Nightmares following a murder that operated as a traumatic event were experienced by a twelve-year-old boy who stabbed to death a boy of six. Following the murder, he suffered from repeated punishment dreams and nightmares in which he relived the event, with various degrees of distortion. The killing occurred when the boy panicked after accidentally injuring the little child while playing mumblety-peg with a penknife. Not realizing how slight the injury was, he had suddenly become terrified that the screaming child would tell his mother, who would not believe the injury accidental. He had conjured up images in his mind of her "grabbing me and slapping me and taking me to the police. They'd beat me and handcuff me and take me to prison, and all the big guys would beat me up and smack me around." In a fit of irrational terror he stabbed the screaming child many times in the head to silence him. Although he was able "when I am conscious" to keep these struggles out of mind, in his dreams he relived many forms of assault and punishment, often awaking in terror or otherwise deeply upset. In one dream, a month after the killing, the dead boy's mother shot him in the head. So vivid was this dream that, after waking up in terror, his head hurt, and he felt that he was really dying from a head injury. In another dream a year later he went before the youth authorities and was discharged from the state correctional institution. Back in his home town, he went to school on the bus, and talked and joked happily with friends. He dreamed that when he got to school one of the boys began to tease him—"bugging" and "ranking," he called it. "We don't want a murderer in our school," the boy said. The patient struck him with his fist and killed him. He was sent back to the institution and entered the gate handcuffed, whereupon he awoke upset and in great fear. In his dreams he repeated the expression of the violent impulses that had led him to kill the smaller child, while at the same time he always imposed upon himself a severe retaliatory punishment. Through the repeated dreams he sought to master this overwhelmingly disturbing traumatic experience, the memory of which afflicted him above all during sleep.

In an adult, a current threatening situation will sometimes become linked with the memory of a traumatic childhood incident, resulting in the production of a nightmare. This was illustrated by the experience of a thirty-year-old man, who learned from a urologist that he must enter the hospital for cauterization under general anesthesia of some small warts at the end of his penile urethra. That night he had a dream in which he underwent the operation, but the warts were cut off instead of being cauterized. When he revived from the anesthesia, still in the dream, his penis hurt and the surgeon said to him, "That's only the beginning. I'll have to do more." The patient awoke in terror; the surgeon's "more" made him think of having his penis or testicles cut off.

As the patient talked to his analyst further about his fear, it became clear that what he feared most was neither the procedure nor castration, but succumbing to the anesthesia and the injections he anticipated in the hospital. The anesthesia meant helpless surrender, in which he could not defend himself, and the injections were associated with the memory of several preventive rabies shots he had received when he was slightly more than two years of age after being nipped by a dog thought to be rabid. He recalled the utter terror and helplessness he felt when his mother brought him to the hospital for these injections, which were probably administered into the abdomen. The overwhelming quality of the anxiety and helplessness he had experienced as a two-year-old, the feeling that he would be destroyed, was relived in the nightmare he experienced as an adult prior to entering the hospital. In addition, he felt distrust regarding "what they're going to do to me," and he experienced the same hatred and rage toward the nurses and other hospital personnel that he had felt toward his mother and the doctors at the time of the childhood injections, which he had interpreted as a betrayal of trust.

INSTINCTUAL ASPECTS.   Nightmares are associated with one of the most intense forms of terror that human beings can experience. In their content, intense, usually violent conflicts are often nakedly revealed. There is no good evidence, however, that this intensity of anxiety is necessarily correlated with a parallel intensity of instinctual drives or wishes provoking the nightmare or occurring during the dream. The ego aspect may be the more important, that is, the ego perceives helplessness and a fundamental threat to existence.

Nevertheless, the instinctual drives generally play an important role in the production of nightmares. The ego in sleep, deprived of reality-testing and supportive objects, tends to link external threats, which have become represented internally, with unacceptable wishes, and to project drives, wishes, or impulses onto the dream's hallucinatory images. These images are then responded to as though they were real creatures or events that actually threaten the individual. As will be discussed in Chapter 4, this tendency to project is especially true of aggressive or destructive impulses, which may find representation in nightmares, while sometimes having given little evidence of their activity during the waking hours. This aggression often has a savage, oral, and sadistic quality, even when it is provoked by conflicts of an oedipal nature or by conflicts occurring in later developmental phases. This suggests the strongly regressive aspect of nightmares.

An illustration is provided by a boy about four years old, in the midst of his oedipal struggle, who had not given up sucking his thumb. His nursery school teachers and his parents were urging him to do so, and he had actually asked for help in giving up the habit, whose pleasure and security had remained compelling. He had been generally naughty and provocative during this period, drawing many angry words and punishments from his mother. He had, for example, broken a little girl's plant, and his mother had threatened to give a plant of his to her. A beloved baby-sitter who had lived with the family was in the process of leaving the home; on one of her last mornings at the house, he would not stay at school, but had insisted upon coming home to be with her. That night he awakened his parents by entering their room, screaming in fear. He could be comforted only by being cuddled by his mother and by being allowed to sleep for a time on her side of the bed. In the morning he reported he had had a bad dream in which he had stepped on a cat that looked harmless enough at first, but then had suddenly and savagely dug its claws into his foot, causing him to awaken in great pain and fear and to rush to his parents' room. Distortions of perception continued. He said his mother had looked like a monster when he first went into the room. As he told of the dream in the morning, he showed his parents the cover of a book he had been looking at the night before, which probably accounted for the dream's manifest content. It showed a tough-looking cowboy astride a huge, fierce bobcat. One of the cowboy's feet, as the child pointed out, was just above and almost touching one of the cat's vicious-looking forepaws, from which extended long claws. The family's own cat was small and extraordinarily gentle. In this example of a nightmare of a normal child in the oedipal phase of development, the role of intense primitive aggression, projected onto the cat in the dream and onto his mother, as well, in the partially awake state, can readily be seen. The most immediate provocations of his aggression were the intense frustration of his oral pleasures in relation to the thumbsucking and the pressure upon him to give it up; the baby-sitter's departure; and his mother's angry reprimands and threatened punishments.

The role of sexual impulses in the nightmares of children and adults is not always clear. The analysis of dreams that seem overtly to be entirely aggressive in content will often reveal the fact that they were inspired by underlying sexual wishes and drives that have become associated with intense conflict and thence deeply repressed. In the case of conflicts involving rivalry over a loved person, where the sexual aim may be genital or pregenital, the aggressive and hostile component of the conflict, rather than the sexual wishes themselves, is most often given expression in the nightmare, as Jones originally suggested. The situation is further complicated by the strongly regressive quality of nightmares. Because of this regressive aspect, a very early and distorted conception of sexuality is revived and given expression in nightmares, a view deeply influenced by childhood pregenital sadistic impulses, as well as by an aggressive-destructive view of the sexual act. Since in nightmares the manifest issue at least is one of survival, with a threat to the very existence of the individual occurring in the dream, it becomes necessary to explain how sexual impulses and conceptions can become associated with destructive and life-threatening perceptions and feelings.

Nightmares lead us once again to consider questions of self-preservation, or what Freud called the ego instincts. The earliest libidinal investment of the infant in its mother is based, not only upon the need for gratification, but upon the need for protection, as well. Any disruption of this vital attachment confronts the helpless child with a threat to his own existence. In the middle phase of his career, during which his ego psychology was evolving, Freud saw aggression or hatred as intimately linked with the self-preservative instincts or functions [11, 12]. According to Freud, hate was also the original attitude of the ego toward an external world filled with unpleasure, thwarting the infant's libidinal aims and threatening its very existence. Hate and aggression, Freud thought at this time, thus served useful self-preservative functions, protecting the helpless infant by fending off disturbing stimuli from an alien world.

The vital relationship of aggression to self-preservation, although readily observable throughout the animal kingdom, was afforded much less attention after Freud separated aggression and libido as the two major instinctual groupings. Instead, self-preservation was then seen principally in relation to narcissism, especially its libidinal aspect. The later development of Freud's theory thus left little room for the self-preservative function of aggression. Nonetheless, in nightmares we regularly see the most intimate association between threats to the survival of the organism and the evocation of an aggressive response. We may agree that the perception of threat—whether it arises from within or without—and the wish to preserve the individual's existence may be based upon narcissism, that is, the *libidinal* investment of the organism in its own survival. However, when its very existence seems to be challenged, which is the case in nightmares, an *aggressive* response may occur and needs to be understood.

DEVELOPMENTAL FACTORS. The analysis of the nightmares of children and adults of various ages regularly reveals the fact that nightmares are likely to be precipitated by impulses and struggles that are appropriate to the current level of psychosexual development, whether this be oral-dependent, oedipal, or any later phase, although in the sleep situation conflicts related to earlier developmental phases are invariably revived. Several such examples occurring in children age thirty-four months to nearly twelve years were given in an earlier publication [10].

A nightmare may give clear expression, for example, to conflicts related to the toilet-training process.

A twenty-eight-month-old boy was in the process of becoming bowel trained—reluctantly. His parents went away on an overnight airplane journey without him and his brothers. He weathered the separation uneventfully, but a few days later, while his parents were out for a drive with his older brother, he remarked to the girl who was taking care of him, "Next time let's all go on the airplane." During this period he was expressing concern about bugs and their biting him, and he liked to "go get" them and squeeze them between his fingers, declaring to his father, "It's a good bug, Dad."

One night a few weeks later he woke up and repeatedly screamed with fear. When asked, he said that a big wind had blown him and an airplane had scared him and gone "bzzz"; also a bug had scared him and gone "bzzz." He was comforted, only to awake once more with the same fears. After this recurred several times, he was taken into his parents' bed and comforted; he continued to wake up but, on finding his parents there, he would go back to sleep without crying. The next day, when asked about the dream, he said that bugs had gone "bzzz," and he pinched his father hard on the chest to show him.

One might not have thought too much of the relationship of this behavior to his conflict about toilet-training but for an incident about two weeks later. He came to his father in distress, pleading to be changed and taken to the toilet. He had half completed his bowel movement and was able to finish it in the toilet, getting praise for his control. Several minutes later he came to his father, rolling a small brown sausage-shaped piece of material between his fingers. "It's a good bug, Dad," he announced. His father examined the object and asked him where he got it. "On the bathroom floor," was his answer. His father smelled it. "Don't eat it, Dad," he warned. He was asked if it was b.m. "No, it's *not* b.m.," he demurred innocently. Then, his face lighting up, he agreed, "It *is* b.m., good b.m.," and again, "It's a no-good bug."

In the nightmare conflicts related to bowel-training, anal sadism, and separation from the parents were brought together economically.

Many examples of nightmares related developmentally to oedipal and superego conflicts are given throughout this book.

Erikson was one of the first psychoanalysts to emphasize specific phases of human development after childhood and adolescence [13]. Significant dreams, Erikson noted, frequently occur at critical developmental junctures in an adult's life and express vividly the conflicts associated with these changes. They can usefully be understood, not only in terms of the infantile origins to which they may be traced, but also in relation to the individual's current struggles and life situation [14]. Severe anxiety dreams, or nightmares in particular, may occur at times of important change in the lives of normal adults and often stand out as landmarks that denote significant undertakings or critical shifts.

An example is provided by the case of a thirty-two-year-old research physician who had a severe anxiety dream several days before he was to present a paper before an important scientific meeting. In the dream, he was sitting in the audience in the hall where his paper was to be given; a speaker on the platform had just finished delivering a paper. He heard the chairman, a senior researcher whose criticism he feared and who he had thought might in fact discuss the paper, announce that the next paper would be his. He felt taken by surprise and realized with horror that he had left his slides and manuscript at home. At first he thought to himself, "Well, I've given this often enough. I can give it off the cuff without my slides." But then the feeling of horror returned, and he thought, "They'll never believe me. I can't prove it. What'll I do? My moment has come, and I've fluffed it." He woke up in a sweat, with tremendous gratitude and relief that the dream had not been true.

His first association was that without his slides he would have *no defense* against the belittling, cutting comments of the senior man. In reality, he had especially resented this particular colleague, whom he regarded as a mean person and undeserving of his renowned position. The young doctor was coming into his own as a research scientist, leaving the status of a promising but untried young man to become a respected worker in his own right. This was the direction of his ambition, and he welcomed the shift, but he also feared punishment for the hostility that underlay his competitive attitude toward his senior colleague. Familiar oedipal conflicts and castration anxiety could be uncovered with further analysis of the dream, but its most immediate significance derives from the struggle of the young man to master the important changes occurring in regard to his position and status. A postscript to the dream demonstrated vividly the internal conflict over ambitious strivings that this man was experiencing. He remembered to bring the slides to the meeting, but forgot to prepare his statistics, despite a reminder by one of his coworkers. He gave the talk without the statistics, which were not essential in this instance. Someone from the audience asked about the statistics; this was embarrassing, of course, but not nearly as humiliating as it would have been had he forgotten the manuscript or the slides.

Fatherhood is similarly a critical period. Becoming a parent may lead to the breakthrough of intense anxiety related to latent jealousy and hostility provoked by the infant. These emotions and the regressive identification with the helpless infant may combine to precipitate a nightmare. An example of such a situation is provided by a twenty-five-year-old intern who reported the following dream when his only child, a son of whom both he and his wife were deeply proud and fond, was eight months old:

I was in a long corridor of rooms. I went into the room where my son was supposed to be, but he wasn't there; the young man who was supposed to be watching him wasn't there, either. I was furious at this young man and extremely frightened and went to look for him. I found him, but not Teddy [the son], and I was angry at him for not watching Teddy. I came to another room where Teddy was strapped to a table; a physician I didn't know was piercing his ears and had some electrodes on Teddy's fingernails and toenails. I think he was trying to make them shorter. I had a vague feeling he was monitoring other aspects of his physiology and taking a cardiogram and brain wave. I was extremely furious, and I started screaming at this doctor, "What right did you have taking him out of the room? Did you have permission to perform this experiment? Why are you piercing his ears?" I was in a tremendous rage, and I was scared. I called a meeting of senior doctors to kick this guy out of the profession, and I told them that this doctor should lose his license. I screamed and screamed, and one of the senior doctors laughed at my screaming and said, "Why should you be so upset?" I started to leave the room, but I came back and screamed even more furiously, swearing at the first doctor, calling him all kinds of names and telling him he had no right to do that and that he should not be a doctor. He smilingly acknowledged that he should not have done this. I woke up petrified with a tremendous terror and still very angry. I was terrified of my own anger.

Of particular relevance for an understanding of this dream are the following facts. The couple was spending the weekend at the home of the wife's parents in a strange city. The child had not seen the grandparents for several months and seemed frightened of these strangers. In these unfamiliar surroundings, the child was unusually irritable, screamed a great deal, and required much comforting. His fingernails had presented a problem, for they had grown unusually long as a result of the difficulty in cutting them. As a consequence, he had frequently scratched his grandparents, which was an additional nuisance. During the night of the dream, the child had slept poorly; the father, concerned over his son's distress at sleeping in a strange crib and room, asked his wife several times if she did not fear that he might suffocate. He felt great tenderness for the infant, and in the past had enjoyed helping with his care. At this time, he identified poignantly with his son's distress and evident helplessness.

Earlier, however, the young doctor had been conscious of other feelings. The couple had made the trip reluctantly; both had thought how nice it would have been to make the trip without the child in order to obtain some relief from the incessant demands he made upon their energies and time. On the night of her husband's dream, the wife also had had an

anxiety dream in which she had "forgotten" to take Teddy with her and
had left him with her husband's parents in their home town. In terror
that she had abandoned the child, in her dream she drove to her in-laws
at breakneck speed over winding roads to save him.

When the couple actually arrived at the in-laws, they found the home
dark, cramped, and terribly inconvenient for caring for the baby; they
resented the fact that the child's anxiety in the presence of the in-laws,
with whom he was not familiar, precluded their taking over as the couple
had hoped. In the course of the evening, the father had several drinks
and talked more openly and intimately than before with his father-in-law
of the father-son relationship. They discussed whether a son should call
his father by his first name. Highly competitive with his own father, the
young man had had a problem in handling both his aggressive and positive
feelings in his relationship with his father-in-law; he wanted this man to
respect and like him. The new father had earlier recognized in himself a
high degree of competitiveness with men, accompanied by intense hostility
toward both superiors and peers, of whom he would often simultaneously
be quite fond. Highly ambitious for success in his profession, he was im-
patient at having to undergo an apprenticeship before taking over and
making outstanding contributions. He had always resented his younger
brother, who had long ago interrupted his exclusive relationship with the
mother. She had continued to indulge this brother, whom he regarded as
less talented and deserving than himself. In spite of his confidence in his
own abilities, which were in fact outstanding, he retained basic anxieties
regarding his masculinity and his relationships with persons in authority.
Earlier on the night of the nightmare described above, he had a dream
in which he was taking a ride with a woman, who told him that she was
married to a man "in order to restore his generativity."

This young man was at a critical period of his life, a time when
his desires for the satisfactions of mature adulthood had brought
him to fatherhood, and he had entered his chosen profession.
He had arrived at the phase of life that Erikson calls "generativity," as his interest turned to the care of the next generation.
Still, he had intense anxiety concerning his capacity to perform
these functions as he would wish. Furthermore, he had powerfully ambivalent emotions in relation to the demands and responsibilities incurred in this new period of adult life, and the
eight-month-old son had become the focus, not only of great
love, but of these negative feelings, as well.

Perhaps no event in an adult's life presents such a demand for
the relinquishment of narcissistic interests in favor of the investment of libido in another person as the birth of a first child. The
degree to which this demand is met with hostility has been little
studied. Although the child gave him much pleasure and satis-

faction, this father also wished to be rid of the demanding intruder who usurped his wife's affection, provoked anxiety about his capacity as a father, and encroached upon his personal freedom. Simultaneously, he was struggling with intense competitive striving, ambition, and insecurity in a new profession in which the satisfaction of real achievement, and the realities of inevitable limitation, had yet to bring about the kind of accommodation and maturation that helps to separate psychologically the professional situation from the residues of the oedipal conflicts. Professional persons in authority were still closely associated for this young man with his father; they, rather than his inexperience, were unconsciously held to be responsible for the delay in fulfillment of his ambitions. Still in the childhood of his profession, he linked his seniors with his own father, and they became the objects of his aggression and consequently of his anxiety.

The study of the dream, as Erikson has demonstrated in the analysis of a dream that occurred at a critical period in Freud's life, must include consideration of the life situation of the dreamer. The nightmare of this young father reflects his interlocked conflicts in relation to the advent of parenthood and his anxieties concerning his new profession. The dream's immediate precipitants are his mounting anger toward the demanding infant son; his sympathetic identification with the baby's helpless and seemingly vulnerable state; and an intimate conversation with his father-in-law, which brought to the surface ambivalent feelings toward his own father. He is, of course, the person responsible for watching his son, although he had hoped to discharge this responsibility upon his in-laws. He also has the wish to be rid of the child; his fear is of the fulfillment of this wish, though in the dream he projects the intention onto another doctor, whom he then furiously blames. This rage becomes linked with the sadistic prerogatives of the medical profession, exerted in a rather brutal manner in the dream upon the hapless child, again by an unknown physician. The anxiety that these destructive impulses occasion for the dreamer becomes linked with the anxieties that the young doctor experiences in relation to the senior doctors.

He is guilty about his ill will toward the child and frightened

that, in retaliation for his hostility, the other doctors will demand his own removal from the profession; in the dream, nevertheless, it is he who is active, who calls the meeting of his seniors,
who demands the ouster of "the other man," and who even ob-
tains his admission of wrongdoing. Despite this manifest vindica-
tion, the dreamer's terror upon awakening makes it clear that
the deeper sources of the anxiety—his own hostility and helplessness—have not been overcome. In the dream, we see the powerful use of projection to disclaim responsibility for aggressive
wishes. We have evidence that the fear of retaliation for hostility
is not the only source of anxiety. Anxiety about potency or "generativity"—or, more accurately, about its loss—is demonstrated
in the earlier dream fragment and again is related to anxiety
about fatherhood. The intense positive identification with the
helpless infant revives very early preoedipal anxieties concerning
suffocation, vulnerability, and abandonment. This combination
of rage and helplessness gives the young man's behavior in the
dream the quality of a temper tantrum, which in some respects
it resembles.

In this and the various other nightmares studied we have seen
how a phase-specific anxiety, or a conflict in a child or adult appropriate to a particular stage in the life cycle, becomes linked
with very early infantile terrors, bringing about the nightmarish
quality of the anxiety. Working in a psychiatric hospital, I have
been impressed by the frequency with which young residents, in
the face of the helplessness they feel in starting their new profession, experience severe nightmares based on the infantile terrors
that their regressed and sometimes violent patients revive in
them.

EGO ASPECTS.   When we direct our attention to the functions of
the ego, we take stock of its relationship to the external world, to
the instinctual drives, and to the self-critical faculties, which include the superego and ego ideal. An intense challenge from any
of these sources to the ego's integrative capacities, particularly a
challenge that induces feelings of helplessness, may contribute to
the occurrence of nightmares.

The role of actual events that are perceived as threatening to the ego appear to play a particularly important role in such nightmares. This fact seems closely related to the aspect of being overwhelmed that occurs in these dreams. Panic or overwhelming anxiety in nightmares, especially in small children, seems often to follow upon a single traumatic event; alternatively, it may be associated with a series of events whose cumulative effect is to inspire an anxiety that cannot be dealt with through daytime activity, the usual ego defenses, or other kinds of dreams. Losses of important persons, separations from love objects, verbal threats by a parent, moves to strange surroundings, hospitalization, surgery or other bodily injury, and deaths of relatives or acquaintances—all seem to be the most frequent disturbing events that overly burden the defensive capacities of the ego and give rise to nightmares. It seems possible that a threat to survival can be perceived in these events, taken to heart, and given expression in a nightmare without our needing to invoke instinctual drives or forces to account for the anxiety that occurs. The judgment of this threat may, of course, be incorrect or exaggerated, especially if the threat is associated with earlier events, with a time when the ego was less mature and more readily rendered helpless.

Some dreams contain images or other features one might think would result in the production of a nightmare—a menacing creature or force, for example, that threatens the dreamer, the seeming helplessness of the dreamer in the face of the threat, and the beginning of an intense fear response—yet a nightmare does not result. In some instances, individuals who were afflicted with nightmares as children have described how the frightening power of their dreams became reduced as they reached adulthood. Gide, for example, wrote that as a child he was "extremely funky; I used to have terrible nightmares from which I would wake bathed in sweat. . . . And suddenly the gland ceased to function. At present I can have horrible dreams, see myself pursued by monsters, knifed, cut in bits . . . but it never becomes a nightmare" [15]. A somewhat different development occurred in the case of Robert Louis Stevenson, as described in Chapter 3.

It is apparent that a variety of ego functions can operate within the dream itself, leading to the mastery of its content and preventing the development of affect of overwhelming proportions. Levitan describes a patient who employed depersonalization to forestall the development of intense affects and traumatization within her dreams; this was characteristic of her defensive patterns during waking life, as well [16].

In very young children, especially under the age of four or five, the inability to establish, even after waking, that the nightmare's oppressors are not real adds to the terror and overwhelming quality of the nightmare experience. One little girl insisted repeatedly to her doctor, while they were playing out the nightmare experience, that the monster was "right dere, next to me. It slept right dere." Even the drawings they made together of the monsters became real for her. One of his tasks in treating this child was to help her establish distinctions between dream, reality, and fantasy play.

The manner in which children struggle to reassure themselves of the nonreality of their nightmares, to tell themselves "this is just a dream" in order to feel less threatened, is well known. At times, children invent quite elaborate devices to combat anxiety in dreams. A nine-year-old girl, who had been suffering from nightmares, assured her doctor that she had come to know, while she was dreaming, that she was having a bad dream and that this helped her not to be afraid. He asked her how she had achieved this. She replied that, when she suspected she was having a bad dream, she approached anyone she saw and announced, "This is a dream." As long as no one contradicted her, she then knew that she was dreaming.

Other ego functions that characterize the individual's areas of strength may be brought to bear in a dream in order to prevent anxiety of overwhelming proportions from developing. This is illustrated, for example, by the dream of a sixty-five-year-old woman who had devoted her life to research in the social sciences. She dreamt one night that she opened a closet and was confronted with a huge and menacing black cat. She began to feel horror, terror, and disgust, which threatened to become overwhelming, but then suddenly had the thought that her son was engaged in psychological research and could deal with the cat without difficulty. However, some anxiety returned as she realized that his field was the study of human beings and that this was a cat. Still dreaming, she thought of the name of a psychologist whose field was animal study and, much reassured, fell into a calm sleep. This lady dealt with the anxiety-laden matter in her dream as she handled many situations in waking life, by treating it as a problem for research.

In the nightmares of both children and adults, the operation of internalized qualities of other persons, especially their aggressive or critical aspects, can be readily demonstrated. In children, current experience with angry persons—other children, teachers, or parents—frequently forms a day residue that finds its way into the dream and becomes represented directly as originally perceived or in exaggerated and distorted form as a terrible noise or a devouring monster or animal (see the case of Sam, for example, in Chapter 4). These raging figures are not, of course, merely representations of aspects of the parents' behavior or qualities, but are infused with the individual's own aggressive impulses and wishes that are projected onto the dream's images.

(It is not only these *recently* internalized, aggression-filled elements that play an active part in nightmares. Threatening figures or angry and critical voices from the past, incorporated into the personality from the time of earliest childhood, may confront the dreamer once again in nightmares, often several decades later, in a manner reminiscent of their earliest appearance to the small child. This is illustrated by the case of the elderly office worker described on page 72.\

(OBJECT RELATIONS. The availability of loved persons during the daytime or the existence of close relationships does not in itself provide immunity from nightmares. One of the principal factors contributing to the occurrence of such dreams is the inevitable separation from the parents or other love objects that occurs with sleep. We see in many of our case examples how the threat of abandonment or separation from love objects can contribute to the production of nightmares in which the dreamer feels lost and unprotected. Children and adults who live in a situation of chronic uncertainty regarding the stability and constancy of their object relationships may suffer from repeated nightmares.\

One result of a nightmare, especially in small children who cry out or come into the parents' bedroom, is to reestablish contact with a comforting person. The dreamer is enabled thereby to gain support in mastering the dream's anxiety and, in certain instances, to find aid in reestablishing reality-testing. It would probably not be accurate to say that this restoring of contact with another person is a motive in precipitating the dream, although in many instances it is possible to perceive in the content of the dream the wish for closeness or reunion with the love object. In Chapter 5 we will see the unfortunate consequences for future development that may result when the parental object is unavailable to the child when he has nightmares.

Nightmares may reflect in themselves the level of object relations. The manner in which the object is represented in nightmares, for example, will give some indication as to the developmental period in which the internalization took place. Children under the age of two will represent threatening aspects of other persons in nightmares as menacing machines, noises, or animals. Biting animals and simple monsters predominate in children from two to five; if human figures are represented, no sexual differentiation is usually made. More sophisticated monsters, machines, and human figures are found in the nightmares of older children and adults, usually with clearer sexual differentiation. However, because of the regression that occurs in dreams and nightmares, figures and images that are characteristic of earlier developmental phases tend to be represented side by side with those of later phases. Because of the relationship of nightmares in children and adults to anxieties and conflicts about destructive aggression, a preponderance of hostile figures is found in such dreams, creatures whose description usually betrays their origins in the ambivalence of the nursery years and in the small child's earliest relationships with the parents.

PHYSIOLOGICAL ASPECTS.   Although various physiological factors have long been known to contribute to the occurrence of nightmares or nightmarelike states, their mechanism and their relationship to psychological disturbances are poorly understood. Only in the past fifteen years has it been possible to differentiate various sleep phases on the basis of extraocular movements, electroencephalographic and electromyographic tracings, and other physiological indices and to correlate these phases with dreaming and other sleep disturbances. Hopefully, these techniques will eventually afford us a greater understanding of the contribution physiological changes during sleep make to dreaming and of the role of drugs, fatigue, fever, or other metabolic and pharmacologic agents in the occurrence of nightmares.

The evidence now available suggests that nightmares can occur at any time in the sleep cycle, although there are indications that the most explosive type of severe night terror attack, with relatively little mental content occurs, at least in adults, in the phase of non-REM, or slow-wave sleep. Fisher [17], however, has noted examples in experimental subjects of REM nightmares in which there was loud vocalization and terror. Since evidence of "ordinary" dreaming can be recovered in a higher percentage of cases from REM than from non-REM sleep, it would be worthwhile to look for additional factors that disturb the sleep-dream cycle itself in accounting for the occurrence of these nightmares. Fisher et al., for example, noted that their adult nightmare subjects tended to have more troubled sleep than normal subjects, with greatly increased frequency of awakenings, increased body movements, and frequent moaning, groaning, and sighing [4]. Both Broughton [18] and Fisher et al. [4] have shown that severe nightmares occur in association with physiological evidence of arousal from slow-wave (non-REM) sleep. As previously noted (page 15), we need still to account for what brings about the arousal or makes any given instance of arousal so terrifying. Fisher [17] was able in one instance to bring about a nightmare experimentally by sounding a waking buzzer; however, this experimental subject was known to be prone to nightmares. Such awakening failed to produce nightmares in other subjects equally prone.

Deliria that interrupt sleep and occur in association with fever, neurological disease, or certain types of intoxication seem in many instances to resemble nightmares that occur spontaneously. Eisenberg describes a characteristic case of a four-year-old boy with a purulent otitis media who developed a prolonged bout of severe nightmare-delirium when his temperature rose to 105°F. [19]. At the height of his fever, he "cried out in terror, striking out wildly to defend himself from monsters he saw attacking him" [20]. He was disoriented during the episode and hardly recognized his parents. I was recently asked to see a thirteen-year-old boy with a septic hip infection who had developed a frightening hallucinatory episode in association with a spiking fever of 103° to 104°F. He woke up at 3:00 A.M., picking at the bedclothes and, although oriented as to time and place, he claimed to see "little men two and six inches tall behind the mirror." He was combative when approached and complained of pain from three penicillin shots he claimed to have received in the head. These symptoms disappeared when his temperature was brought to normal. Although the systemic septic condition had induced the delirium, the hallucinatory state did not occur at the height of the fever, suggesting that a toxic agent associated with the septic illness and not simply the fever itself may have brought about the delirium. The fact that similar nightmare-deliria can occur in the absence of toxic or febrile states suggests that these agents trigger or augment fundamental psychophysiological mechanisms, but may not be sufficient causative agents.

Adults recovering from anesthesia after life-threatening surgical procedures will often report nightmarelike experiences in which death is represented symbolically. Similarly, patients with medical illnesses, especially heart disease, who come near to death from circulatory or respiratory failure during sleep will often report nightmares the next morning. An example of this occurred in the case of a forty-eight-year-old man, who experienced a cardiac arrest while sleeping. Resuscitation procedures, which included pounding on his chest, were successful. The next morning he could recall nothing of the experience except nightmares in which "all those huge giants were chasing the little people and stepping on their chests." Without knowing more precisely the time relationship between the dream and the cardiac arrest, one can only speculate as to the mechanisms involved in the precipitation of the dream. We may suspect that the ego perceived even in sleep the catastrophic danger associated with the heart stoppage and the resuscitation measures and that this perception, together with the cardiorespiratory difficulty, acted as a preconscious stimulus in the dream's formation. In this example, the dreamer's position of weakness and helplessness in the face of huge, powerful, and threatening forces is evident; the struggle for life is represented in terms that are typical of early childhood conflict—little people are threatened by the giants. There are other possibilities, however. The anxiety-filled dreams could, for example, have precipitated the cardiac arrest rather than followed it. Only all-night sleep records of such patients, furnishing frequent reports of dream content, could establish the exact relationship between such nightmares and the occurrence of life-threatening episodes.

Informative work regarding the role of a drug in producing nightmares has been done in relation to psychoses following withdrawal from alcohol [21, 22]. Chronic alcohol intake produces a severe alteration of all sleep phases. In each example studied by Gross et al. [21] the acute psychosis began at night; in several instances it was a continuation into waking of a severe nightmare that had interrupted sleep. Interestingly, in contrast to spontaneously occurring severe nightmares, these nightmares of alcoholics erupted during the REM phase that had built up to a high percentage of the total sleep time as a result of the effect of the alcohol prior to withdrawal [23]. Gross and Goodenough suggest that, rather than being simply a rebound phenomenon, the high percentage of REM time may be the result of the action of alcohol in building up or enhancing the REM state, while simultaneously inhibiting its discharge. This work and other studies of sleep and dream physiology pertaining to nightmares will be discussed further in Chapter 6.

REGRESSIVE ASPECTS.   Many of the phenomena observed in a nightmare or in association with the dream are usefully brought together by considering the various types of regression that occur in relation to it. If reference to the concept of regression does not explain the phenomena observed, it is at least a valuable way of ordering our thinking about many of the most characteristic features of these dreams.

Freud emphasized the topographical regression that occurs in dreams, the shift of cathexis from the motor to the perceptual end of the psychic apparatus, thereby endowing the latter with particular intensity [24]. Perhaps nowhere are perceptions, especially visual ones, endowed with such vividness or apparent reality as in severe anxiety dreams. To the small child the dream images are so compelling in their perceptual actuality, "so real" as the child on page 58 complained, that it is difficult to persuade him that what he dreamed has not actually occurred. In considering the loss of reality orientation and testing that occurs in these dreams, it is important to take into account this extraordinarily heightened vividness of perception. One important determinant affecting the ego's ability to distinguish objective reality from dream perceptions is the perceptual and affective intensity of the dream images themselves.

Instinctual regression, usually evident simply through inspection of the manifest dream content, is perhaps the most obvious type of regression that can be studied in nightmares. Whatever developmental levels of functioning the child or adult may have achieved, conflicts tend to be represented in pregenital—especially oral—terms; expressions of the most primitive forms of infantile rage and aggression are clearly evident in the nightmares of adults and children. As the dreamer turns away from objects in the outside world and temporarily abandons his investment in other persons, he simultaneously returns to a narcissistic state in which there is a great heightening of self-protective or self-preservative needs. The regression in the level of object relations to that which is characteristic of the early infantile relationship to the mother can be seen in analysis of the dream itself, which frequently reveals powerful longings for fusion and protected closeness with the mother. The reaction to the dream in children, who very frequently insist upon being cuddled by the mother after they awake in terror, also gives evidence of this regression.

Various types of regression of ego functioning occur in nightmares and contribute in significant ways to their clinical characteristics. Regression to a state of intense infantile helplessness in the face of overwhelming anxiety is a cardinal feature of nightmares. This is accompanied—Freud ascribed this to dreams in general—by a return to developmentally earlier modes of thought that he called the primary process. This type of thinking is characteristic of small children who, in their absorption with their own bodies and body sensations, draw upon familiar elements in the external surroundings to represent what they perceive of other people or feel in their own bodies. Symbolization, condensation (the representation of several ideas by a single perceptual element), displacement, distortion, projection, and other characteristics of primary process thinking are found in nightmares, as in other types of dreams. Nightmares seem to show an extreme range from the most literal representation of identifiable threatening elements of the outside world, with minimal symbolization, to the most bizarre and distorted or disguised symbolic representations. Although the reasons for this great range are not clear, it may be related to the unevenness of functioning of ego defenses in these dreams. Closely related to primary-process modes of thought is the regression of ego defenses that occurs in nightmares. These same phenomena of symbolization, distortion, condensation, and projection have also operated in the past as early defense mechanisms to which the dreamer may return once more in his desperate effort to deal with the elemental conflicts that confront him with the threat of annihilation in the dream. Although "failure of repression" has been a short-cut expression for designating these phenomena, it has probably also included what could be thought of in terms of the regression to earlier modes of ego defensive functioning.

We have already spoken of the loss of reality-testing that occurs within dreams of all sorts. Of all the types of dreams, loss of reality-testing seems most frequently to persist after awakening from nightmares. Although schizophrenic patients (see Chapter 5) have the most difficulty in reestablishing a firm reorientation to reality after awakening from a nightmare, normal children and even healthy adults may suffer for several minutes with persistent hallucinations and perceptual confusion in the same circumstances. This is probably the result of several factors. In the first place, the intensity of affect (especially terror) that is attached to the dream ideas and perceptions provides them with a heightened actuality that confronts the waking ego with a most difficult challenge. Secondly, ego regression in the dream may occur to a state characteristic of early childhood, when external and internal realities were not distinct. The restoration of more mature functioning following a nightmare may be difficult for a normal person and impossible for an acute schizophrenic during the psychotic period.

Finally, regression occurs in nightmares with respect to the representation of human objects in them. The parents or other important persons are represented, not as they are viewed by the more mature waking individual, but by their qualities as these were perceived in the preoedipal period in accordance with the highly ambivalent attitudes of this time, strongly colored by primitive aggression. The frequency with which fierce animals appear even in the nightmares of adults is related to this tendency to represent aspects of the parents as they may have appeared to the child when they were angry. The projection of the child's own hostility onto these images intensifies their apparent threat to him. Regression in nightmares may also affect portions of the personality that have seemed to function independently from the original objects. Personality structures that were formed from the internalization of object representations that have been built into apparently stable ego identifications temporarily undergo regressive transformations. Regression in this situation results in a kind of segregation or resegregation, in which structures such as the superego, which have come to function automatically within the personality, seem to become fragmented. The early object representations, especially hostile ones, then confront other portions of the ego in the dream in their original elemental form as an angry voice, noise, or other threatening or accusatory image.*

---

* Freud once likened the structure of the ego as it is formed in the course of de-velopment to a crystal whose boundaries, though invisible, are sharply laid down When pathological regressions occur, the lines of cleavage between the various fragments of the ego become evident to the observer. Although we must be cautious lest we invite an analogy to substitute for a fact instead of to serve as an illustration, this analogy seems particularly apt in representing the way nightmares can illuminate the lines of cleavage within the personality without necessarily resulting in its becoming shattered into the component parts, as seems to occur at times in certain psychotic states. (See Freud, S. 1933. *New Introductory Lectures on Psychoanalysis*. Standard Edition, 22:58–59.)

Three Additional Clinical Illustrations

Illustrations of the various determinants and characteristics of nightmares described in the preceding pages can be seen in the three clinical examples that follow.

RECURRENT NIGHTMARES IN AN EIGHT-YEAR-OLD GIRL. Recurrent nightmares were one of the principal reasons her parents brought Laura, an attractive and capable child, for treatment when she was eight years old. According to her parents, Laura had first had nightmares at the time of the birth of her baby brother when she was two years and nine months old, and these had become more intense at Halloween, a few weeks after the baby's birth, following a disturbing incident. She had gone trick-or-treating with her mother, and a child at one of the houses she visited appeared in a skeleton costume. Terrified, she had clung to her mother and was inconsolable even when the other child took off the costume and revealed her true identity. Laura continued to be a somewhat fearful child who suffered intermittently from nightmares. An important aspect of the nightmare experience was the fact that her mother came to her bedside and sometimes took her into her own bed. To this had been added the additional pleasure of telling mother about the dreams, which created a closer and more intimate relationship. In her treatment, Laura revealed an intense fear of separation from her mother; she needed, for example, always to have someone present in or near her room in order to go to sleep. The mother had found it difficult to give affection to the child during the child's first two years and had felt that the later clinging and difficulty with separation was an effort on both their parts to make up for this earlier lack.

Shortly before her treatment began, Laura had visited the planetarium and had become frightened when it was explained and demonstrated that the sun might become larger and brighter until it collided with the earth or encompassed it, destroying all life. Shortly after this trip, and about two months before she related the dream to her doctor, her mother reported that Laura had begun to have a recurrent nightmare in which a large yellow monster that resembled the sun came down the street, devouring the children at the houses along the way. As the creature approached her house, her mother sent Laura out in the street to turn off the garden hose, thereby bringing her into confrontation with the monster, at which point she awakened and screamed for her mother. Just before she began to have this dream, Laura had overheard her mother angrily berating her younger brother for turning on the garden hose without permission. She also had been reading a book on Greek mythology, which told how Mother Earth had eaten her children. Another story that seemed to intrigue her concerned the Oedipus myth, especially Oedipus' killing his father and tearing out his eyes.

When Laura finally was able to tell her doctor the dream, she told him of a huge stuffed toy snake she took to bed with her, holding his body between her legs and cuddling his head against hers. In addition to his obvious erotic properties, the snake also had a vital protective function, blowing away the bad dreams with his great breath. According to Laura, sometimes he attended parties, as her parents often did at night, where he consumed ice cream, candy, and hot dogs and become so tired that he neglected his protective role; the nightmare then recurred. She stressed how vital it was for her mother or father to pick her up and carry her into the parental bed when she had a nightmare. Another device she employed to reduce the anxiety content in the dreams, both in the analytic session and at home, was to elaborate it creatively into stories of enslavement and piracy in which she was no longer a helpless victim, but became instead the master story teller, fully in charge of the situation.

Laura's father's work required that he be away from home a great deal; in the course of her treatment, her intense attachment to him and the highly stimulating activity in relation to him that occurred in the parental bed when he was home became evident. Within herself, the most immediate source of the aggression that underlay the dream's content was the hostility she felt toward her mother. This hostility, which had both oedipal and preoedipal roots, was very threatening to Laura; she came to see the nightmare as a punishment for the hitherto unconscious aggressive wishes toward the mother.

Feelings of helplessness, which were of extreme intensity in the nightmare, were also a major issue in the treatment. As Laura had felt overwhelmed and powerless in the face of the devouring sun in the dream, in her treatment she revealed a similar sense of helplessness in the face of her mother's tendency to control and regulate her behavior and to demand, however subtly, compliance and goodness. The difficulty Laura experienced in controlling the hostile impulses which these demands called forth added further to the sense of powerlessness that dominated the dream. When her parents left her for the evening, she felt particularly helpless. On one such occasion she was left with a male teen-age baby-sitter, whose presence she found threatening. She experienced a sense of impotent rage; to reverse the feeling of impotence, she took her father's sword, which she said he had wrested from a German in combat, and playfully chased the baby-sitter around the house with it to scare him. The need to prevent separation from the mother and to seek closeness to her served also to offset the magical power of the hostile wishes toward the mother that arose in the context of the oedipal triangle. Laura was actively caught up in intensely conflicted oedipal relationships and was experiencing considerable anxiety over the erotic and aggressive impulses associated with these relationships. The recurrent nightmare took place following a series of external events that were meaningful and threatening because of their specific correspondence to the structure and content of her conflicts.

Several types of regression occur in Laura's nightmare and in the behavior and verbal content associated with it. Instinctual regression is clearly evident in her experiencing of the oedipal struggle in terms of being eaten and in her representation of her parents' pleasure with each other as a party at which much good food is consumed. Her relationships with her parents, especially with her mother, return in association with the nightmare to the cuddling type of closeness more characteristic of an earlier period of childhood. Ego regression to an earlier childhood state of helplessness or powerlessness is evident in the dream; Laura employs defenses outside the dream to offset these feelings. Finally, there occurs regression to early forms of symbolic thinking, in which the threatening parent is represented by such elemental cosmic symbols as the sun or the earth mother.

Fourteen months after the dreams of the yellow monster, Laura had another nightmare, which occurred in the context of her doctor's approaching vacation and the reduction in the number of her visits prior to termination of the analysis several months later. Through this dream, connections were established between anxieties regarding the processes of sexual intercourse and childbirth and earlier fears from the period between two and three years over separation from the mother and aggressive impulses toward her and the baby brother.

In the session prior to the one in which she reported the dream, Laura expressed curiosity about how babies were made and how two persons could be formed from one. With a mixture of hostility and curiosity, she broke the doctor's ballpoint pen in two in order to examine the dark fluid contained in the cartridge. Perhaps in this fluid, she thought, she might find an answer to the mystery of how babies were made.

After this session, Laura took the remains of the broken pen home and tried to remove the ink from the holder. She made a mess and stained her blouse, whereupon her mother angrily threw the cartridge away, despite the child's protests. Laura then went to bed and dreamt that she was in her room with her father and brother. In the dream, she said, "We have a real skeleton, and my mother is taking the bones apart. By the end of the dream they are all apart. It was very scary, and I woke up." She called to her mother, who came to her room and comforted her.

In her associations to the dream, Laura recalled the rage she felt toward her mother when she discarded the valuable fluid. Laura had been afraid to express this anger because "It's not right to talk back to your mother." She then picked up a knife on the doctor's desk and began to cut objects in two, resuming her exploration into the matter of how the baby comes out of the mother's body; she had actually been told at one time that both she and her brother had been delivered by Caesarian section. Laura then remembered the time when her mother went to the hospital to give birth to her brother, shortly after which she became so terrified at Halloween by the boy dressed in a skeleton costume. Although she was left in the care of her grandmother, she remembered being anxious about when her mother would return and what harm might befall her in the hospital. She remembered, too, the mixture of jealous anger—totally unacceptable to her mother—and interest she had felt toward the baby boy.

In the sessions that followed the skeleton dream, Laura continued to explore the mysteries of love and sexual union, the role of the male genital organ and fluids, and her understanding of conception and childbirth. Laura's sexual curiosity was first inhibited about the time of her brother's birth by the severe anxieties she experienced in relation to her mother's pregnancy, hospitalization and childbirth, and the arrival of the new baby in the home. Doted upon by both parents, this intrusive rival, who arrived endowed with the penis of which she had been deprived, aroused intense rage in Laura toward both the baby and the mother. However, she was forced severely to restrain this anger lest she run the risk of incurring her mother's retaliatory wrath, withdrawal of love, and abandonment. The intense anxiety contained in this conflict first broke through in the fear of the skeleton costume when she was two years and nine months and was revived again at nine years of age in the skeleton dream.

We have seen that Laura developed sexual interests and curiosities appropriate to her level of development between the time of the skeleton episode and the skeleton dream. With each of these interests, however, she experienced inevitable disappointments, additional foci for her hostility, and new fears. Laura's nightmares in the nine-year-old period were precipitated by the conflicts associated with current sexual and aggressive impulses. However, the fears that had originally been associated with destructive wishes toward the mother and baby brother in the period just before three were readily revived in the regressive dreams. Along with the anxiety associated with her interest in the penis, a persistent destructive attitude toward the male genital was demonstrated in Laura's play and also contributed to the anxieties of the later period. This may have originated at the time of her brother's birth. Laura's nightmares thus provided links, which were most valuable for her therapy, between the anxieties of the later developmental period and those of the earlier time that had remained active in her unconscious.

NIGHTMARE PERSISTING AS A DAYMARE OR HALLUCINOSIS IN A FOUR-YEAR-OLD GIRL.   Why some nightmares persist into the daytime as hallucinatory states has not been studied extensively. This phenomenon was more clearly recognized when the term *daymare* was more popular. In the recent literature, the focus upon the hallucinatory experience as such [25–27] has diverted attention from the important differentiation between those hallucinatory states, usually visual, that arise directly out of a nightmare and those that occur spontaneously during waking hours. It is likely that the former situation indicates a more temporary ego regression, limited to the area of dream-reality differentiation, one more closely related to acute conflicts and anxiety-provoking situations.

An illustration of a nightmare that persisted as an hallucinatory experience was provided by Sarah, a child described more fully in another context [10]. Sarah was slightly over four years old when her parents brought her for treatment because of the persistence of a fearful hallucination of a snake that had been following her about day and night for two days.

The hallucination was derived from a nightmare from which she had awakened screaming at approximately 3:00 A.M. while sleeping at an aunt's house, her parents having gone away for the weekend. In the dream, a garden snake had climbed up her shoulder, and she had picked it off and thrown it to the ground. Then a big snake had come out of the wall until it was bigger than the room and had bitten off both her arms and legs. She dreamed that she was with her aunt, that her parents returned and went to her funeral, but that monsters came and killed her father after also tearing off his arms and legs. Soon everyone in sight was killed, including her mother; she awoke in terror and continued for two days to be convinced that the snake was still following her.

Sarah's history revealed that for many months, with her mother's cooperation, she had been engaged in an intensely erotic relationship with her father, who literally preferred to sleep with her than with his wife. At one year she had awakened one night screaming in terror; the parents discovered that a live rat had gotten into her bed and awakened her. Although she appeared to be uninjured, she balked at going back to bed and awoke during the night, evidently from nightmares. For the next several years, Sarah had frequent separations from her mother, who had undergone numerous hospitalizations for surgical procedures, especially in the abdominal and genital regions, and for various other medical disorders; this brought about further opportunities for intimacy between Sarah and her father, which he did not forego. For about one year before coming to the clinic she had been masturbating actively despite frequent chastisement. Her intense interest in her father's and brother's genitalia was accompanied by highly aggressive behavior. Spying either one naked, she would cry out, "I see a penis"; she once grabbed her father's groin, showing pleasure when he registered pain. In her play she demonstrated further her intense aggressiveness, erotic excitement and curiosity, and marked anxiety that was focused upon the danger of phallic attack; in turn, this had become fused with projections of her own savage impulses to stick, bite, and attack others.

The most stricking fact about Sarah's case was that the hallucinations, which were themselves transitory, were not accompanied by any other lasting regression of ego functioning or suggestion of psychosis. A treatment program that emphasized obvious changes in the parents' behavior with the child, in addition to play therapy sessions with her, produced in a few months such improvement that the program could be terminated. Although Sarah had no conscious memory of the trauma involving the rat at one year of age, an experience that was itself accompanied by nightmares, it seems not unlikely that it served as a fixation point for later nighttime ego regression to a time when the capacity to differentiate dream perception from perceptions of external reality is practically non-existent.

The capacity to differentiate between dream and reality is a hard-won struggle for children and readily subject to regression in the face of anxiety and conflict, such as Sarah was encountering in her oedipal relationships. The frequent *actual* separations from the mother, experienced by Sarah as abandonment, together with the mother's submission to surgical procedures and the mother's *actual* retirement from the oedipal struggle served to increase further the child's problem of differentiating between powerful wishes and real events or consequences. In Sarah's case, lasting disruption of reality-testing occurred only in relation to a sleep experience —on a night when she was actually separated from her parents—in which regression of ego functioning regularly occurs. Havens [28] and Beckett et al. [29] have written of the role of actual early, severely traumatic events in the hallucinatory psychoses of adult life. In small children, transient hallucinatory episodes persisting after severe nightmares may be related to single or multiple traumatic events that undermine the child's newly won capacities for reality-testing, especially in the sensitive area of dream-reality differentiation. These events seemingly confirm the effects the child imagines will result from his or her destructive wishes and impulses.

NIGHTMARE OF A SIXTY-FOUR-YEAR-OLD WOMAN WITH DEPRESSION. The way in which the dreamer may be confronted by hostile or critical qualities of the parents much as they once appeared to the child before being incorporated into the structure of the personality was illustrated by the case of an elderly woman who was admitted to the hospital following a serious suicide attempt. The patient, a sixty-four-year-old single female office worker, had survived a potentially lethal overdose of barbiturates after several days in coma. On admission, her clinical picture was one of moderate-to-severe depression characterized by agitation, continued suicidal preoccupation, somatic complaints, feelings of hopelessness, and multiple self-reproaches and expressions of self-devaluation. The patient had lived all her life with her mother, now nearly ninety-five. Frustrated and often unhappy over the years, the patient experienced increased depression, precipitated by changes in her mother's state. Rather than appreciating her daughter's servitude, the mother had become more demanding and incapacitated and inveighed against the patient with such remarks as "Well, you won't have to wait long now before I'm gone and you can enjoy yourself." These comments provoked a great feeling of guilt in the daughter. She rationalized that, as her mother had nothing to live for but herself, by taking her own life she could enable her mother to die. The death wishes that underlay this thought were not evident to her.

As an only child, the patient's earliest years were relatively happy ones. This contentment was shattered suddenly when her father, of whom she was deeply fond, was killed in an accident when she was five years old. Raised in protected isolation by her restrictive mother, the patient clung in secret to a few treasured and idealized memories of her father. In her treatment, she became aware of a lifelong wish that her father instead of her mother had survived; she believed that then she would have had more freedom and would have been less sexually prudish and unfulfilled. Sometimes her father appeared in her dreams as gazing down upon her from heaven with a disapproving look. As a young woman, she had broken off several potentially close relationships with men because of guilt inspired by their too direct sexual interest. She had grown up with an anally devalued view of her body, herself, her sexual impulses, and the sexual act itself. Later in life she had had an actual affair, but only under circumstances she found degrading.

Shortly after her discharge from the hospital, it became necessary for the patient to place her mother in a nursing home despite the latter's strong protests. The mother insisted that her daughter would thus kill her. The hostile and destructive implication of any wish for separateness from her mother had kept the daughter tied to the old lady through self-sacrifice. The actual separation highlighted the conflict, particularly as the patient enjoyed her newly found freedom.

In her treatment, the childhood sources of her hostility toward her mother became increasingly evident. Unpleasant though she was, it was not the elderly sick woman in the nursing home, but the childhood mother, who had survived the beloved father, at whom the daughter increasingly directed her reproaches. The mother's qualities while the daughter was still a child were fully internalized in the form of a severe conscience that allowed the patient little pleasure and reproached her equally for her sexual and aggressive wishes. Longing since her father's death for a love relationship that would replace the one she had lost, the patient brought the full intensity of her thwarted erotic needs into the transference relationship with her young male doctor, which brought about further feelings of shame and guilt.

The patient had been treated in biweekly psychotherapy for five months when she had a most distressing dream in which a large Buddha—a cousin, of whom she was very fond, was currently sending picture postcards and letters from Thailand—abruptly lost its facial serenity and began to jeer at the patient, accusing her of being "deceitful, dishonest, crude, and cheap" and above all "lustful and lewd." The doctor was in the dream, laughing and saying, "Try and get out of that one." The dream continued in another setting, in which she was high on stilts in a room with no exits. A "fire starts down underneath" and threatens to consume her. Her associations to the dream led back to childhood nightmares in which she was suffocating in a small room that was contracting about her. Although she had a trusting relationship with the doctor, she complained that the therapy was an unwelcome intrusion, a painful penetration of her private thoughts. Her mother, she felt, would be opposed to it. At other times she saw the doctor as tyrannical or cruel, describing him in terms similar to those she had used to describe her mother or her own conscience. In the session before the one in which she reported the following dream, she talked of her father's birthday, which had occurred several days before, said she had looked at an early picture of him, and spoke of how she still clung to the childhood belief that father was in heaven, watching her with approval or disapproval. That night, after her session, she had the following nightmare.

It was one of those nights when I couldn't go to sleep. When I finally did go to sleep, I had been sleeping only a short time and I had the most frightening dream—it woke me right up and then I was awake again—and I couldn't go to sleep again, and it was almost 6 o'clock before I ever went to sleep. . . . I was in a car that seemed not to be moving—must have been a convertible—because it was open (the doctor's car was a convertible). There was this young man who kept coming from I don't know where, running up to the car and putting his arms around me and trying to kiss me. Now, you wouldn't think that would be frightening, but there was something very menacing about the whole thing. . . . I just sat there. So, finally, the last time this happened he had something in his mouth—a long sharp toothpick—and he tried to force it down my throat. That is when I woke up and my heart was beating and I was so frightened and I had been trying to fight him off in the dream and I was writhing around in the bed. It was funny. I was pushing my head back in the pillow, and you know I told you last week I had a bad time—I don't recall dreaming that night when I got up the next morning—this was the night of my father's birthday. When I got up the next morning, the hair on the back of my head was standing straight up in the air and I remember I said to myself, "You must have been having a battle in the night with somebody." But I don't remember dreaming that night. The very same thing happened this time, too.

Her first thoughts after reporting the dream were that what had begun as a seemingly affectionate approach had turned into an attack of a sexual nature. Then she spoke of severe guilt in relation to her mother, whom she wished never to visit, and connected this guilt with her mother's severe attitudes toward sexuality and with her own intolerance of what she called wishes for "animal satisfaction and pleasure." She described how she had become more tolerant of loving and sexual feelings, recognizing that "most people have it on their minds a lot more than I ever realized."

In the months that followed the nightmare, the dual themes of the patient's heterosexual erotic wishes and her savage pregenital rage toward her mother evolved further in the transference relationship. The doctor was perceived on the one hand as an erotically idealized figure conceived in the treasured image of her father. These powerful erotic feelings, which had a strong sadistic and destructive cast, brought intense guilt and violated her strict moral code based on internalized precepts of both parents. On the other hand, she experienced the doctor as an outrageous intruder, forcing out her thoughts with his words and presence and penetrating her carefully guarded mental life, much as her mother, in her anxiously overprotective zeal, had invaded the privacy of her thoughts and body when she was a child. Ultimately, her destructive rage toward the mother and her wish to be rid of her were revealed as the deepest source of the patient's guilt. This conflict was most clearly demonstrated in her associations to another dream in which she represented her mother as a madwoman in a mental hospital, "mercilessly" beating another patient with "superhuman strength." So badly did the mother behave in the dream that she had to be taken "away somewhere" where "I won't be able to see her any more." The patient experienced enormous relief in the dream and then, upon awakening, felt horror that she should have felt such relief at having been rid of her mother.

In the nightmare, the structure of the patient's depression had become dissected into its component elements. In the dream one week before the nightmare, a variety of internalized attitudes, derived from critical parental figures of the past, were projected onto the images of the Buddha and the doctor. The "toothpick" nightmare further revealed the instinctual impulses that had inspired this severe internal criticism and also had supplied the superego with its power.

The dream may be understood on several levels, although these are closely interlocked. Both derive from the patient's unresolved oedipal conflicts. In her relationship to the man, her erotic wishes are revealed as highly masochistic. However, her impulses are again projected onto a sadistic attacker whose aggression then threatens her life so that she awakes in terror. The genital wishes and excitement are regressively displaced in the dream so that the sado-masochistic coitus occurs at the mouth, as the attacker forces his "long sharp toothpick" down the patient's throat. Her immediate associations reveal the link with her beloved father, of whom she had been thinking that night. We may ask why the relationship with the man is conceived of in such savage and aggressive terms. Nothing in her associations, or for that matter in her treatment, revealed aggression of this intensity toward her father or other men. However, toward her mother, who had thwarted her every wish, she came increasingly to reveal aggression and murderous rage, based both on oedipal and pregenital frustrations. It is toward the mother, as revealed so clearly in the mental hospital dream, that the oral sadistic and annihilatory wishes are primarily directed.

Why, then, does the attack come from the man? If we look to the enormous guilt that both the hostility toward the mother and the persisting erotic wishes toward the father bring about in the patient, we are given a helpful clue. As she expresses the sexual and aggressive impulses in her dreams, the punishment for these wishes is meted out simultaneously. It is the work of her conscience, of her superego, that turns her aggression upon herself and all but exacts the death sentence in the nightmare, a sentence that the patient had in fact pronounced upon herself when she had decided to commit suicide several months earlier. Paradoxically, since dreams usually depend upon visual representation, the agents through which the instinctual wishes are expressed are also the creatures that represent the variety of internalized objects and attitudes that comprise the superego.

A nightmare such as this is therefore in one sense a punishment dream in which the internal tribunal has decided that mere criticism and a feeling of guilt are insufficient expiation for the crimes at issue. Capital punishment, an attack that threatens total destruction, has been found necessary, and the executioners dispatched by the court have gone into action. In the situation of the nightmare, the multiple internalized attitudes of early objects, whose largely unconscious criticism the patient had previously experienced subjectively as a state of depression or lowered self-esteem, receive a new component of aggression with which to attack the ego.

In the deeply regressive dream, a situation similar to that of the small child in relation to early perceptions of the parents is revived. The parent figures that were precursors of the superego —and perceived as external by the small child—confront the ego once more from "outside" in the adult nightmare, much as they did in childhood before some degree of homogeneity in the personality was achieved in the form of a well-internalized superego. Once more, the parent figures have gained the intense aggressiveness with which they were originally endowed by the child, partially on the basis of projection of the child's own aggressive impulses. Naturally, the introjects are not the identical ones of childhood. The experience with objects after childhood and the changes of later psychosexual development leave their stamp upon the images of the adult's nightmare. Nevertheless, it is striking how the adult nightmares of a patient can resemble those of his childhood and how often associations lead directly from the former to the latter, as in this lady's case (see also Brunswick's descriptions of the wolf-man's wolf dreams as an adult [30]). I know of no better example of the preservation in the adult of the unconscious components that were once the elements of a childhood conflict.

Nightmares Occurring During Psychoanalysis

In the course of psychoanalytic treatment, severe anxiety dreams or nightmares, remembered from childhood or evoked in the transference relationship, may contribute in a manner perhaps not equaled by any other psychological phenomenon to the reliving and ultimate understanding of the early childhood fears and defenses that produce the adult neurosis. This is particularly true of those conflicts that first took root as the result of environmental threats or traumatic experiences and produced intense emotions that were originally experienced as overwhelming by the child.

In the regressive psychoanalytic transference situation the painful emotions the small child experienced when he had a nightmare or "bad dream" may be relived in relation to the analyst, especially at times of vacation or other separations, without the recurrence of actual nightmares in the analysis. At such times the adult patient may experience intensely once again, especially at night, the feeling of aloneness, the dread of abandonment, and the longing for closeness with the parent (or analyst) as he had originally felt these emotions in association with a nightmare as a small child. Although oedipal anxieties deriving from erotic wishes for intimacy with the parent of the opposite sex, and fear of retaliatory anger on the part of the parent of the same sex, may be evoked in the transference relationship, it is the preoedipal terror of helplessness that seems to be revived most vividly and to resemble most closely the original childhood nightmare situation. At such times the adult ego may seem temporarily to disappear and an ego state similar to that of the small child may be reproduced in the transference relationship, with a strong sense of need for the analyst-parent's immediate presence and comforting, to remove the fear and to offset the malevolent powers of the ghosts, monsters, and witches that seem once more to populate the night.

The psychoanalytic situation provides in addition a unique opportunity to study the interrelationship between the feeling of helplessness and terror in nightmares and the external traumatic influences, sexual excitements, primitive hostility, and other determinants that combine to produce these dreams. Through nightmares that occur in the transference setting a link can be established with the most severely traumatic anxiety-filled experiences, relationships, and conflicts of early childhood, especially through association to actual childhood nightmares.

A thirty-year-old woman had several severe anxiety dreams or nightmares during the course of her psychoanalytic treatment. Occurring at critical times in the transference relationship, these dreams were linked to childhood nightmares and thereby made possible an understanding and working through of the patient's most profound early anxieties and conflicts. A prominent concern in the analysis had been that the doctor would break down the edifice of her personality, that her private world would be invaded and destroyed. Symbolizing these concerns, she had many dreams in which buildings crumbled or were threatened with destruction. These fears had a sexual meaning relating to fears of men and concerns about rape; however, through nightmares their link with very early threats to her existence, especially in relation to the mother and other mothering figures, became clearly established. In association with her concerns about rape, she had several severe anxiety dreams in which snakes, immobile and frozen at first, had suddenly become active and "unthawed," chasing her until she awoke in great fear.

In the context of exploring her early childhood sexual curiosity, for example, the patient had a severe nightmare. The day before she reported this nightmare, she had a dream in which she received a very poor grade for not correctly answering all the questions in an examination. This was associated with her wish to have all the answers to her childhood sexual questions and to her fear of her mother's disapproval should she ask such questions. The night before the examination dream, she had been fixing a dress to make it more attractive and hunted for the "king thread" that would lead the whole thing to unravel. Unable to find it, she had felt desperately frustrated and had the impulse to take the curved, sharp-bladed knife with which she was fixing the dress and jab it into her abdomen, eyes, or face. The following night, after she had reported this in her treatment hour, an alien voice told her to masturbate and she did so, joylessly and reluctantly, with the conviction that she was being watched. She fell into a deep sleep and had the nightmare she reported the next day.

The start of the dream was accompanied by a number of circumstantial details. Then she dreamed that she would take a nap. A girl said, "Now I see why you washed your hair," with the critical implication that it was done to attract a boy. She protested angrily that she was trying to take a nap. In the dream she went to sleep, but awoke sensing that someone, a woman, was in the room. The bed was gigantic, long and wide, with "tubes arching" and spindles and "highly wrought." The woman was in her fifties, sophisticated in air and manner, a woman of the world dressed in a tailor-made suit. She was sitting on a stool and said to the patient, "I was waiting for you to wake up." In a casual but suggestive tone, she invited the patient to go on a trip, and she knew the woman was trying to seduce her. In the dream, the patient said, "She looked at my body; I was naked from the waist down, and I knew that she knew it. I got very nervous and said, 'I must study for orals' "—she had been reading a psychoanalytic article on "orality" in relation to her work. "The woman strolled around the bed, pulled her skirts up beyond her thighs, and crossed her legs. I became more and more panicky, and I knew that she would not leave. So I wrapped a sheet around me and suddenly what I feared began to happen. She put her hand up my thigh until she reached my genitals and made cooing noises. I felt I was falling back over a great black anxious space and I screamed, 'It's not real—I've never been seduced by a woman,' and I woke up. For two seconds it was so real, I couldn't believe that I was awake."

Her first associations were to masturbating before going to sleep, to the voice, and to reading about "the oral period." She stressed how *real* the horror of the voice and the dream had seemed after waking. The dream reminded her of her fears of rape by a man; she noted that in her dream she had been wearing the sort of pajamas she used to wear in bed as a small child, recalling the guilty pleasure she then derived from the sensation of rubbing against the sheets. The woman reminded her of a friend of her mother's, a person the patient looked upon as sexually free as she would wish to be, except that the other woman was slightly mannish. The patient's parents looked upon her as immoral. According to her mother, this woman had once frightened the patient when she was still in her carriage. She had leaned over upon the patient while wearing a bulky fur coat. In connection with her childhood masturbation, the patient recalled the thwarting of childhood sexual curiosity and railed against parents who so frustrate their children. She did not recall seeing her mother naked until she was eight; she then felt that somehow the black pubic hair was unclean. She thought how frightening a man's big penis is to a little girl, and she recalled the horror she had felt when as a child she saw a man's penis at a museum, swollen out of proportion as a result of disease. This swollen penis made her think of the pleasure a friend's two-year-old child took in poking his mother's breasts and of a previous dream about her mother, who had delivered her brother when she was 20 months old, with her abdomen swollen with child and then deflated after delivering the baby.

Over the next few days this seduction nightmare became vividly associated with a childhood nightmare from age six that had occurred to her several times before in the analysis. In this dream she was in a large room whose floor, walls, and ceiling were padded with a soft leatherlike material. It had impressed areas with buttons in them, such as an upholstered piece of furniture, which sank in when she stepped on the floor. In the center of the room was a huge ball that reached to the ceiling and almost filled the room. In a corner of the room was a toilet, also made of the same soft material. The ball chased her about the room, and she tried unsuccessfully to escape into the corners of the room until it squeezed her against the floor, and she was unable to breathe. She woke up in terror, screaming. Her parents came into her room and placed her on a couch, and her mother lay down next to her to comfort her.

The patient recalled the intense anxieties of her toilet-training experience, particularly her fear of displeasing her rather overprotective and controlling mother, who had seemed enormous to her, at the same time retaining her soft and comforting qualities. Above all, the dream was linked with a huge, hated grandmother who had first come to visit when she was four and had lived with the family at that time. This woman was in reality an obese, sloppy, and gluttonous person whose crushing embraces the patient found disgusting, hateful, and frightening, representing everything devalued that the patient did not want to be. Once, the grandmother had given the patient and her brother three large rubber balls as gifts, which she did not want to keep because they came from the grandmother. The largest ball, encased by netting, reminded her of the ball in the dream, which was associated with the grandmother.

This nightmare was associated with other terrifying dreams the patient had as a child until she was about nine, in which a savage man with a spear, a bear, or a snake attacked her. So disturbing were these dreams that she sometimes feared going to sleep. These nightmares characteristically occurred after she had read jungle stories, which both fascinated and terrified her, or after she had attended horror movies, usually with her mother, in which violence and threatening murderous monsters were plentiful. After reading about pythons that devoured their prey, for example, she dreamed of huge jungle snakes that swallowed her or crushed her to death. In the movies, she covered her eyes in horror and then peeked in fascination. In one film that furnished the content of a nightmare, a white man and woman were on the floor. Quivering spears had been stuck in them by savages. She recalled the fear of being murdered or suffocated in other nightmares. She particularly enjoyed stories about children in the jungle who faced the dangers of the wild and mastered them, sometimes shooting and killing wild animals.

To deal with her anxiety, as a child she also had become an expert on the habits of various snakes, the way their jaws and salivary glands worked, which ones actually attacked humans, and how to tell whether a snake had eaten in order to know if he was likely to attack. She read books that told what to do if one encountered a lion and which animals climbed trees, and she and her brother played out imaginary pursuits and attacks in the jungle. The aim was to avoid helplessness and destruction. In the analysis, as she became less frightened of her aggressive impulses, especially toward men, she turned the tables on her nightmare attackers and in her dreams sometimes beat them savagely.

The patient slept in her parents' room until she was three, her mother naively assuming that a child that small would not notice anything. She did not recall directly observing her parents' sexual relations, but retained a vague association of intercourse as a battle in the dark; feelings of excitement had become combined with helpless terror as she lay awake in the parents' room. Efforts to remember this period aroused nausea, diarrhea, and an intense feeling of pressure in the head that seemed to block out thoughts and memories. After she was moved to her own room, she recalled, she would wander toward her parents' room, eager to go in and see what was going on. Her father reprimanded her if he caught her in the hall or anywhere outside her room at night. Once, when she was four years old, she slept in the same bed with her father, while the mother slept with her sickly brother in another bed. According to her recollection, neither she nor her father moved during the night. He slept turned away from her and expressed no affection. The first nightmares she recalled as a child occurred at this time and were of a huge hulking creature, not clearly male or female, with a knife with which he attacked her.

The patient was the older of two children, very special and pretty as a baby, doted upon by her physically affectionate mother and by the mother's relatives. Until the mother became pregnant and delivered her baby brother, she enjoyed her mother's exclusive love. The brother was sickly as an infant and required extra care by the mother, who shifted much of her attention to the baby. The reconstruction of this period in the analysis brought about in the patient very intense depressive feelings and rage toward the mother and brother. When she was about three, her efforts to turn to her father for love were met with coldness, awkwardness, and rejection. This was not because he did not love his daughter, but rather because, like King Lear, his selfishness and inability to give affection paralyzed his responses to the child. An arrogant and angry man in reality, he was made to appear doubly so to the patient by the mother, who warned the patient to placate him and, in effect, to avoid him. Rejected utterly in her efforts to seduce her father during the oedipal period, the patient was forced to turn back to her mother for love. The *danger* associated with this regressive retreat to the early intimacy with her mother came to be understood through nightmares, such as the one described above, in which seduction by a woman occurred. To submit to such homosexual seduction meant the destruction of her heterosexual hopes, which she had not relinquished.

The terror associated with these nightmares proved to have another, equally profound meaning. The regression to the preoedipal attachment to the mother brought with it the arousal of the full force of the patient's infantile destructive rage toward her that had been stimulated by the inevitable frustrations of the early years, at first by the birth of the brother and the toilet-training experience, and later through the mother's effort to keep her away from the father. This rage, which came increasingly to be represented directly in her nightmares, was often expressed in oral destructive terms, as in the devouring-snake nightmares. Having found little love or protection in her relationship with her father, the patient found her early murderous wishes toward her mother especially threatening. If these impulses, to which as a small child she had ascribed magical power, were actually to result in the mother's destruction, she would be utterly alone and would have no one to love her or care for her. This conflict was vividly revealed through exploration of her nightmares. Even disapproval or criticism by the mother could be terrifying, as it might result in retaliation or at the very least could mean the loss of the mother's love. Thus, the destructive creatures in her nightmares, often poorly differentiated sexually, signified not only the dangerous, sexual man, but represented also the early mother, made profoundly threatening as a result of the patient's projection of her own infantile aggressive impulses.

As the patient grew out of childhood, her mother described her childbirth experience to her as bloody and tearing her body apart, and she spoke to the patient with disgust of the father's sexual advances. Apart from the seductive aspect of such confidences, they served to heighten the patient's view of heterosexual relations as destructive and threatening and tended to revive the childhood conflicts. In response to the inevitable unfulfillment and frustrations of the analytic relationship, the patient had several, severe anxiety dreams, the common feature of which initially was her feeling of helplessness in the face of attack by some savage man, on one occasion a doctor with a hypodermic needle. In one dream, a threatened assault by a swarm of biting locusts that died and left disgusting husks provided a link between the patient's feeling of hostility toward the male genital and her degraded view of the genitalia of both sexes that derived from the anal period, this view having received later reinforcement by the mother's attitude.

This patient's nightmares—both those that occurred in the transference setting and those recalled from childhood—were especially valuable for exploring systematically the various levels of her conflicts. Above all, they provided the indispensable link between the fear of adult heterosexual intimacy and the associated threat of a regressive return to the early, homosexual, and highly ambivalent preoedipal and infantile attachment to the mother. The ultimate danger was that of being overwhelmed by or fused with an early parental figure viewed as destructive, partially on the basis of actual parental threats that had been internalized and partly on the basis of the child's projected aggression.

The overwhelming quality of anxiety in the nightmares of both the adult and childhood periods was the result of revival of an early childhood ego state of frozen helplessness in the face of threatening figures in the external environment and powerful aggressive impulses and sadomasochistic excitement arising from within. In the case of the most disturbing of the patient's adult nightmares, the seduction dream, ego regression with respect to reality occurred, with conviction of the dream's "realness" persisting for several seconds after waking. This aspect, together with many of the projective phenomena seen in association with these nightmares, such as the conviction of being watched and the hallucinated voice urging her to masturbate, suggest a resemblance to paranoid psychotic states. Many of the pregenital conflicts described in association with this decidedly nonpsychotic patient's nightmares have great prominence in the content of acute psychoses. The profound resemblance to and the important differences between nightmares and acute psychoses will be discussed in Chapter 5. One difference that can be noted in this patient's case lies in her handling of the nightmare anxieties in childhood, in the effective defenses she was able to mobilize in order to deal with the terror. As many of us try to do as adults in relation to particular fears that often remain unconscious, she became an "expert in the field." In order to master her terror of the devouring creatures that haunted her dreams, she became something of a jungle naturalist, familiar, like Kipling's Mowgli, with the creatures of the wild and their habits. She also was able to *dramatize* her fears in play, enlisting her brother's aid. Eventually, through the use of knowledge and creativity, she was able to limit the regressive power of her night fears.

References

1. Coleridge, S. T.   The Pains of Sleep (1803). In Coleridge, E. H. (Ed.), *The Poems of Samuel Taylor Coleridge*. London: Oxford University Press, 1912. Pp. 389–390.
2. Gardner, G. E.   Night terrors and the mutilation threat. *Psychoanal. Rev.* 19:182–199, 1932.
3. Hadfield, J. A.   *Dreams and Nightmares*. Baltimore, Md.: Penguin Books, 1954.
4. Fisher, C., Byrne, J., and Edwards, A.   REM and NREM Nightmares and Their Interrelationships. Lecture delivered to the Department of Psychiatry, Mt. Sinai Hospital, New York, Apr. 10, 1968.
5. Sackett, G. P.   Monkeys reared in isolation with pictures as visual

input: Evidence for an innate releasing mechanism. *Science* 154: 1468–1473, 1966.

6. Foulkes, D.   Dreams of the male child: An EEG study. *J. Abnorm. Psychol.* 72:457–567, 1967.

7. Freud, A.   *Normality and Pathology in Childhood.* New York: International Universities Press, 1965.

8. Hirschberg, J. C.   Parental anxieties accompanying sleep disturbance in young children. *Bull. Menninger Clin.* 21:129–139, 1957.

9. Nagera, H.   Sleep and its disturbances approached developmentally. *Psychoanal. Stud. Child* 21:393–447, 1966.

10. Mack, J. E.   Nightmares, conflict and ego development in childhood. *Int. J. Psychoanal.* 46:403–428, 1965.

11. Bibring, E.   The development and problems of the theory of the instincts. *Int. J. Psychoanal.* 22:102–131, 1941.

12. Freud, S.   Instincts and Their Vicissitudes (1915). In *The Standard Edition of the Complete Psychological Works of Sigmund Freud,* tr. and ed. by J. Strachey with others. London: Hogarth and the Institute of Psycho-Analysis, 1957. Vol. XIV, p. 138.

13. Erikson, E.   *Childhood and Society.* New York: Norton, 1950.

14. Erikson, E.   The dream specimen of psychoanalysis. *J. Amer. Psychoanal. Ass.* 2:5–56, 1954.

15. Gide, André.   In O'Brien, J. (Trans.), *Journals.* Dec. 20, 1924. New York: © Knopf, 1948. P. 365.

16. Levitan, H.   Depersonalization and the dream. *Psychoanal. Quart.* 36:157–171, 1967.

17. Fisher, C.   Personal communication, Apr. 18, 1968.

18. Broughton, R. J.   Sleep disorders: Disorders of arousal? *Science* 159: 1070–1078, 1968.

19. Eisenberg, L.   Hallucinations in Children. In West, L. J. (Ed.), *Hallucinations.* New York: Grune & Stratton, 1962. Pp. 198–209.

20. *Ibid.* P. 203.

21. Gross, M., Goodenough, D., Tobin, M., Halpert, E., Lepore, D., Perlstein, A., Sirota, M., Dibianco, J., Fuller, R., and Kishner, I. Sleep disturbances and hallucinations in the acute alcoholic psychoses. *J. Nerv. Ment. Dis.* 142:493–514, 1966.

22. Greenberg, R., and Pearlman, C.   Delirium tremens and dreaming. *Amer. J. Psychiat.* 124:133–142, 1967.

23. Gross, M. M., and Goodenough, D. R.   Sleep Disturbances in the Acute Alcoholic Psychoses. Paper presented at 133d Annual Meeting of AAAS, Washington, D.C., Dec. 17, 1966.

24. Freud, S.   The Interpretation of Dreams (1900). *Standard Edition.* 1953. Vol. V, pp. 533–549.

25. Brenner, C.   A case of childhood hallucinosis. *Psychoanal. Stud. Child* 6:235–243, 1951.

26. Esman, A. H.   Visual hallucinoses in young children. *Psychoanal. Stud. Child* 17:334–343, 1962.

27. Wilking, V., and Paoli, C.   The hallucinatory experience. *J. Amer. Acad. Child Psychiat.* 5:431–440, 1966.

28. Havens, L.   Projection and the Concept of Ego Defect. Paper read at Fall meeting of the American Psychoanalytic Association, New York City, Dec. 5, 1964.

29. Beckett, P. G. S., Robinson, D. B., Frazier, S. H., Steinhilber, R. M., Duncan, G. M., Estes, H. R., Litin, E. M., Grattan, R. T., Lorton, W. L., Williams, G. E., and Johnson, A. M.   The significance of exogenous traumata in the genesis of schizophrenia. *Psychiatry* 19: 137–142, 1956.

30. Brunswick, R. M.   A supplement to Freud's *History of an Infantile Neurosis. Int. J. Psychoanal.* 9:439–476, 1928.

3   Nightmares and Creativity

BECAUSE OF THE CAPACITY of nightmares to reveal the inner regions of man's mental life, especially the forces that produce conflict, writers and artists have frequently drawn upon these dreams to dramatize such struggles or have turned to their own nightmares for creative inspiration. Nightmares thus provide us with an opportunity to examine several aspects of the creative process.

In this chapter we will look first at the use writers have made of nightmares in their work, expecting that they will have anticipated the insights that we have so laboriously arrived at through a clinical approach. After this, examples of nightmares that have given rise to specific works will be discussed; this will be followed by a consideration of creativity and madness as two possible alternatives to the conflicts that initially brought about the dream. Finally, I shall present examples of creative responses to nightmares in small children, stopping short of claiming to have discovered therein the origins of creativity.

The Use of the Nightmare in Literature

Dreams can be valuable for a writer in his work because of their freedom from the bounds of logical thought, the access they provide to unconscious motivation, and the richness of symbolic expression that they may contain. More specifically, nightmares can be of unique value in conveying the conflict over murderous impulses and primitive sexuality and in capturing an individual's feeling of helplessness in relation to forces within himself and in the outside world that threaten to overwhelm and destroy him. These characteristics, together with the tendency of nightmares to be accompanied by at least a temporary loss after waking of the capacity to distinguish inner and outer reality, account for their frequent association in literature with the supernatural and with works in which the characteristics of the dream life are projected into the outside world and treated as actual. In ghost stories, for example, the central character often knows not whether he sleeps or wakes, is having a nightmare, or is living in a distorted world filled with horror. The macabre atmosphere of ghost stories, whether or not explicitly related by the writer to a nightmare of one of his characters, is similar to the atmosphere that is created for an individual who, upon awakening from a frightening dream, has become confused as to whether the demonic forces that torment him are real or imagined.

Dostoevsky, because of his profound preoccupation with the dark forces in man's psychology, made effective use of dreams, especially nightmares, in his novels. As Ruth Mortimer has pointed out, Dostoevsky, who often used a dream to release tension at a point of climax in the story, carefully integrated the dream into the work as a whole, fitting it to the dreamer's character, the range of the story, and the overall artistic purpose [1]. Elements from preceding passages of the story were incorporated into the dream, much as occurs in living dreams that draw upon past memories and elements of current experience. In the early pages of *Crime and Punishment*, as he led Raskolnikov inexorably to the murder of the pawnbroker, Dostoevsky observed: "In a morbid condition of the brain, dreams often have singular actuality, vividness, and extraordinary semblance of reality. At times monstrous images are created, but the setting and the whole picture are so truthlike and filled with details so delicate, so unexpectedly, but so artistically consistent, that the dreamer . . . could never have invented them in the waking state. Such sick

dreams always remain long in the memory and make a powerful impression on the overwrought and deranged nervous system." [2].

Raskolnikov, forced to give up his studies because of extreme
poverty, fastens upon the old woman as the cause of his abject
condition. She drains him of his last few possessions for a few
kopecks that are quickly spent; in his view, she has "sharp malignant eyes." He struggles with his wish to murder her, break into
her strongbox, and steal back what she has stolen from him and
others. A long letter from his mother, to which he reacts with a
mixture of fury and guilt, informs him that, in order to help him
financially, she is sacrificing his beloved younger sister—the last
item he had pawned was a little gold ring that had been a parting
gift of hers—to an older man, who will exploit her. His resolve to
murder the pawnbroker hardens: "A month ago, yesterday even,
the thought was a mere dream: but now . . . now it appeared
not a dream at all, it had taken a new menacing and quite unfamiliar shape, and he suddenly became aware of this himself"
[3]. Raskolnikov's incapacity to deal with his sister's violation is
symbolized by his own rescue, then abrupt abandonment of a
helpless girl he encounters in the street being pursued by a lech-
erous man. "Let them devour each other alive. . . . What is it
to me?" he thinks. After spending his last thirty kopecks on
vodka and a piece of pie, he heads toward his home to sleep, but
is too exhausted to reach it, turns into some bushes, sinks on the
grass, and falls asleep. He then has the dreadful nightmare.

In the dream, he is seven and accompanied by his father. They
are heading toward a church he loved. In the churchyard are
buried his grandmother, whom he had never seen, and a baby
brother, whom he does not remember. On the way to the
church, he and his father pass a tavern where drunken towns-
people are engaged in some kind of hideous celebration. Near the
tavern he sees a strange cart drawn by a thin little sorrel nag
instead of the heavy cart horse it required. One of the peasants
loads the cart with his drunken friends and then showers murderous blows upon the helpless animal in a crescendo of beating.
Horrified, the boy turns to his father, who tells him not to look,
for "they are in fun." The boy runs to the mare, but is helpless to

protect her. The crowd urges the brutal peasant to greater efforts; with tears streaming, the boy watches helplessly as the little mare is whipped across the eyes. In an orgy of sadistic violence, the peasant and the crowd beat the mare with a long thick shaft from the bottom of the cart and then kill it with a crowbar. The boy puts his arms around the dead mare's bleeding head and kisses it on the eyes and lips. He strikes out in a frenzy at the murderous peasant, but his father tells him, "It's not our business." He puts his arms around his father, but feels choked. As he tries to draw a breath to cry out, Raskolnikov wakes up, gasping for breath, his hair soaked with perspiration. Standing up in terror, "He felt utterly broken; darkness and confusion were in his soul." Although relieved that it "was only a dream," he recognizes that the murderous impulses really emanate from within himself and that the dream reveals his intention to murder the old lady. " 'Good God!' he cried, 'can it be, can it be, that I shall really take an axe, that I shall strike her on the head, split her skull open . . . that I shall tread in the sticky warm blood, break the lock, steal and tremble, hide, all spattered in the blood . . . with the axe. . . . Good God, can it be?' " [4].

Following the dream, he reviews all of his justifications for murdering the old lady: that she was rich, that she bled the people, that she did not deserve to live, that her removal would help humanity—a kind of rationalizing that is not uncommon in murderers studied clinically. "His casuistry" having "removed all rational objections," Raskolnikov completes his plans for the murder and proceeds to kill the pawnbroker with an axe and her sister, as well, when she intervenes unexpectedly.

Dostoevsky has used the nightmare as a deliberate invention to dramatize his hero's profound struggle to deal with terrifying murderous wishes. The dream reflects Raskolnikov's failure to forestall the violence with love, and the balance swings with finality in the direction of actual murder and a kind of madness wherein what had been but a daydream has progressed to a nightmare and then has ceased to be a dream at all. The nightmare leads here to a temporary resolution of conflict, a decision in the direction of action, of violence, of murder. After the nightmare, Raskolnikov could "suddenly breathe more easily. He felt he had cast off that fearful burden that had so long been weighing upon him, and all at once there was a sense of relief and peace in his soul . . . It was as though an abscess that had been forming for a month past in his heart had suddenly broken. Freedom, Freedom! He was free from that spell, that sorcery, that obsession" [5].

It is often not profitable to interpret the latent meaning of a dream in a fictional work beyond specific evidence provided in the work itself. In view of the violent aggression directed toward the old woman in the novel, it is, however, of especial interest that Dostoevsky's Notebooks for Crime and Punishment, recently published in English, set forth explicitly Raskolnikov's hostility toward his mother and sister, as the work itself does not [6]. In the Notebooks, Dostoevsky repeatedly refers to how burdened Raskolnikov was by his mother's attentions and demands and above all by her unattainable expectations of him. Although I do not believe that the evidence justifies the conclusion that the pawnbroker represented Raskolnikov's mother, intense aggressive feelings toward his mother, similar to those experienced toward the moneylender, are attributed to him in the Notebooks.

Milton Horowitz has recently pointed out, on the basis of his own biographical researches, that the beating of the little mare was associated by Dostoevsky with the death of his beloved mother when he was seventeen, and that it was followed closely by the death of Pushkin, of whom he was also deeply fond [7]. En route to the site of the duel in which Pushkin had been fatally wounded, Dostoevsky watched a young coachman relentlessly beating a horse in response to blows that he had received from a courier. The memory stayed in his mind to be represented later in such scenes as the beating of the mare in Raskolnikov's dream. Furthermore, as Mortimer has shown, women in Dostoevsky's works are often seen as animals for hire, beasts of burden to be sacrificed to man's cruelty. These observations make more understandable Raskolnikov's powerful feelings of empathy toward the little mare in his terrifying dream and show us how effectively Dostoevsky has captured, through the use of the nightmare, the various dimensions of his ambivalence. Ras-

kolnikov has several other terror-filled dreams in the course of
the novel, all conveying his struggle with powerful destructive
drives, primitive guilt, and loss of control of murderous impulses.

Shakespeare departed from the conventional use of the dream
for prophecy in Elizabethan drama and employed it in addition
to recapitulate the past, enabling him thereby to construct the
dream from actions of his characters and thus to make it consistent with their natures and motives [8]. In some of his plays, he
drew upon images of sleep and dream to create the atmosphere
of evil or of menace that he desired. *Richard III* and *Macbeth*,
for example, "are plays of usurpation and murder and of troubled
sleep" [9]. Thus, the nightmare of the Duke of Clarence in
the first act of *Richard III* not only anticipates his murder at
the hands of Richard's henchmen, but expresses in addition a
deeper psychological reality as it links his terror to the vengeance
of conscience for the desertion of Warwick, his father-in-law,
that led to his death, and the murder of Edward, the Lancastrian
Prince [10]. The dream is a punishment dream and also a classic
nightmare with monstrous distorted creatures and forces that
terrorize the dreamer with horrible cries and vicious threats so
vivid that, even after waking, Clarence "for a season after could
not believe, but that I was in Hell—Such terrible Impression
made my Dreame" [11].

Later in the play Shakespeare again makes use of dreams to
"inform" the action as he balances the affliction of the sleep of
Richard, whose "conscience hath a thousand severall tongues"
[12], with the "sweetest sleepe and fairest boading dreames" of
Richmond, who is at peace with his conscience [13]. In Richard's
terrifying punishment dream the ghosts of Prince Edward, of
Henry VI, of Clarence, of Anne, and of all those others he had
murdered confront him in his sleep and accuse him. These
"shadowes" strike "more terror to the soule of Richard than can
the substance of ten thousand souldiers" [14].

In the dream, the intactness of Richard's personality begins to
give way. Portions of it war against one another, and he himself
perceives the elements of the inner conflict that severe anxiety
dreams can so uniquely convey [15]:

"What? do I feare my Selfe? There's none else by,
Richard loves Richard, that is, I am I.
Is there a murtherer heere? No; Yes, I am:
Then flye; What from my Selfe? Great reason: Why?
Lest I revenge. What? my Selfe upon my Selfe?
Alacke, I love my Selfe. Wherefore? For any good
That I my Selfe, have done unto my Selfe?
O no. Alas, I rather hate my Selfe,
For hatefull Deeds committed by my Selfe."

It is illuminating to compare Shakespeare's construction of
Richard's dream with the account given in Holinshed's chron-
icle, from which the historical material for the drama was drawn
[16]. In Holinshed, there is the "terrible dreame," "the diverse
images like terrible diuels," the troubled mind and "dreadfull
imaginations." However, the emphasis is upon Richard's fear of
the coming battle and of the enemies that lie in wait for him.
"The pricke of his sinfull conscience" is discussed, but only as a
kind of hydraulic balance, its "sting" being in proportion to "the
heinous and unnaturall" degree of his deeds. The depiction of
the internal structure of conflict, of the warring elements within
the personality, and of the dissection of the inner "conscience"
into various hate-filled voices, attitudes, and qualities of objects
from the past that assault the subject's ego—these are the
unique product of Shakespeare's creative insight.

Three centuries later in the play *Serjeant Musgrave's Dance*,
the contemporary British dramatist John Arden made similar
use of a nightmare to convey forcefully a critical psychological
turning point in the bizarre career of his central character, Serjeant Black Jack Musgrave [17]. Musgrave, an army deserter, has
come with several other fugitives to a stricken coal-mining town
in the north of England in order to turn the people away from
violence by confronting them with a spectacle of horror that will
force them to change. Musgrave, however, carries within himself
the burden of his own past destructiveness, of having killed and
beaten people "in the streets of their own city" to "keep order."

The night before the principal action of the play is to take
place, Musgrave is disturbed in his sleep by the reliving of one
such episode. In the dream he shouts out, "Fire, fire! Fire, fire,

London's burning, London's burning! Burning. Burning. One minute from now, and you carry out your orders—get *that* one! Get her! Who says she's a child! We've got her in the book, she's old enough to kill! You carry out your orders. Thirty seconds. Count the time. Twenty-six . . . Twenty-three . . ." (a woman tries to interrupt his shouting) "Be quiet. Twenty . . . Eighteen . . . I'm on duty, woman. I'm timing the end of the world. Ten more seconds, sir . . . Five . . . three. . . two . . . *one!*" He lets out a cry of agony and falls back on the bed [18]. The nightmare is a way station in Musgrave's progress to madness. His insane "logic" of multiplying violence gains momentum, leading to the crumbling of his own personality and a crescendo of violence on the stage.

On occasion, a writer will deliberately employ a nightmare or other dream to work himself out of a dilemma. In the musical comedy-drama, *Fiddler on the Roof*, for example, Joseph Stein places his central character Tevye, the impoverished dairyman, in a most difficult position [19]. He has bargained a "good" match for his beloved daughter Tzeitel with a comfortably well-off but middle-aged butcher. Although his wife is thrilled, his daughter, who loves the tailor, Motel, is miserable. Tevye is upset and conflicted but, being flexible, gives in to his daughter's pleas; but what will he tell his wife, Golde, whose anger he dreads? He pretends to have a nightmare.

In his sleep he groans and screams out for help. When his wife shakes him to find out what is the matter, he tells her, "It was terrible," and the nightmare-solution is then enacted on the stage. A "celebration of some kind" is taking place. Golde's grandmother, Tzeitel, dead thirty years, enters and is pleased to see her great-granddaughter and namesake being married to the tailor. When Golde corrects her, saying that she must mean the butcher, she flies into the air, screaming angrily. They argue, and she becomes still more enraged when Tevye tells her of his bargain. The argument is interrupted by the appearance of the butcher's deceased wife, who is furious about the match and her husband's "handing over my belongings to a total stranger." She threatens that, three weeks after such a "fatal wedding," she will

come at night, "take her by the throat, and . . . this I'll give
your Tzeitel, that I'll give your Tzeitel, this I'll give your Tzeitel"
[20]. She then begins to choke Tevye, laughing wildly. Golde
says it is an evil spirit, brought on by the butcher, and that, if her
grandmother Tzeitel came all the way from the other world to
plead for the tailor, it is for the best that her daughter marry him.
Tevye's problem is resolved, and his wife is convinced in his direction.

Nightmares as a Source of Creative Inspiration

Not infrequently writers or artists tell us that a nightmare or
other dream has furnished the source or inspiration for the creative product, if it has not actually provided the literal content of
the work itself. Henry James' story, "The Jolly Corner," is based
on a nightmare, as are several of Robert Louis Stevenson's tales,
and most likely many of Poe's stories [21, 22]. It should not
surprise us that this would be the case. Rochlin has stressed the
similar function of dreaming and creativity in making restitution
for what has been lost, or for transcending discontents, depriva-
tions, and limitations [23]. Both are attempts to achieve an integration between a present reality or experience, on the one hand,
and past, largely unconscious, wishes, desires, conflicts, and
memories, on the other. Thus, if the creative process is an attempt to resolve a conflict, fulfill a wish that has not been grati-
fied, restore what has been lost, or convert limitation and inepti-
tude into mastery, it has readily available to it in nightly dreams
the products of a fundamental psychological activity that is itself
regularly devoted in part to the pursuit of these aims. Furthermore, dreaming, with its vivid and powerful emotional elements,
its rich and flexible use of symbols, its reliance on concrete sense
perception, and its access to unconscious mental content, has
made use of the very psychological mechanisms that are essential
to creative activity. The dream has, in effect, done a part of the
job. What remains for the writer or artist is to employ his
technique to transform the crude, overly personal, and largely
narcissistic dream into shared perception and illusion, to make it

into a coherent work in which larger audiences can find expression, some resolution of their own conflicts, and gratification of their unfulfilled emotions [24].

Terrifying dreams or nightmares seem in particular to give rise frequently to stories, paintings, and other works of art. In these instances, we often find that the external reality that gave rise to these dreams was too painful, the wishes and conflicts that were revived too intolerable, or the childhood memories and emotions regressively reexperienced in sleep too overwhelming to permit a successful dream-resolution. Nightmares are in certain respects unsuccessful efforts to deal with conflicts. Under these circumstances the impetus to creative activity would be particularly intense.

An author may himself be aware that a particular work represents an effort to master a conflict that has been revived in a dream. Henry James' story, "The Jolly Corner," derives from a "dream-adventure" of age thirteen, "the most appalling yet most admirable nightmare of my life" [25, 26]. Both nightmare and story are concerned with a confrontation, a terrifying life-and-death struggle between a man and a ghostly apparition that haunts or menaces him. The story is about a repatriated middle-aged gentleman, Spencer Brydon, who returns to America, to the town of his youth, to examine and renovate his property. He finds the house stalked by a threatening creature, a ghostly presence that represents what he might perhaps have been had he not been so filled with fears [27]. In the nightmare of age thirteen, James was able, despite his "unutterable fear," to turn the tables on the "just dimly-descried figure that retreated in terror before my rush and dash" [28]. Although in the tale, written in his sixties, the confrontation has become far more intricate and complex, the essential elements of Brydon's relationship to the awful stranger—probably a composite of James' older brother William and warded-off aspects of his own personality with which he had never been able to come to terms—was contained in the adolescent nightmare. Courage or cowardice, weakness or strength, aggression or passivity, triumph or defeat, murder or annihilation—these possibilities confront the dreamer and the story's hero alike as they struggle to reconcile conflicting aspects

of their natures. Although James' art elaborates and transforms
the conflicts that were contained in the nightmare, it does not
resolve them. They are preserved in the story with a vitality that
half a century of elapsed time had not reduced [29].

At times, as in the case of Kubla Khan, the poet claims that
the work *is* the dream, which he snatched from sleep and wrote
down. This is, however, unlikely. It is probably true that the
dream may contain what John Livingston Lowes called, "Those
mysterious elements out of whose confluences and coalescences
suddenly emerged the poem" [30]. An additional essential part
of the creative process would also be the transformation of these
elements—the images, feelings, and memories of the dream that
inspired the poem—into a unified, coherent work of art.

Although we have numerous instances in which writers or artists state that they have converted their dreams into creative
work, we have few examples in which they tell us of the process
by which they claim to have achieved the transformation. An
exception is Robert Louis Stevenson. So accustomed was he to
draw upon his dreams for his tales that he called the mind of the
person asleep "that small theatre of the brain which we keep
brightly lighted all night long, after the jets are down, and darkness and sleep reign undisturbed in the remainder of the body"
[31]. The child Stevenson was "an ardent and uncomfortable
dreamer," given to nightmares in which "sooner or later the
night-hag would have him by the throat, and pluck him, strangling and screaming, from his sleep" [32]. Gradually, as he grew
up, he was able to master the terror of his dreams, and he noted
that they became "more circumstantial, and had more the air
and continuity of life." Nevertheless, his stories continued sometimes to "come to me in the form of nightmares in so far that
they make me cry out aloud" [33]. Eventually—Stevenson is
here speaking of himself in the third person—"he began to read
in his dreams—tales" and learned that these dream-founded stories could bring financial reward. Upon going to sleep, he would
deliberately set his mind to manufacturing dreams that could be
made into stories.

One story he set down "exactly as it came to him" in a dream,
but did not publish because it had "unmarketable elements." It

concerned the son of "a very rich and wicked man" who secretly murdered his father in a quarrel, succeeded to his "broad estates," and moved in with the dead man's young widowed second wife. An unacknowledged love grew between the young man and his stepmother—the mother is nowhere mentioned—who guiltily kept distant from one another. The young man learned that the woman had discovered an object of "deadly evidence" against him, but she would not denounce him. Unable to bear his guilty torture any longer, he confronted her, whereupon she declared her love and the dreamer (Stevenson) awoke "with a pang of wonder and mercantile delight" [34]. Commenting upon this dream-story, Stevenson pointed out the psychological realism, the craftsmanship, the dramatic timing, and other aspects of its form and construction that were present in the dream itself. He did not, however, comment upon its meaning except to note how well-kept were the guilty secrets prior to the confrontation. However, we may suspect that it was precisely the meaning, the transparently incestuous aspect of the story, that accounted for the fact that "his mercantile delight was not of long duration." One requirement, then, of a "marketable" dream-based story is that the unconscious impulses that inspire the creative activity must undergo sufficient modification to be acceptable to the author's judgment and censorship.

Stevenson attributed much of this creative activity in dreams to what he called "brownies" or "little people," which he distinguished from the "I" or "conscience ego." The brownies "have not a rudiment of what we call conscience"; they "are somewhat fantastic, and like their stories hot and hot, full of passion." In these respects, they are akin to Freud's concept of the id. However, they also are inventors and performers, share in the dreamer's financial worries, and "do one-half my work for me while I am fast asleep" [35], unconscious functions perhaps more properly ascribed to the ego. They also served as a device to protect the writer from responsibility for the unconscious content of his works. The above story, for example, "was not his [Stevenson's] tale; it was the little people's!" The "I," on the other hand, corresponds to the conscious ego. It is "a creature as matter of fact as any cheesemonger or any cheese, and a realist buried up to the ears in actuality" [36]. The "I" is an "excellent adviser," pulling back, cutting down, holding the pen, dressing the whole "in the best sentences that I can find and make"; he makes up the manuscript, pays for the registration, and takes too large a share, considering the creative activity of the brownies, in the profits. Finally, the "I" takes part in the invention and imposes its conscious intentions during the dream itself as a kind of prospective producer-director at an audition or rehearsal, seeking good story material while at the same time encouraging and guiding the performances. "Even when fast asleep I know that it is I who am inventing," Stevenson claimed, "and when I cry out it is with gratification to know that the story is so good" [37]. Compare this thorough mastery in adult creativity with the helplessness of Stevenson in childhood: "The night-hag would have him by the throat and pluck him, strangling and screaming, from his sleep."

We can recapitulate the steps Stevenson has told, whereby he converted nightmares or other dreams into stories. Initially, like every child, he was beset with nightmares that, with maturity, gave way to some degree to less threatening dreams, although nightmares continued to inspire some of his work. These dream images were concerned with familiar impulses, with love and hate, incest and murder, and in themselves reflected Stevenson's effort to master through symbolic expression the conflicts related to these forces. He then discovered that he could further impose upon these images and make them into stories, modifying and shaping them in the service of external reality—financial necessity and reward, communication with readers—and internal requirements—further mastery of conflict, pleasure in the creative activity itself. Much of the creative invention, the elaboration of images and the depiction of scenes and events, went on as an unconscious function, ascribed to "little people" in order to disavow personal responsibility for the original impulses. Final molding of the dream into a tale was the work of the "conscience ego" that both directs the creative transformation during sleep and gives final shape to it after waking.

Often the mood or atmosphere of menace, destruction, and terror of a nightmare are carried directly into a story. In this situ-

ation, the creative modification and elaboration are applied more
to the structural elements and psychological possibilities and less
to the emotional atmosphere, which retains its nightmarish qualities. When this occurs, the result is a tale of horror or a ghost
story in which the terror the dreamer once had to bear alone is
shared with or inflicted upon the story's readers or hearers.

Henry James' "Turn of the Screw" is perhaps the best known
of such ghost stories, based probably upon a nightmare [38]. In
this story, James has woven a complex tale of the supernatural,
which contains such psychological elements as destructive possessiveness, forbidden sexuality, and terror of abandonment. Furthermore, in his blurring of the margin between purely psychological and external realities—including details that violate the
laws of nature—he has brought to our attention another central
aspect of the nightmare. In actuality, the images and emotions
of nightmares give way perhaps less readily before the clarifying
force of the waking ego than those of any other type of dream.
After waking, the dreamer seems to be held longer in a state of
uncertainty as to whether the dream was real, suspended thus in
a kind of brief psychosis. This uncertainty, in turn, deepens the
experience of terror as the dreamer seems briefly to have lost the
mastery of his own reality-testing faculties. In his story, James
seems to emphasize precisely this uncertainty. Our interest in the
content of the narrative is continually challenged by our uncertainty as to the mental state of the governess. We are kept unsure—and thus forced to share in the nightmare—as to whether
the governess is alone in the threats she perceives. Do others see
the same images? Does she really see them herself? Is she hallucinating? Does she dream? Is she mad? Often what she sees is
not in itself so terrifying. Rather, the anxiety lies in the uncertainty over whether she sees it, whether it is "really there" or not.
Thus, we are drawn into an identification with the governess'
psychological situation and come ourselves to experience one of
the cardinal features of the nightmare, the uncertainty over
whether what one perceives as menacing is real or otherwise.

One might conclude from this discussion that James, if he did
indeed derive this story from a nightmare, was merely imposing
his anxieties and conflicts upon his readers. As the readers are

forced by the writer's skill to take part in his frightening vision, however, they are also permitted to derive some comfort from being members of the wider community to which the story is addressed. Heywood Broun made this discovery after a reading of "The Turn of the Screw" plunged him into a state of "sinister horror" [39]. He was living at the time in a "lonely roost in the high Alps"; the realization that thousands of other readers of this story had surely suffered similar emotions rescued him from his distress. "Any one of us," he observed, "was in mortal danger— all of us together were a comic and protected company." One of the reasons, Broun suggested, that James wrote the story might have been to enable his readers to discover the value of "protected company" in mastering anxiety. "We can do anything," Broun concluded, "we must do anything, rather than try to go it alone, with our helpless and terrified loneliness clutching at us in the night" [40].

Creativity, Nightmares, and Madness

Creativity and madness are two alternatives, two possible responses to nightmares or, more accurately, to the critical conflicts that give rise to them. Although madness and creativity may coexist, even simultaneously, in the same individual, for a work of art or literature to be successful, the artist's hold on reality, his capacity to relate to the world outside his own mind, must be sufficiently maintained to communicate the quality of shared illusion. Art, as Kris has pointed out, is linked to the intactness of the ego [41]. In Chapter 5 we will see in case examples some instances in which no such capacity existed or where it was insufficient to master the conflicts or to aid in the integration of the personality. In these situations, nightmare progressed to psychosis. Creative ability can be a powerful integrating force. The fact that psychosis can exist in a writer or artist despite his creative effectiveness only testifies to the power of the conflicts or to the inability of the artist in those instances to deal with them through his work. One may often discern clearly that a man is wrestling with the same problems in his work as in his madness, only more successfully in the former.

Justin Kaplan has recently provided a beautiful description of how the ability to write stories specifically saved Mark Twain from utter madness in his later years [42]. At sixty, when he had been burdened with an accumulation of business disasters of his own making, Twain received a cable that his favorite child, Suzie, had died unexpectedly of meningitis while he was apart from her. Looking back on this time ten years later, he considered it remarkable that a man could have received "a thunderstroke like that and live." Devastated by grief, guilt, and rage after Suzie's death, Twain became increasingly occupied with his dream life, with his own fantasies and illusions. In psychoanalytic terms, he underwent a severe narcissistic regression. Hitherto forbidden sexuality emerged in his dreams, and a liberated "dream self" would go to "unnameable" places and do "unprincipled" things "which the waking self would never dare." However, even the dream self, responsibility for which Twain disavowed, lost its "way in caves and in 'the corridors of monstrous hotels' " [43]. The dreams seemed to become nightmares as the hold on reality after waking was increasingly lost, and their content became more terrifying.

With his creative stock waning and his mind dominated by images of fire and conflagration, symbols he applied to his emotional response to Suzie's death, Twain turned to these dreams for creative material. He transformed his personal struggle over the distinction between dream and reality into an intellectual and literary challenge. He wrote story after story about men whose dreams turned into reality, a displacement that preserved the distinction for himself. Whereas in his early story, *The Prince and the Pauper*, the prince awoke from his bad dream, in the later tales the protagonists do not know whether they dream or wake; they undergo severe dislocation of perception, place, scale, and psychological time. They are, in other words, mad. Twain's characters in the stories struggle with the questions that threatened to overwhelm *him* completely, problems of guilt and responsibility, of disgrace and disaster, of the destruction of identity, of the distinction between dream and reality. While Twain noted that he was "never quite sane in the night," his characters underwent a still more severe mental disruption. As Kaplan has phrased it, "fearing madness if he became the creature and not the master of his past, he worked like a man pursued of furies" [44]. Although he emerged from this traumatic time with his literary powers weakened, by turning the dream life into a source of literary activity, he saved himself from madness. The dream, which in itself may work in the service of integrating current traumatic experiences and earlier painful memories that these revive, may be an insufficient safeguard against madness if the external reality is too devastating. In these instances, the integrating power of creative activity, as in Mark Twain's case, may prevent the inevitable insanity of the night from leading to a pervasive madness in the daytime, as well.

The successful transformation into a creative product of nightmares that emerge in the course of a severe psychological regression may result in work whose originality exceeds that which has gone before. Goya at forty-six and at seventy-three underwent two bouts of severe undiagnosed illness that brought him close to death [45]. During these illnesses, the first of which left him deaf, Goya, in addition to central nervous system symptoms suggestive of an encephalopathy, suffered from a profusion of tormenting nightmares that confronted him with a dark inner world of violence, sadism, and cannibalism. In response to these sinister and overwhelming fantasies, which remind one of nothing so much as the inner world of a schizophrenic, Goya produced the "Caprichos" and *pintas negras*, works of powerful originality. These paintings, whose content Wolfenstein has linked to several severe early losses in the painter's life, demonstrate Goya's use of art in the face of the disorganizing experience of the nightmares. The paintings derive their subject matter—monstrous creatures of the night, predatory men and women, witches and demons of all sorts—from the nightmare visions themselves. They are not, however, merely literal transcriptions of this chaotic world; this would be little more than a visual reproduction of the experience of madness. Rather, Goya organized the perceptions of these visions into an aesthetically satisfying composition. Furthermore, as Wolfenstein has pointed out, he generalized his inner experience. He related his suffering to that of all men, embodied his demonic forces in a mythology, and externalized his private horror in the form of a social protest against the violence men inflict upon each other.

Goya's successful transformation through art of a painful inner reality contrasts with the examples Kris has provided of the creations of psychotics in which private meaning and unconscious conflict are not integrated into an aesthetically satisfying or socially and historically relevant whole [46]. For example, the eighteenth-century German sculptor Messerschmidt was, like Goya, visited by "demons" in the night. He tried to ward off and intimidate these creatures, which he seems to have regarded as actual, through concentrating on sculpting grimacing faces. Instead of transforming the projected inner "demon," however, these physiognomies were empty of feeling other than a relatively unmodified "insane" rage, which overly distorted and unbalanced the work. In this instance, the artist failed to surmount his psychopathology through his work, which was dominated by it. In Kris' terms, the ego could not control the regressive process essential for artistic creativity.

Children's Dreams and the Beginning of Creative Activity

Genius, wrote Sartre, is the way one invents in desperate cases [47]. Small children provide us with many opportunities to observe their invention at "desperate" times. An example of this sort was provided by a twenty-one-month-old boy who, from the time he was thirteen months old, tended to react with intense fear to machines that made loud noises, especially vacuum cleaners, reliving in nightmares the terror associated with his daytime encounters with such machines. At twenty-one months, a man worked in his house for three days with a screaming floor sander. During the days the child stayed away from the man and his sander, which obviously frightened him. On the third night, after they were finally gone, the boy began the enactment of a drama, performed before his parents, in which elements of the man driving his sander were woven together with a pleasurable imitation of his father driving a car and scenes recollecting an unhappy afternoon he had passed with older cousins who had treated him roughly, pushing him around and shouting at him. "Man," he would say, as he made a gesture like the man with the sander pushing the machine or his father driving a car. With increasing excitement mixed with intense agitation, he played out the sander man in action with gesticulations and grimacing, finally interrupting the play with an anxious cry or by throwing himself to the floor with a yell. Attacks by the man with the machine and counterattacks by his victim were featured. With increasing pleasure and diminishing tension, he played out the drama on three successive nights, throwing in phrases like "the man" and "daddy car" to indicate what he was doing. Also, what had begun as a solitary activity became shared play in which he allowed his parents to take various parts. Gradually, the traumatic experience of the sander man's invasion of the house was mastered, and the nightmares ceased. A happy by-product of the episode was that the fear of vacuum cleaners ceased, overcome apparently with the help of the dramatic production. The play had many elements of creative theater: plot, action, imagination, and communication with an audience. For the child, a terrifying experience in which he had been a passive victim was converted into an active one in which he was the master. Furthermore, it would be difficult to argue that the anxiety related to the sander did not stimulate the development of symbolic processes and the capacity for creative elaboration.

Kaplan and Rank have observed that a small child faced with separation, loss, or some other severely disruptive experience may respond by phobic mechanisms (avoidance), by direct expressions of anxiety, or by efforts at conflict-resolution that have the germ of creativity [48]. They studied the adaptations of normal children to the birth of a sibling and moves to new surroundings. In one case a twenty-one-month-old boy, in despair after the arrival of his baby sister, created an alter ego who was an empire builder where he felt downtrodden, who became the excluder where he had been excluded. A potential defeat was turned into a kind of success. In the view of these authors, an important part of the success of these mechanisms was a loving identification with the mother-as-creator who encouraged the child's talent.

Greenacre has stressed the particular innate equipment of the artist and the special degrees of sensitivity and qualities of perception that they possess from childhood [49]. This may be the case, but, as Rochlin has pointed out, such sensitivities and the process of creativity occur inevitably in most children, including those who do not later become writers or artists. There remains the job of studying the later fate of these processes, the later development or loss of creativity in children, in order to understand what determines why some become creative persons and some do not.

Few "cases" are more desperate for a small child than a nightmare; in relation to such dreams we may regularly observe creative forces in operation. Frequently children will convert their dreams, especially the frightening ones in which they feel helpless, into stories in which they direct the action and its outcome. One seven-year-old boy in psychoanalytic treatment had frequent nightmares that were related to a terrifying episode at age four in which he had fallen into the water and almost drowned. When he reported these dreams to his doctor, it became clear that he had converted them into stories. The original nightmares were discovered to have been thinly disguised symbolic representations of the traumatic event, the child being victimized in the dreams by swirling, suffocating forces and by primitive aggressive and devouring monsters. The stories, which he reported as "dreams," based on these nightmares, though similarly concerned with violence, life-and-death struggles, and self-preservation, were much more intricate, elaborate, and coherent, with a richer use of symbols. Unlike the original nightmares, in these modified "dreams" he was rarely himself the victim. The positive relationship with the doctor, the conversion of a private horror into a shared communication, were a vital part of the mastery achieved in this transformation of nightmares into stories.

The Punch and Judy tales, whose history goes back to ancient Egypt, give expression, both in their content and atmosphere, to the conflicts in children's nightmares [50]. Puppeteers in many countries have presented these plays through the centuries in various costumes, but the basic plot has remained the same. A little villain puppet, Punch, mistreats his family and friends and may even go so far as to vanquish Satan himself. However, a time comes always when, as in the nightmare, he becomes himself the frightened victim and is to pay for his misdeeds by losing his own life. The puppet dramas, which are usually watched by groups of children, provide a shared experience that helps the children master the anxieties they hold in common, especially if the show is constructed and enacted with imagination. They can take advantage of the displacement the puppets provide to identify either with the criminal or his punisher, the victim or his attacker.

Edmund Gosse described the powerful impact "the internal troubles of the Punch family" had upon him as a child [51]:

The momentous close, when a figure of shapeless horror appears on the stage, and quells the hitherto undaunted Mr. Punch, was to me the bouquet of the entire performance. When Mr. Punch, losing his nerve, points to this shape and says in an awestruck, squeaking whisper, "Who's that? Is it the butcher?" and the stern answer comes, "No, Mr. Punch!" And then, "Is it the baker?" "No, Mr. Punch." "Who is it then?" (this in a squeak trembling with emotion and terror); and then the full, loud reply, booming like a judgment-bell, "It is the Devil come to take you down to Hell," and the form of Punch, with kicking legs, sunken in epilepsy on the floor,—all this was solemn and exquisite to me beyond words. I was not amused—I was deeply moved and exhilarated, "purged," as the old phrase hath it, "with pity and terror." [Later Gosse came to the opinion that] with a little more tact on the part of Mrs. Punch and some restraint held over a temper, naturally violent, by Mr. Punch, a great deal of this sad misunderstanding might have been prevented [52].

In another Punch and Judy show, seen recently by the author, Punch was chased by a white ghost, with big teeth, for throwing a baby down a flight of stairs, as well as for other crimes, while an audience of small children watched with delight and apprehension. Running in terror from the ghost, Punch was confronted by a Devil, whom he ground into sausages. Then a policeman in a menacing voice accused Punch of being bad and enumerated his various crimes. He sent an alligator to visit Punch which opened its great jaws wide and snapped at him. The alligator's jaws closed on Punch and devoured him. In the last scene, Punch's body could be seen disappearing into the alligator's abdomen. The author's five-year-old son commented that he was not scared because the puppets were made of wood and were not real. Anyway, he added, he had a wolf in his bad dreams, not an alligator.

Anxiety dreams seem frequently to lead to the invention of stories and to provide a further stimulus to the imagination of even very young children.

Carl, a normal three-year-old boy, was troubled for several months by a series of nightmares so frightening to him that he became afraid to go to sleep because "the bad dream will come if I do." In the dream, a frightening creature he dubbed "Aw," a monster with combined characteristics of alligator, dog, and man, came through the window at night to bite or kidnap him.

A child characteristically reluctant to part with instinctual pleasures— he had retained his nighttime bottle to age three—Carl had prolonged his toilet training, begun at age two and several months, until a few months before these particular dreams began. The fear of being "taken away" dated from the onset of his toilet training, which was followed by an actual brief separation from his parents. He became concerned at that time about the disappearance of his stool, not wanting to part with it. About the time the nightmares began, Carl had become openly worried about his mother's lack of a penis and possible dangers to his own organ, from which he was deriving considerable pleasure through self-masturbation and being bathed by his mother. He would insist that, when he looked at his mother's "bottom," he saw a penis, although he found no contradiction in his own suggestion that perhaps "she doesn't have one *yet*." In one nightmare his castration fears became condensed with the moral dictates he was absorbing in relation to his toilet training. Fearful of bugs since his toilet training began, he worried that spiders or bees would get under his covers at night. He awoke from the dream holding his hands over his lower abdomen and continuing to hallucinate. His body rigid from fear, he cowered and screamed that a "bee" was on him and was about to bite him. Earlier that day he had been scolded for soiling and also had listened to a favorite record that entreated children to be good "do be's." ticking off a list of shoulds and shouldn'ts, of "do be's" and "don't be's." Also, he held his hands over his ears when his older brother pretended that a balloon that released air with a sound like gas escaping was the "do be." Bees and other "bugs" were clearly associated with feces in his mind, for he was sure that, if his "bottom fell off, the bees will fly out." After this particular nightmare, he imagined that a bee was on his penis and was about to pull it off, and he worried that he would hurt it if he sat in a hot tub. He told his father teasingly that *his* penis had come off and offered to give him one. He was also confused about where the bowel movement came out, thinking for a time it came out of a hole in the penis.

About this time Carl became deeply identified with the little boy in the story, *Where the Wild Things Are*, whose room at night becomes a fearful jungle filled with toothy, gnashing "wild things" he eventually subdues [53]. Max, the boy in the story, was being punished by this nightmarish experience for being himself a "wild thing" and chasing a dog with a fork. Although he found it exciting, Carl was clearly anxious about Max's wild behavior and disapproved of it strongly, particularly as he had himself been tormenting the family cat. If the wild things were to come to his house, Carl boasted, he would eat them all up, a solution identical to that which he had recently offered in order to keep his father from going away on trips and his mother from leaving the room at bedtime. Carl's nightmares, with their helplessness, terror, and victimization by devouring or mutilating creatures, became markedly less frequent when he learned to convert them into stories. The following tape-recorded excerpts of a conversation with his father demonstrate this transformation, which is aided by the father's participation:

FATHER: Who is Aw?
CARL: He's an alligator. And he bites people and Billy's [older brother] going to kill him some day. . . . I budged him with his head off.
FATHER: How did you do that?
CARL: I threw him in the bushes and I tickled his head and he ran into the bushes and called his mommy, and a new neck growed on, so I threw him down again, and a bear ate him, and he wouldn't come out.
FATHER: Does Aw come when you're awake or after you go to sleep?
CARL: When I'm asleep.
FATHER: What does he look like?
CARL: Well, he looks like an alligator, but he's really a dog and an alligator. He looks like a cat because he has the whiskers, and he has some eyes like a cat and a dog.
FATHER: Are you scared of him?
CARL: Yeah, because he has sharp teeth. He bites. He's very small, but he used to have big teeth when he was big, but now he doesn't have any. Now he can't bite because all of his teeth is out.
FATHER: They're all out?
CARL: Yeah, and he's in the bushes prickled. I get something and I push the thing down on him.
FATHER: What's the scariest thing Aw ever does?
CARL: He used to bite me. Once he bit my finger, but a new one growed on me. They took a thumb, they took another finger that somebody had, but that was all right, because she had a thing on her finger, she had two fingers on—the girl that helped him.
FATHER: The girl?
CARL: Yeah, the girl helped me take Aw away to her mommy alligator. So the alligator ate Aw up.
FATHER: When was the first time you met Aw?
CARL: I first met Aw last summer. I went driving with my mother. And mommy killed Aw. 'Cause mommy has a gun with me.
FATHER: A gun?
CARL: Yeah, and I asked of her to call the police to take Aw.
FATHER: Did that really happen?
CARL: Yeah, but I turned on the . . . I pushed the button, and the police came and took Aw away, put him in jail, 'cause he took me with him in the car, and I watched him, and he bite my finger off.
FATHER: Why did he do that?

CARL: 'Cause he was hungry. 'Cause he didn't have any food.
FATHER: Why wouldn't his mommy—
CARL: There was a mommy, but there was no daddy 'cause daddy was shopping.
FATHER: Why was Aw so hungry? Do you know why?
CARL: No. He had breakfast, and he wanted a drink, so he pretended my finger was a drink. He ate a radio, so he couldn't talk. Mommy and daddy was away, but a sitter was there, another lady was there to help him.

The story unfolds readily in response to the father's questions and is designed partly to entertain him. Although he remains a biter, Aw is disarmed and subdued in a variety of ways and is transformed into a hungry creature whose aggression is made rational and satisfies ordinary needs. The tables are turned in the story; it is no longer Carl who is attacked, but Aw. Carl becomes active, aggressive, and masterful, not helpless and victimized. He is allied with strong women, who help him. However, Aw's fate, which is inseparable from his own, is not as grim as Carl's in the nightmare. Vital body parts regenerate or are replaced, and Aw is not denied the help that Carl allots to himself. A terrifying period in Carl's life is mastered in part through the creative activity and pleasure of storymaking.

Greenacre has pointed out, with respect to creative activity in adults, that it may relieve, but not solve conflicts [54]. Perhaps we need to claim no more for such activity in childhood. The conflicts are embodied, as in Carl's case, in the "imaginative product" only in derivative or displaced form. One may still wonder, however, whether mental conflicts are ever truly solved, and we should perhaps instead measure psychological health by a capacity such as Carl's to achieve fruitful accommodations. We may expect of Carl, as we do of ourselves, that he will continue throughout his life to do battle with the instinctual forces from within and the threatening realities from outside that are symbolized in these early stories.

References and Notes

1. Mortimer, R. Dostoevsky and the dream. *Modern Philol.* 54:106–116, 1956.
2. Dostoevsky, F. *Crime and Punishment.* (Trans. by Constance Garnett.) New York: Random House, 1944. P. 55.

3. Ibid. P. 47.
4. Ibid. P. 61.
5. Idem.
6. Wasiolek, E. *The Notebooks for Crime and Punishment.* Chicago: University of Chicago Press, 1967.
7. Horowitz, M. Discussion of paper by Lower, R. B. On Raskolnikov's Dreams in Dostoevsky's *Crime and Punishment.* American Psychoanalytic Ass., Boston, Mass., May 11, 1968.
8. Arnold, A. The recapitulation dream in *Richard III* and *Macbeth. Shakespeare Quart.* 6:51–62, 1955.
9. Ibid. P. 57.
10. For a psychoanalytic discussion of this dream, see also: Fliess, R. *The Revival of Interest in the Dream.* New York: International Universities Press, 1953.
11. Shakespeare, W. *The Tragedy of Richard the Third.* New York: Random House, 1931, I, iv, 62–63.
12. Ibid. V, iii.
13. Ibid.
14. Ibid.
15. Ibid.
16. Holinshed, R. *Chronicles of England, Scotland and Ireland,* London, 1808. Vol. III, p. 483.
17. Arden, J. *Serjeant Musgrave's Dance: An Unhistorical Parable.* New York: Grove Press, 1960. P. 64. Copyright © 1960 by John Arden.
18. Idem.
19. Stein, J. *Fiddler on the Roof.* New York: Crown, 1965. Copyright © 1965 by Joseph Stein. Used by permission of Crown Publishers, Inc.
20. Ibid. P. 61.
21. Edel, L. *Henry James. The Untried Years, 1843–1870,* vol. 1. London: Rupert Hart-Davis, 1953. Pp. 75–76.
22. Marie Bonaparte, in her psychoanalytic study of Poe, has aptly observed that Poe's works "fall into that category of literature which presents dream and nightmare characteristics in high degree." *Life and Works of Edgar Allen Poe.* London: Imago, 1949. P. 654.
23. Rochlin, G. *Griefs and Discontents: The Forces of Change.* Boston: Little, Brown, 1965.
24. Marie Bonaparte has also discussed the relationship between dreams and creative works. "The same mechanisms," she wrote, "which in dreams or nightmares govern the manner in which our strongest, though most carefully concealed desires are elaborated, desires which often are the most repugnant to consciousness, also govern the elaboration of the work of art." (*Life and Works of Edgar Allen Poe,* p. 209) What psychoanalytic writers often fail to stress are the differences in the two, the nature of the ego functioning that enables a writer or artist to transform a dream into a creative work.
25. Edel, L. *Henry James. The Untried Years, 1843–1870,* vol. I. London: Rupert Hart-Davis, 1953. P. 76.
26. James, H. *Autobiography.* New York: Criterion Books, 1956.
27. James H. The Jolly Corner. In Edel, L. *The Complete Tales of Henry James,* vol. 12. Philadelphia: Lippincott, 1965.

28. James, H. *Autobiography.* New York: Criterion Books, 1956. P. 196.
29. Saul Rosenzweig in his essay, The ghost of Henry James (*Character and Personality* 12:79–100, 1943) has observed that "unlike the ghosts of other writers, the creatures of James' imagination represent not the shadows of lives once lived, but the immortal impulses of the unlived life." Pp. 92–93.
30. Lowes, J. L. *The Road to Xanadu.* London: Constable, 1927. P. 357.
31. Stevenson, R. L. *Across the Plains.* New York: Scribner, 1909. P. 206.
32. Ibid. Pp. 208–209.
33. Hammerton, J. A. (Ed.) *Stevensonia.* London: Richards, 1903. P. 85.
34. Stevenson, R. L. *Across the Plains.* New York: Scribner, 1909. P. 223.
35. Ibid. P. 225.
36. Ibid. P. 226.
37. Hammerton, J. A. (Ed.) *Stevensonia.* London: Richards, 1903. P. 85.
38. Katan, M. A causerie on Henry James's "The Turn of the Screw." *Psychoanal. Stud. Child* 17:473–493, 1962.
39. Broun, H. Introduction to *The Turn of the Screw* by Henry James. New York: © Random House, 1930.
40. Ibid. P. ix.
41. Kris, E. *Psychoanalytic Explorations in Art.* New York: International Universities Press, 1952.
42. Kaplan, J. *Mr. Clemens and Mark Twain.* New York: Simon & Schuster, 1966.
43. Ibid. P. 342.
44. Ibid. P. 345.
45. Wolfenstein, M. Goya's dining room. *Psychoanal. Quart.* 35:47–83, 1966.
46. Kris, E. *Psychoanalytic Explorations in Art.* New York: International Universities Press, 1952. Pp. 87–168.
47. Sartre, J. *Saint Genet.* (Trans. by Bernard Frechtman.) New York: Braziller, 1963.
48. Kaplan, S., and Rank, B. Communication and transitory creativity in response to a trauma. *J. Amer. Acad. Child Psychiat.* 1:108–128, 1962.
49. Greenacre, P. Discussion and comments on the psychology of creativity. *J. Amer. Acad. Child Psychiat.* 1:129–137, 1962.
50. Finis, and Annamay. *Punch and Judy for Everyone.* Waterloo, Iowa: Finis and Co., 1961.
51. Gosse, E. *Father and Son.* London: Heinemann, 1913.
52. Ibid. P. 75.
53. Sendak, M. *Where the Wild Things Are.* New York: Harper & Row, 1963.
54. Greenacre, P. Discussion and comments on the psychology of creativity. *J. Amer. Acad. Child Psychiat.* 1:133–135, 1962.

4

Nightmares and the Threat of Aggression

NIGHTMARES OCCURRING at various ages have in common the feature of violence, or the threat of it, which inspires terror in the dreamer and thus forces waking. Furthermore, persons of all ages and phases of development are burdened by internal aggression, by impulses of hostility or hatred that threaten their relationships with valued persons in their environment. In this chapter, the relationship between these two observations, between the violence in nightmares and destructive aggression, will be examined. The intense inner struggle that young children experience in trying to deal with hostility, the manner in which severe anxiety dreams reflect such conflict, and the efforts of the ego to resolve that conflict will receive particular emphasis. The failure to master these conflicts over aggression in early childhood may account in part for the continuation of such dreams into adult life.

In recent years, many writers have noted the varying ways in which the term *aggression* has been used. Accompanying the development of psychoanalytic ego psychology, there has been increasing interest in the modifications of aggression, its value for adaptation, the possibilities for its transformation and sublimation, and the conversion of its destructive implications into less dangerous channels. Interest in the relationship between destructive aggression and a broader conception of aggression—

111

which includes self-assertion, dominance, ambition, or qualities of initiative or "drive"—has led to an extension of at least the use of the term "aggression," if not its definition.

Students of ethology have retained a more limited definition of aggression, restricting the term to some sort of fighting behavior [1, 2]. Tinbergen, for example, has specified that aggression, in *behavioral terms*, "involves approaching an opponent, and when within reach, pushing him away, inflicting damage of some kind, or at least forcing stimuli upon him that subdue him" [3]. A psychological definition that can be usefully applied to human beings must, however, also include its inner purpose—what psychoanalysts, who regard aggression as a primary instinct, call its *aim*.

In this chapter, I will employ the term aggression to designate impulses, wishes, and fantasies and associated behavior that are primarily destructive in their aim. This inner destructiveness presents a danger throughout the course of human life and, in the sense to be described, is uniquely human. Its mastery or deflection into nondestructive forms of behavior is one of the principal tasks of the civilizing process. I will try to show how the intense conflicts that are associated with the effort at various ages to modify aggression may find expression in nightmares. Many such examples have already been provided in earlier chapters of this book. If the reader questions this limited definition of aggression, he may note that it is by no means certain whether such qualities as human initiative, reaching out, ambition, self-assertion, pleasure in mastery, and the like exist from birth as distinct potentials or "instincts" side by side with destructive aggressiveness or whether they occur as particular expressions of some broader aggressiveness. Anyone who has worked closely with small children will recognize the difficulty in determining on clinical grounds whether destructive aggression itself derives from the thwarting of self-assertive behavior or whether the latter represents the adaptive modification of destructive impulses.

Nightmares seem to be most clearly related to aggression in its destructive aspect, although they seem also to arise in relation to the effort of the small child to master new skills. Often, however, nightmares appear to occur in connection with the mastery of a developmental task or a drive toward independence in early childhood, or in adult life accompany the aspiration toward some other ambition; in such cases, a deeper exploration of the dream will often reveal that these initiatives are associated for the dreamer with destructive impulses he experiences as dangerous. These dreams are, in my view, small but intense dramas that demonstrate the assignment with which a human being is burdened throughout the course of life: to inhibit, modify or transform the hatred and hostility that may at any time disrupt his relationships with those persons whom he loves or upon whom he has become dependent.

Although a developmental approach will be employed, it should be recognized that the expression of aggression does not conform to regular sequential phases in the same sense as sexuality. It is also doubtful whether there is any real "latency" period in aggression to the extent that this concept holds true for sexuality.

Psychoanalytic Views of Aggression

Following Freud's lead, psychoanalysts have generally agreed to regard aggression, together with sexuality, as one of two fundamental instincts. Freud did not derive his later theory of the duality of the instincts, of aggression and libido, from the empirical fact of the ubiquity of aggressive behavior. As psychoanalysts have pointed out, aggression as an instinctual drive and aggression as a description of an act of behavior must be distinguished, since manifestly aggressive behavior may derive from motives other than hostility or hatred toward the object. Instead, Freud supported the existence of aggression as a primary instinctual drive in human beings on the basis of the irrationality of masochism and the tendency to unreasonable repetition—the "repetition compulsion" [4, 5]. Observing these phenomena, he found himself unable to explain certain behavior that seemed to operate destructively against the best interests of the individual, to fly irrationally and repetitively in the face of the pleasure principle. Some destructive urge, Freud felt, must be at work, and he postulated an instinct of destruction, or death instinct. Aggression aimed at the destruction of others he saw as motivated by narcissism, the subject's wish to direct his own aggression away from himself and toward other objects in order to preserve the self. Thus, Freud's derivation of an instinct of aggression was not based primarily on clinical or empirical evidence of externally directed aggression. However, the phenomena on which Freud's derivation was based—masochism and the repetition compulsion —can be explained at least in part on other grounds, such as unconscious guilt, the effort to master anxiety, and the search in disguised form for various satisfactions. Thus, there is little direct clinical support in Freud's writings for a primary instinct of destruction.

Waelder, who does not accept the death instinct as Freud postulated this theory, recognized an instinct of primary destructiveness, "an inborn propensity operating without provocation and basically independent of ego and libidinal activities" [6]. Unlike Freud, Waelder found his support for the existence of this instinct in observable phenomena such as extreme forms of assaultiveness, the suicidal drives of mental patients, or the insatiable hatred of dictators such as Hitler that strike one as irreducibly destructive. Nevertheless, the quantitative intensity of observed behavior does not in itself provide support for its instinctual origins. The behavior could, as Cannon and James pointed out long ago, proceed from other motives or emotions such as fear or reflect markedly aberrant personality development [7]. Psychoanalytic findings have not provided adequate supporting evidence for the assumption by Hartmann et al. of a "constant driving power [of aggression] comparable to that of libido" [8] if, as these authors state, the primary aim of aggression is destruction of the object.

Direct observations of infants also do not support the existence of an instinct to destroy. Spitz, for example, has written of the angry weeping and screaming that can be observed when an infant is deprived of its mother [9]. Although the infant certainly looks angry, we have no evidence of a mental representation of anger or aggression that would fulfill the psychoanalytic definition of an instinct or a drive representation. We would probably do well to accept Wolff's caution in questioning whether any psychoanalytic "core concepts," such as drive and defense, "can be tested meaningfully (either confirmed or disproved) by the data of infant observation alone" [10].

This does not mean that aggressive impulses do not play an important role in the individual's development; neither can one argue with Freud's assertion of the ubiquity of aggression or the statement by Hartmann et al. that "aggression is dangerous because it involves the individual in conflicts that are difficult if not impossible to solve, since they threaten the very object on whom man depends" [11]. What seems to remain unsettled is the degree to which such aggression exists in the infant or young child as an instinct or force that seeks to destroy others before the individual has developed relations to other persons. This is to be contrasted with another possibility: that there exists a potential for hostility or violence, mediated most likely by hypothalamic centers, that is elicited in response to the demands and limitations of developing human relations. Although this question cannot be settled in this chapter, the relationship between nightmares and the problems of aggression that arise in the anguish-filled development of human relationships in childhood and thereafter will be explored.

Aggression and the Development of Social Life in Man

Studies of aggression from other than psychoanalytic sources, especially animal behavioral researches, also provide little support for a primary destructive drive [12–14]. In fact, there seems to be general agreement that, among most animals, intraspecific aggression under normal conditions serves particular species-preserving aims such as territorial defense, sexual selection, and protection of the young. Its aim is the fulfillment of these functions, not the destruction of another animal [15].

Whether or not we may regard aggression as a primary instinct, whatever that may imply, the arousal of aggressive impulses or the eliciting of an aggressive response will depend in man, as in other animals, upon an interplay of internal biological and environmental influences. Tinbergen has recently observed that the distinctions between innate and acquired patterns are becoming less clear in the study of animal behavior and that patterns thought to be innate "may contain elements that at an early stage developed in interaction with the environment" [16]. Although the simplistic environmentalist view that aggression was brought about only by environmental frustrations can no longer be supported, some form of thwarting or privation in early childhood seems to be an essential factor in the development of aggressive impulses and behavior in human beings [17–19]. Robey and Brazleton have found that, among the isolated Zinacantecos Indians of southern Mexico, overt fighting behavior or violence is almost nonexistent [20]. They thought that this might be attributable to the fact that, whenever an infant under two or three years of age shows any discomfort, he is immediately picked up by his mother and held to her breast until his distress subsides. Such conditions could not, however, possibly be reproduced in Western society. For the infant developing in our culture, pain is inevitable and, as the English psychoanalysts Joffe and Sandler have phrased it, "the normal response to pain is aggression, directed at whatever is thought to be the source of the pain" [21]. Ernest Jones has expressed a similar view, observing that "it is extraordinarily difficult to detect spontaneous activity of the aggressive instinct in isolation" [22].

What the foregoing arguments imply is that destructive aggression in human beings is largely the product of social life, of what von Bertalanffy has called "domestication" [23]. As Rolde has recently observed, "To define aggression as an action aimed at hurting another implies some concept of the existence of the other" [24]. Hatred arises as a sustained aggressive attitude toward another person who is regarded as the cause of pain. It presupposes considerable prior interaction with other persons and the capacity to carry internally a mental image of the other person when he is not present. Freud wrote of hatred: "The relation of *unpleasure* seems to be the sole decisive one. The ego hates, abhors and pursues with intent to destroy all objects which are a source of unpleasurable feeling. . . ." [25].

The purpose of this discussion is not to argue for or against the existence of a primary destructive drive. Rather, it is to stress the intimate association of destructiveness with the development of human relationships. In summary, we may conceive of aggression as a phylogenetically transmitted drive or drive potential serving, in man as in other animals, species-preserving functions and, in response to the provocations, demands, limitations, and other complexities of social life, becoming associated with destructive aims and with hatred.

Aggression and the Clinical Occurrence of Nightmares

Hostility or hatred in relation to other persons presents an inner threat to the human child and arouses anxiety as he experiences its danger for him. It is imperative that he find ways of modifying the harmful potential of hostility, replace destructive acts with destructive thoughts, and then learn the difference between the two or be faced with object loss, loss of love, and abandonment or annihilation through retaliation. The first nightmares that can be documented in early childhood seem to occur in relation to the child's earliest struggles with aggression as it arises within himself or is perceived as emanating from angry persons in the outside world or from more impersonal destructive forces. Aggression that is associated with a demonstrably destructive *aim* can occur probably only after some degree of awareness of other persons as distinct from the self has occurred. In the second year, when such differentiation has certainly begun, aggressive behavior may be seen in the context of developing relations with other persons. The mechanism of identification with the aggressor can already be observed, that is, destructive behavior resulting from the child's need to identify out of fear with the other person's aggressive qualities in order to avoid being destroyed. A complex interplay of destructive impulses and introjected and projected aggression has thus already begun to develop in the second year, and has particular relevance for the understanding of nightmares and anxiety dreams.

There has been insufficient study of the parent's actual qualities and behavior in shaping the child's aggressive drives and activity, especially the element of destructiveness [26]. It is striking, for example, how vividly the angry voice or some other aggressive quality of a parent is represented as a hostile element in a child's or, later, in an adult's nightmare. Often in a nightmare the projection of the individual's own aggression appears to be less critical than his effort to preserve himself from a cruel attack from another person or creature. Furthermore, we know little about the distortion or intensification of aggressive drives that occurs when a child perceives himself to be constantly under attack or hated by the parents. Anna Freud has discussed the mechanisms by which destructive urges are modified or bound in the course of development, especially in the third or fourth years [27, 28]. She stressed in particular the necessity for libidinization, for fusion of aggression with libido, in order that the child's destructiveness will not remain isolated. She regards the failure to achieve such fusion as responsible for the pathological aggression of small children. However, it is not clear from her writings what the conditions of such fusion of aggression with libido must be in order that a constructive modification of aggression and not an enhancement of sadism will be the result. Anyone who has observed the wanton assaultiveness and annihilatory destructiveness of small children, especially boys between eighteen and thirty-six months, will realize what a universal developmental problem such aggression represents and will recognize that major internal changes and structural reorganization of the personality must occur in order to bring these impulses under control.

Clinical Investigations

THE TWO-YEAR-OLD'S TERRIBLENESS. Under ordinary circumstances, during the second year of life a mutually satisfying relationship is established between the mother and child based on love, affection, and constancy. Once established, the stability of this much-valued attachment is threatened for the child by the upsurge in the intensity of his aggressive impulses and the increase in the capacity for physical violence. Furthermore, with the achievement of this attachment to the mother, other persons such as the mother herself, siblings, or the father, who would limit or interfere with the exclusive claims of this relationship, become more specifically the target of the hostility; this, like the love it accompanies, becomes more unequivocally object-directed. This may mean that the child's aggression will now present for him a threat of much greater magnitude.

The following account describes over an eight-month period the earliest struggles of a normal two-year-old boy to master the violent aggression that burdened his immature ego and threatened his developing relationships with his parents. This period coincided approximately with his toilet training. During this time he had several nightmares that, together with his play, revealed the intensity of the child's conflict and provided information as to its nature and the psychological processes involved in its mastery and resolution. It is likely that this boy's struggles are representative of the usual developmental situation of the two-year-old; he is described in detail here to highlight the issues of aggression, nightmares, and normal development at this age.

Sam, the youngest of three children, had developed unremarkably during the first two years of his life. He was a lively, happy child. At two years and two months his mother had begun to place him occasionally on a potty chair, although he had watched with interest his older brothers using the toilet. At this time he began a game in which he grabbed his father's nose with his fingers and then pretended to toss it to the floor. "Where's my nose?" his father asked. "It throwed away," Sam answered. "Oh! Oh! Help! Help! I need my nose," his father cried out. Then Sam got down on the floor, sometimes groveling as if to look for something, exclaiming finally with delight, "Here it is." He then put it firmly "back on" his father. He then repeated with pleasure the whole sequence over and over. Sometimes he played the same game, with visibly less pleasure, disposing of and recovering his own nose in a similar fashion.

About six weeks after he began to play this game, Sam had his first documented nightmare. For several days he had had an aversion to sleeping while wet and especially to lying down on a wet spot on the sheet, insisting his mother get him a dry one, and she had been encouraging him to use the potty chair. Also, for several days before the dream he had been particularly destructive, especially on the day before the nightmare, knocking over lamps and wantonly tearing up plants. His mother had reached the end of her patience and had punished him, angrily closing him in his room on two occasions. That night, one to two hours after being put to bed, Sam awoke, crying out in fear and asking for his mother. When asked what frightened him he said, "De thing" and "De thing gone" and pointed to a wet spot made by his sweat and tears on the sheet at the head of the crib. When taken into his parents' room, he continued to hallucinate, trembling in distress, pointing and repeating, "De thing gone." He was reluctant to return to his crib, and cried a little before he went back to sleep. Two weeks later he had a similar nightmare, disclosing somewhat more content. During that day his own behavior had been relatively calm, but he had taken considerable knocking about from his brothers. He had heard his father yelling at them when they misbehaved. Before going to sleep, he had watched excitedly with his brothers the "Bat Man" TV program, a show filled with violent assaults. During the night he awoke, screaming for his mother. "De buggy's on de wall" and "Dere," he cried, pointing to the wall by his crib and to the doorway. "It hurt me dere on de back and on de tummy," he insisted. During the week after these dreams, Sam expressed considerable interest in parts of his and other person's bodies and concern with dogs that bite. Concomitantly, he showed a greater inclination and ability to represent his conflicts in symbolic play. He found rubber dolls and identified them as members of his family. In one bit of play, he repeatedly kissed and hugged the father, older brother, and "me" dolls in turn and had them fall down and hurt "his foot." He put each in a car to sleep, but stuffed the "daddy" under the mattress. Open interest in parts of the body increased markedly and came to include, not only noses as two months earlier, but also hands, thumbs and other fingers, feet, and the penis. He repeatedly expressed concern with these parts coming off or falling off. The nose game with his father described above was played with greater enthusiasm than before, and now he added the hands and feet. He grabbed at his father's hand or nose with particular energy and threw it to the floor and then returned the part to its owner with pleasure and relief. In a variation, he took his father's nose and put it on himself and put his nose on the father. Once when he saw him urinating, he pointed to his father's penis and said, "Daddy's bott (bottle); bott in dere." Then he pointed to his own penis and said, "Bott; bott in dere. It's all vett." Several other times he wanted to unzip and show his penis to his father or have his father show his to him.

During these weeks he continued to resist the toilet, retaining his urine until he could let it go in the bathtub. He defiantly took off his diaper and urinated standing up in his crib. On one such occasion he held his penis proudly and announced to his father, "I vett my bed." "What will Mother say?" asked his father. "No, no poopah (his brother's word for feces); no, no poopah," came the answer, accompanied by repeated delighted blows of his fists on his father's chest and then against his own. A week later at the supper table, after playing the nose game, he pinched his father's ears and said they were "out." Then he poked his fingers in his father's eye, grabbed his tie, and said, "Dis is Daddy's tie." Then he went to his mother and the baby-sitter and, pointing and yanking at imaginary ties, declared, "Dis is Mommy's tie" and "Dis is Margie's tie," following this with, "Dis is my tie" as he pulled at his own tieless neck region.

The next two weeks saw a rampage of aggression and destruction on Sam's part, alternating with affectionate and clinging behavior with his mother. He attacked his brothers' toys and tore up their drawings. He dumped food on the table and threw it and his silverware at others and about the room without provocation. He squeezed the contents of tooth-paste and other tubes on clothes and carpets, threw his parents' belong-ings on the floor, and scribbled with marking pencil on their bedroom wall. Disapproval did little to check the behavior but, if firm enough, could elicit a teary, "Sorry." His anxiety in relation to this aggression, based on the expectation of retaliation, was made particularly evident one night when, while sitting on a bed with his father before bedtime, he looked out the window and announced anxiously and playfully, "Derz a wolf out dere—ooh—he whack me right dere on de face." A moment later he said, "I whack you, Daddy" and hit his father on the face. Then, more seriously than before, he pointed to the window and said, "Dere's a wolf out dere—he kill me down—he kill me down" and gestured to smack his own face.

The third and last of Sam's nightmares in this period occurred three weeks later when he was two and a half. Before the dream he had had no bowel movement for five days, clearly withholding in response to his mother's wish that he use the toilet. In the evening before the dream he had considerable physical as well as psychological distress over his simul-taneous need and reluctance to pass his stool. Anxiously, he asked to be held by his mother and father. Finally, after much holding by his parents and a great deal of pain and anxious straining, he passed a huge stool while sitting on his mother's lap, followed by two more in the course of the evening. Thus relieved, he went peacefully to bed. About 1:30 in the morning he awoke crying loudly, was inconsolable and said, "Get de thing off," pointing to his diaper area. He continued to be so frightened that only taking him to the parents' bed gave him any relief. He con-tinued to sleep fitfully, crying out from time to time. At breakfast he seemed still to be under the influence of frightening hallucinations, cried loudly, and demanded to be held by his mother. Through his sobs he said a lion had come into his bed during the night to bite him and had "died." It had fallen down and was "broken." His parents played with him a game in which they dismissed the lion by saying, "Good-by, lion" and waving it away. With increasing pleasure he asked for this to be repeated over and over until his severe distress was gone. In the evening he was his usual self again, calling his father "daddy-pooph" (feces).

A month later (two years and seven months) he introduced a new fig-ure into his play, a hand puppet sea serpent named Erby. Erby, whose ag-gression was completely under Sam's control and manipulation, bit Sam's parents, giving the boy great pleasure. After this he spontaneously scolded and slapped Erby with the words, "Don't you bite Daddy, Erby." Forget-ting that he had disclaimed responsibility for his own aggression by the invention of Erby, he had Erby bite Sam to punish him. Another time, after he had been scolded for particularly destructive behavior, Sam was discovered with Erby, hitting him angrily and scolding, "You a bad boy, Erby. I gonna hit you, I gonna cut you" (he got a scissors and started to cut the puppet). His father asked what Erby had done, "He bite me and he bite Tommy (Sam's brother)—he a bad boy—he a big man—a bad man—I cut his mouth."

Sam made it clear that the aggressive insects and animals were closely associated with his stool, which he would sometimes animate directly. One evening, for example, he made a small bowel movement in his pants at the dinner table, rather than use the toilet, as he was becoming accustomed to doing. His mother reminded him that he should use the toilet, as other members of the family did. He repeated her words, but then patted the diaper with the bowel movement in it. "It goes quack-quack," he repeated over and over. Then he said that a wolf came and scared him at night, and he woke up and said, "Hello, Daddy." "Margie" (the babysitter), he continued, "is a bad lady. She comes in my room and scares me. She goes 'grrh, grrh.'" Then he discovered a "bad bug" on the floor (perhaps he saw a small insect). He invited Margie over to look at the now entirely imaginary bug. Squatting, he spit at the bug saying, "It's dead; it'll die; it'll cry." Spitting at it over and over, he called it a "lady bug" and returned repeatedly to attack it.

Over the next two months Sam's toilet training was virtually completed. His mother noticed changes in his behavior, particularly in the way he dealt with his aggression. He acted charming or coy, trying to avoid punishment. He denied his "crimes" or through argument sought amelioration of punishments. He declared dramatically, "I'm sorry, Mommy" in a placating tone, as if he really meant it. Although he could sense that his mother was upset, felt bad about that, and wished to appease her, there was as yet no evidence that he felt internally troubled over his own behavior.

One day, at two years and ten months, his mother found him at the bathroom sink, smelling of cosmetics and struggling, like Lady Macbeth, to erase from his hands the evidence of her lipstick he had just smeared in her room. He tried to hide the red on his hands from her and said, blinking his eyes nervously, that he was "too sleepy" to show her where he had gotten the lipstick. "I'm sorry, Mommy," he conceded finally, as if to say, "Don't punish me."

Sam showed through his play and dreams the intensity and multifaceted nature of his struggle as a maturing two-year-old to deal with aggressive impulses. This aggression occurred in the context of the earliest efforts to impose civilizing restraints and demands upon him, including toilet training, and was in part a rebellious response to these efforts. The aggression in turn opposed the civilizing process and impeded its progress. This aggression was also, however, perceived as a danger for the child, threatening the treasured relationships with those he loved. He was forced, therefore, to find ways of modifying its destructive potential.

Much of Sam's destructiveness seemed to be a response to thwarted anality. Anal erotic pleasures, the desire to pass or withhold the stool on the child's own terms, where, when, and under what circumstances he alone chose—these certainly were important during this period of Sam's life. His parents' efforts to curtail this freedom, to have him pass his excreta where they directed, were intensely frustrating to him and called forth powerful aggressive responses and emotions of hatred. There does not, however, seem to be sufficient evidence for drawing a direct parallel between the two or for finding a sufficient causal relationship between the anal frustrations of this period and the violent aggression that seemed to characterize it. Other developmental factors appeared to be at work, associated with growing physical and motor capability, and the intensity of destructiveness seemed to be gathering in relation to the growing significance of the particular people who stimulated, loved, thwarted, and even seemed at times to attack the child in a great variety of ways. In the two-year-old boy aggression seemed to reach a relatively great biological and psychological intensity in comparison with the ego functions that were responsible for mastering it. In relation to particular persons, it was manifested as hostility or even hatred and was expressed through physical attacks, notably with the mouth (spitting), teeth, hands, feet, and organs of excretion.

Sam made clear that he had a very great investment in his body and its parts, especially his stool, penis, fingers, and other appendages that gave him pleasure and that he had reason to regard as especially vulnerable, particularly as these parts were themselves the implements of his aggression. He was concerned with possible injury or loss of these parts, and the fact that he could now actually be forced to give up his stool, which was then flushed down the toilet, made this anxiety more acute. His own aggression became increasingly a liability for him because, in the same fashion as he wished to destroy others and their property and saw the result of his attacks, he had good reason to believe that the same or worse could happen to him. Another serious problem for him was the possibility of losing the love of those he valued most and the pleasure and security this love gave him. He learned very early that his destructive aggression and hatred elicited angry scolding, scowls, and even slaps from his parents and still readier retaliation from his less tolerant brothers, thus threatening his relationships with these important people.

Sam's nightmares provided the most dramatic, vivid, and clearest evidence of the intensity of his conflicts over aggression and their life-and-death quality. The content of the dreams, though limited in detail at this age—or at least as far as he could tell us—was concerned with aggressive attack aimed chiefly at himself. His own destruction seemed imminent before his awakening prevented it. Much love and affection must be given when such a small child awakens from a frightening dream to balance its awful force, and even then it is difficult to assure the child that there is no real danger. The most striking fact about these dreams is that Sam, though highly aggressive in waking life, *was always the victim and never the aggressor in the dreams*. The hallucinated "thing" or "buggy" or lion threatened to bite or destroy him, not the reverse. It is true that in his last dream he said that the lion was broken, but this was reported the next morning, and there was no suggestion that he regarded himself as responsible.

It was in relation to conflicts surrounding destructiveness that some of the earliest ego defenses began to form and served to prevent these conflicts from becoming overwhelming and disruptive to emerging skills and human relationships. Through an increasing array of symbolic displacements, Sam began to master his immediate struggles. In his play he displaced his concern with the flushed stool onto the "throwed away nose" and it was his father's organ, not his own, that was thrown on the floor. In these few months the variety, elaborateness, and mobility of these symbolic displacements could be seen to increase markedly as body parts readily came to stand for one another and Sam's play and fantasy life made use of bugs, lions, wolves, sea serpents, and neckties.

Whereas displacement transposed the body parts that are the instruments of aggression, as well as the vulnerable objects of potential retaliation, disavowal of responsibility for the impulses themselves was accomplished through projection. It was not Sam, but the puppet sea serpent Erby, who was the biter. It was not he, but Margie who growled; not he, but the wolf who killed. Related to and combined with these mechanisms of displacement and projection, was the use of denial in fantasy as described by Anna Freud [29]. Concerned, for example, that ladies lack a penis, Sam yanked imaginary "ties" at their necks that he asserted they had just as his father did. Another valuable defense for Sam derived from his increasing capacity to assume roles in his play, to take on through identification the aspects of persons who were strong, active, masterful and unafraid, rather than weak, vulnerable, passive, and thus endangered. Through identification with his brothers he became a full-fledged member of a band of western killers. Through play activity such as this the boy began to achieve the mastery of motor functions and the elaboration of fantasy life that may later serve as the basis for effective sublimation. Humor and clowning, which are not given sufficient attention in discussion of the psychology of two-year-olds, begin as imitations of and identification with aggressive objects and serve also as effectively modified and socially engaging means of discharging aggression in play.

It would not be accurate to regard the displacement and projection that occurred in Sam's dreams as arising entirely out of the defensive needs of the child in the same fashion as, for example, his blaming of Erby for assaults. Displacement and projection are essential aspects of dreaming and are determined in part by the dream process itself. The child nevertheless makes use of dreams in giving expression to various conflicts. He can use the projections, displacements, and symbolic transformations of the dreaming process to express aggression without acknowledging that he harbors such aggression toward other persons. Why must he become himself the victim of the attack and bring assault upon himself in such terrifying ways? His psychological development is not sufficiently advanced that he would experience a need for punishment based on the demands of his superego, at best a rudimentary structure at this age. The beginning internalization of inhibiting parental voices and attitudes is reflected in the content of the dreams, playing a part in the attacking images. However, this does not tell us why, when the child appears to struggle so actively against such parental limitations in waking life, he should victimize himself with them in his dreams.

One possible answer to this question may lie in the extreme danger for the small child of harboring murderous wishes toward those persons upon whom he is dependent, not only for love, but for his very existence. The child, as in Sam's case, turns his aggression against himself to spare the object because he could not bear the anxiety that would accompany the direct expression of such impulses toward other persons. The danger lies, not only in the possibility of retaliation, but also in losing the valued person should the aggressive wishes be fulfilled.

Dreams depend heavily upon concrete visual representation and upon the implementation of thoughts and feelings in actions occurring in the dream or seen as already accomplished. A small child such as Sam could not, for example, bear to see himself in a dream destroying his mother or father or even to see a representation of one of his parents as irrevocably dead or gone. It is my impression that, even among adults, the direct fulfillment of murderous wishes in a dream occurring outside of a therapeutic context tends to occur primarily in emotionally disturbed individuals.

The parental prohibition and punishment of Sam's aggression contributed to the intensity of his conflict and likewise provided him, through the eventual internalization of effective inhibiting attitudes and controls, a means of mastering it. At the stage of his life that we have found him, Sam perceived these restraints as threats to his freedom and dangers to his person, and they confirmed his fear of loss of love. Through frustration, these prohibitions increased the intensity of his hostility and thereby also the danger he perceived from his impulses, increasing further his fear of injury and loss of love. At the close of this account, he had begun to internalize some of these externally imposed limits and himself to play the part of the scolding parent ("You a bad boy, Erby"). He was taking responsibility for his behavior to the extent of scolding himself, but he had not yet learned real remorse for his aggressive misdeeds, although he could feel so sorry for his mother and her unhappiness over what he had done that he even tried to appease her. Perhaps this concern for another person's feelings is a prerequisite for the effective internalization of external prohibitions; an interest in appeasement may precede real internal modification of aggressive attitudes toward other persons. Without such love of another person, the child's opposition and contempt for the authority imposed from without would prevent its acceptance and effective internalization. We can say that Sam had begun to develop a super ego, but that it was far from a fully internalized agency that could play a major role in the civilizing process and in regulating behavior.

In summary Sam, like any child of two, faced as one of his principal developmental tasks the mastery of the intense aggression and hatred that was aroused in conjunction with the socializing demands of those upon whom he was dependent. Since the aggression and destructive wishes were directed toward the very persons whom he was coming to love most, he was faced with the danger, not only of retaliation and injury to his own body and its parts, but also of the loss of the love of these people. In response to these conflicts, early ego defenses—displacement, projection, denial in fantasy, internalization, and various identifications—began their development and will come to serve, along with later super ego formation, an important civilizing role. Nightmares in small children such as Sam are sensitive indicators of their internal struggles and reflect in particular their desperate conflict over aggression and hatred, perceived in the dreams in life-and-death terms. The fact that the little child is himself the victim and almost never the aggressor in his dreams is a telling indicator of the totally unacceptable and intolerable nature of aggressive impulses and death wishes toward valued people, wishes whose full acknowledgement even on the part of mature adults rarely occurs. Although the dreams express murderous attack against himself, it is possible that they protect the dreamer from something worse, namely experiencing, or taking responsibility for, murderous impulses toward those he loves and upon whom he is so dependent physically and emotionally.

SIBLING RIVALRY AS A PROTOTYPE. Rivalry with another child for the parents' love is one of the most ubiquitous and frequent instigators of aggressive impulses. Such rivalry is, of course, not confined to any particular developmental period; it arises as soon as the child is able to perceive that he is not the exclusive object of the parents' interest and continues throughout the individual's life. Hostility and hatred arise toward both the rival child and toward the parent who shares his or her favors with the rival. A child may thus become doubly burdened by aggressive impulses that arise in this way. Such hostility toward siblings seems to be one of the most frequent precipitants of nightmares in childhood. Frequently the birth of a sibling will precipitate frightening dreams in a child in whom they have not been noticed before. The association of the dreams with the heightened aggression aroused in the child by the advent of the unwelcome intruder can easily be demonstrated.

Harry, the oldest of four children, was three years and four months old when his third sibling and only brother was born. His mother said he had always been an overactive, aggressive child who had even "bit" on her nipples when she nursed him and regularly had attacked his sisters after their arrival; it was only after the birth of his third sibling, however, that she became concerned over his assaultive behavior. At that time he became increasingly aggressive with his sisters and brother, demanded their toys and bit, kicked, tripped, and punched them, took putty off windows, or played in doorways to force people to step over him. Toward the end of her last pregnancy, Harry began to tell his mother that he hated her and intended to kill her and cut her stomach in order to remove the new baby and then cut it up. Sometimes he punched his mother in the abdomen so hard that it hurt her. The parents dealt with his behavior by scoldings and punishments, such as spankings and putting him in a chair in the corner, but also let him come into bed with them when he arose and walked around at night. After the baby's birth, the mother noticed that Harry seemed unhappy, smiled little, began again to suck his thumb, and cried easily; whereas his toilet training had been complete a year before, he now began to have frequent incidents of soiling and wet every night and frequently during the day.

About one month after the baby's birth Harry, who had not been known to have sleep disturbances, began to have nightmares. He awoke from these in terror, convinced that the events he described actually had occurred. Typically, he dreamt that a girl had come to hurt him or that a woman had killed him. It was very difficult for his parents to comfort him.

Ten weeks after the baby was born, his parents brought Harry for treatment. In his interviews with the child psychiatrist, he revealed the preoccupations with aggression and violence that have been reported in the history. He tore open bags of candies with his teeth and ate them voraciously, spoke of tigers and other wild animals that eat people, and told of another "boy" who bit his back as he in fact had done to a neighbor's child. He drooled and enjoyed making a mess, although he was careful to clean up. He thrust a thermometer into a doll's genital region and then said that he had been struck by a car and hurt in the eye; he had in fact been hit, but not injured. He expressed worry about blood and had other concerns about possible injury.

Harry's mother had wanted to have sixteen children, but she found that having only four in a little over three years created stresses for the family and especially for Harry that were greater than she had anticipated. Although Harry gave evidence of being in the phallic phase of his development, the frequent pregnancies and new infants helped to keep alive or to revive the oral and anal aggression and sadism that had originated in the earlier phases of his development. Even before his baby brother was born, his behavior toward his mother left little doubt that this latest intruder was especially unwelcome. The disfavor and punishments that his sadistic assaults engendered in his parents brought home to Harry the fact that he must curb his hostility or risk serious retaliation and loss of their love. His play revealed especially the additional danger of bodily injury from his phallic-aggressive wishes and attacks. Harry's nightmares revealed with particular vividness the conflict between these aggressive impulses and the need to inhibit them. As in the play where a "neighbor boy" bit him, thus reversing the direction of his aggressive actions, so in the dreams the girl or woman killed Harry, similarly reversing the direction of the hostile intentions. Rather than be the attacker of his mother or sisters, by projection the girl or woman hurt or killed him. To be the victim in this way, though terrifying, was perhaps less dangerous or disturbing than to bear a thought, which his immature ego would have difficulty distinguishing from the real deed even if he were awake, of destroying the person he loved most and upon whom he remained so dependent.

An experience that confronts a child with the reality of his own vulnerability, with the fact that loved ones can really disappear or die, is likely to precipitate severe nightmares, especially when the child has borne aggressive wishes toward the other individual. This phenomenon is well illustrated by the case of a girl brought for treatment at five who began to have severe nightmares when she was three, just after her thirteen-month-old sister had died of a fulminating viral infection three days after entering the hospital. Unable to deal with their own grief, the parents removed from the home all evidence of the dead child's previous existence and did not speak of her. The patient was told only that her sister had gone to the hospital and died. When the child was four another baby sister was born, and, though jealous of the baby, she was permitted no aggressive expression toward the infant. The patient, an unassertive and inhibited child, began at five to have the fantasy that an angry bear clawed her baby sister in her crib. She abhorred toilets and feared that a baby might be flushed down the bowl. She spoke of a "friend" who went to the hospital and never returned. To the doctor, she clearly expressed hostile wishes toward both the living and the dead sister, although her behavior at home was exemplary. A typical dream at five was that a lion was entering the window to eat her up. Awaking in fear, she went to the foot of her bed, where she felt safe. In another dream an elephant came to her room, took off all her clothes, and threw her in a mud puddle. In association with this last dream, she expressed the wish to throw mudpies at her father and her doctor.

This little girl's nightmares, expressed in the terms of her active oedipal conflicts, were the product of her intense fear of the aggressive wishes that she had harbored toward her rival mother and toward both her living and her dead sister, whose internal representations had become fused. Her experience with the sister's actual disappearance and death had confronted her with the possibility that her murderous wishes might indeed have a fatal result and also with the fact of the vulnerability of her own existence. Her aggression in combination with her perception of her own vulnerability produced her nightmares. In the dream she became the victim, and the other person or creature was the aggressor.

PHALLIC AGGRESSION IN NIGHTMARES. In children and adults of both sexes, it is not unusual for aggression associated with frustrations of the phallic phase of development to erupt with violent intensity in nightmares. Such nightmares occur frequently in children, but may also occur at critical points in the analysis of adult patients, providing valuable insight into deep-seated childhood conflicts over repressed hostility and hatred. The following example from a woman undergoing psychoanalytic treatment illustrates the manner in which the full intensity of phallic aggression that is intimately linked with earlier pre-oedipal conflicts may burst forth in a nightmare. The familiar lines of the seventeenth-century playwright, William Congreve, "Heaven has no rage like love to hatred turned, Nor hell a fury like a woman scorned," seem especially apropos in this connection [30].

A thirty-one-year-old single executive secretary sought psychoanalysis because of her inability to form a lasting and satisfying heterosexual relationship. She had been in analysis with a male analyst for three years when a severe anxiety dream that represented a critical turning point in her treatment occurred.

The patient's father, a playboy, was already on his way to becoming an alcoholic in her infancy, yet she had early positive memories of his taking her to a lake shore. The mother was socially prominent, involved in her social ambitions, and wanted children for the prestige they could give her, but she did not want the responsibility of taking care of them. Whenever there was difficulty or inconvenience for her or the family during the patient's early childhood, the mother packed the patient off to her grandfather's and later sent her to boarding school. The patient felt that her mother had consistently failed to support or protect her and in the analysis gave many examples of the mother's emotional if not actual desertion. Characteristically, the mother promised gifts or rewards and then withdrew them.

Because of her husband's drinking and failure to support the family, when the patient was eight the mother and the grandfather arranged to leave, taking the children. The patient felt deeply disappointed at what she felt to be the abandonment of her father by the family, a feeling that was shattered when the father quickly married an alcoholic woman she could not respect. He subsequently had two further marriages to alcoholic women and numerous affairs. Just prior to the divorce, the mother gave birth to a baby girl, who died four days later. When the patient was twelve, her mother remarried, and the following year gave birth to a boy.

In her adolescence and early adult life, a pattern of promiscuity and seduction of men developed, and the patient had the fantasy of herself as a prostitute. She sought men close to her, especially her own bosses or those in positions of authority; persuaded them to go to bed with her; and then demanded exclusive possession of them. Inevitably, after several months or even years, she cast them off, often humiliating them. During sexual intercourse she was herself frigid, but kept the light on so she might see the excitement in the man's face and thereby appreciate her own success and dominance. On a number of occasions she performed fellatio, which made her gag or retch; such retching also occurred when she ate certain foods. On two occasions she became pregnant and underwent abortions with her mother's strong encouragement.

The dream that follows occurred at a point in her treatment when she had been reexperiencing with intense emotion her childhood disappointment with her father and was beginning to acknowledge the full force of her hostility toward him. In this context, she interrupted the analysis for several sessions to attend the wedding in another city of her favored half-brother to a very attractive young girl. The night of her return she had the nightmare, which she reported the following morning:

"I was away at my brother's wedding and was in a ballroom, and for some reason the ladies were prevented from going to the ladies' room, so that they just urinated all over the floor, and no one seemed very concerned about it. But I had a piece of toilet paper in my hand and didn't know how to dispose of it and was embarrassed. I left the party with my mother. It was late and quite dark. My brother came out and was immediately set upon by four men with four long solid butcher knives. They de-

manded his money, but he had paid for the party and hadn't any on him. I knew this, but they didn't. I rushed across the street and told my mother to stay where she was because I knew she wouldn't be of any use in the situation. I got between my brother and the men and with the back of my arm I broke off all four points of the knives (the patient demonstrated this as she spoke, using a sweeping motion with her arm similar to that which she had used to dismiss, with a gesture of contempt, the erect and sometimes venereally infected penises of men with whom she had had relations). The knives were still dangerous, and I tried to scream to my mother for help. As I was screaming, I had a fork in my hands. I didn't know where it came from, and I was smashing the men's hands to a pulp; they were all lined up in a row, and I woke up screaming."

Her first associations were to several examples of the angry use of urination to express the attitude, "Piss on you." She then stated with envy how men can stand erect, swing their penises, and spray a urinary stream, while women must squat or dribble in a ridiculous way. The knives made her think of attacking penises, but she soon saw that the one she wished to attack was herself. The fork also was associated with "fucking" and with the fact that women get injured, pregnant, and have abortions. Of her brother's marriage she remarked with anger, "It's just like my father—all the women he had, and there's my useless mother over there just standing around." She then recalled that the last time she had visited her father he was in a hospital being treated for thrombophlebitis. The sheet had fallen off, and she saw his penis "just hanging out and he didn't do anything to cover it up." She felt disgusted and furious and said, "You mean that here I've been screwing around all these years because I wanted to smash that bastard's penis to a pulp?" She then understood that one factor in her inability to go through with her pregnancies had been her disappointment and anger that the babies were not sired by her father. The frightening dream, terrifying because of the intensity of her hatred, had brought out for the first time the full force of the aggression toward men that had prevented heterosexual fulfillment.

The theme of rivalry with the brother in the dream also provided the link with the more deeply unconscious pregenital hostility toward her mother, against which she had guarded herself by assuming a protective attitude toward her, even in dreams. Previous expressions of anger toward her mother had always been at least to some degree inadvertent, as on one occasion when, while taking a shower, she stopped up the drain with a face cloth and "by accident" flooded her mother's bedroom. Not only did she experience a hostile oedipal rivalry with her mother for capturing her father's penis and baby, but a lifelong rage toward the mother for failing to protect her also came into awareness. Her mother had disappointed her infantile "only child" wishes by having more babies, and, in the view from childhood she still retained, had let one baby die. At a deeper level, this memory of the baby her mother had "allowed to die" was associated with an earlier feeling of maternal deprivation and with the murderous hostility that had arisen when she felt herself to be unwanted. Her violent aggression toward men was linked with her savage, biting impulses toward the breasts of the ungiving mother whom she was afraid she would destroy, impulses she had previously guarded against through reactions of disgust, nausea, and vomiting.

From the standpoint of the analysis, this nightmare represented a critical turning point. The terror in the dream reflected the emergence into awareness of the full intensity of the primitive hatred toward both the father and mother that had remained buried until this time. Although she had been aware of her aggression toward her parents, it was only through the vivid experience of the nightmare that the patient was able to appreciate fully the intense force of the hostile feelings toward them that had warped her relationships with both men and women. Furthermore, as we have seen repeatedly in other examples, the nightmare provided the essential link between impulses and anxieties belonging to the oedipal period and the preoedipal infantile hostility and terror in relation to the mother dating back to the oral phase of development.

Three months after she had the above dream, the patient had a second anxiety dream that further clarified the conflicts that had begun to become clear in the first. She had continued to explore her hostile feelings toward her mother; on the day before the dream she experienced a severe bout of vomiting associated with a flu syndrome, after which she could not brush her teeth without gagging. On the anniversary of her first abortion she had the following dream:

"*I had four puppies to look after. I explained to two other girls how you feed them with one can of dog food mixed with a little milk; there seemed to be too little milk. The puppies were in a paper bag, and all were doing fairly well, but I was convinced these girls wouldn't feed them right. Then I went out to clean their boxes in my room. I opened my bureau drawer; there were hundreds of dead puppies in it, and I woke up alone and crying.*"

Her associations led directly to an abortion, which had been done in her room, and her cleaning up of the room afterward. She recalled with an intense rage, of which she had not heretofore been aware, how, when she had come to her mother pregnant, her mother had sent her away to be aborted, saying, "We don't want to let your grandmother know." To the patient, this meant that good relations with the grandmother were more important to her mother than whether she lived or died. When she returned, her mother, instead of giving love and support, angrily criticized the patient's "disgraceful" appearance. She was pale and washed out from the physical and emotional strain of the abortion. Again she associated to the child of her mother's who had died, but this proved to be a displacement from her own dead fetuses and her guilt that she had permitted them to die, indeed, had brought about their deaths. The girl who did not feed the puppies represented her view of herself, and the dead puppies were her own dead babies. At a deep level, the dream expressed her own deprivation and thwarted wishes for mother's milk and love. Through the dream she expressed her wish to mitigate her guilt. Through it she was saying, "I have not received enough milk for myself. I cannot be expected to keep my babies alive." The terror in the dream, from which she awoke

"alone," was of abandonment. Identified with the lost, impoverished puppies, she relived her infantile agony that untended and unloved she, too,
like her mother's second baby, would die. The first nightmare had provided the link with the deeply repressed oral longings, associated hostility,
and terror of abandonment in relation to the mother. The second dream
brought her to a fuller realization of the intensity and pervasive quality of
these earliest and most disturbing of human emotions.

NIGHTMARES IN ASSOCIATION WITH AGGRESSION IN THE OEDIPAL
PERIOD.   The traditional view of the nightmare in both adults
and children was that it represented a form of circumscribed anxiety hysteria, reflecting the dreamer's concerns over incestuous,
oedipal impulses. Later studies, which were based on direct observations of children, emphasized pregenital impulses and conflicts. The focus has remained, however, upon the libidinal factor, with less attention devoted specifically to the problem of the
child's aggression. Nevertheless, Hall, in her classic study of a
boy's night terror attacks, demonstrated clearly that the child's
frightening dreams occurred at times of rising aggressive impulses toward his father [31]. The fact that such dreams deal so
frequently with murder deserves to be considered in this regard.
This is not to deny, of course, that the hostility in question may
be inspired by jealousy, frustrated erotic excitement, or the wish
to be rid of a rival for a highly prized libidinal object. It is his
aggression and its feared consequences, however, that provide
the most severe threat to the individual's security and are revealed in dreams. In the example that follows, a terrifying nightmare brought out unmistakably the enormous burden that intense hatred of his father presented to a five-year-old boy caught
in a highly disturbing oedipal situation.

Andy, an only child, was just five when he was referred for treatment
because of increased irritability, aggressive behavior, poor tolerance of any
frustration, and difficulty in sleeping. His difficulties were of a year's duration and coincided with his father's leaving the home after the mother
discovered that he had been staying out at night with another woman.
Before the above personality changes occurred, Andy had been a lively,
bright, vigorous, and imaginative child. He had been in analysis for two
months when he announced to his analyst, at the start of a session, that
he had had

*"a very bad dream last night and you're the person to tell it to." He had
often used volcanos in his play to represent whatever force or person in*

the outside world he perceived to be violent, dangerous, and potentially overwhelming. Now he drew a volcano as it had appeared in the dream and a wavy line to indicate himself climbing up the left side of the cone-shaped mountain. He said he was "warm" in the dream. He had started down the right side and reached a kind of halfway ledge or way station when the volcano suddenly erupted, and he was unable to return to the safe starting place. Great torrents of fire and lava spewed out of the top and also "cut through" the side of the mountain; he was tumbled off his perch on the ledge and crushed at the bottom under a great weight of rock. He was terrified as "this was the end of me." Andy repeated with violent gestures the cutting through of the flame and the eruption of the volcano. He said he knew, when he woke up, that it was not real, but he remained frightened, and "I cried until she came"—he seemed to feel it was unnecessary to say that he meant his mother.

After describing the dream, Andy said that he had had a very bad week-end with his father, with whom he had gone to stay overnight at his grandparents' home. The grandparents were away, and father had brought his new fiancee to stay with him, and also an adult male friend with whom Andy did not like having to share his father. The boy had found the situation overwhelming and had asked his father if he could return to his mother to spend the night. A "terrible argument" ensued; Andy said that his father angrily insisted that he stay, and he helplessly submitted. Although it was not certain that he actually saw any of his father's sexual activities with the other woman, he found sleeping at the house disturbing and wished to return to his own home to be with his mother. "It was bad, bad, bad. My whole life is bad. Everything is bad," Andy complained. In the office he played out his rage and hatred toward his father in multiple ways, attacking puppets and doll figures so violently that it became necessary to use clay models. He sawed and hacked these figures to bits and said he felt like crushing his father into powder until "he is no more." He also feared his father's wrath—according to the mother, the father at times had in fact taken a harsh and punitive attitude toward the child—and played out imaginary tortures to which his father might subject him, such as striking a nail, spike, or sewing machine needle against his chest in a rapid in-and-out motion. He declared, however, that the point would bend and not enter or hurt him because he had "super powers." Andy's hatred of his father was not unmixed with love, and he reproached his father bitterly for leaving the family when he needed him most. Although he was affectionate toward the doctor, he seemed unable to avoid certain demonstrations of aggression, such as digging his heels into the doctor's genital region when trying to sit in his lap.

In the weeks of treatment that followed, Andy continued to explore the disturbing mystery of his father's sexual activities with the new woman, which he represented in his play as the dangerous colliding of a planet into the sun. Furthermore, he was forced to contend simultaneously with visits to the house of new men whom his mother was seeing, and he played out his anger toward these rivals and his sadistic concept of all heterosexual relations.

It is not my purpose here to explore the full complexity of the structure of this child's neurosis. Rather, I wish to emphasize the enormous burden that the intense anger and hatred toward his father placed upon his developing ego as we learn of these emotions through the nightmare. This hatred had multiple determinants. These included the father's abandonment of the boy, the child's continuing oedipal rivalry with him for the mother, the father's actual harshness and, more immediately, his exposure of Andy to a situation in which he was excluded, yet found intolerably exciting. In the dream Andy made himself the victim of destruction in precisely the fashion in which he wished to destroy the father. The separation from his mother which he feared became a reality as he found himself unable to return to her on the safe side of the mountain. The volcano embodied a destructive rage, which Andy also feared and turned upon himself, as if this were less dangerous than to direct it at his father. There was little evidence of real guilt or a need for punishment on the basis of superego demands. Instead, Andy felt justified in his rage and hatred but, finding it too intense and threatening, turned it upon himself. At another level, we see the child's fear of the passive feminine position and of penetration by the father. He dealt with this fear, and the wishes that underlay it, through magic and omnipotence, declaring that his super powers would make the needle bend against his flesh. These wishes, however, were in part a defense against aggression, a submission out of fear, adopted to protect him from the horrible potential of his own hateful impulses, which he perceived as all-powerful.

It is not unusual for children who are deeply immersed in an intense oedipal struggle to begin to have nightmares when a turn of events serves to heighten these conflicts. The dreams may appear to the parents as virtually the only indication that the child is having difficulty. The following case of a five-year-old boy illustrates how nightmares can reflect the struggle of a young but healthy ego to master an increased burden of aggression, aroused in this instance by the father's abrupt departure for an overseas assignment in a combat zone.

Timmy, the younger of two children, was brought for treatment by his mother because of nightmares that had begun two months earlier when he was almost five, just after his father, a career army officer and paratrooper, had left for Vietnam. During these two months he awoke during the night twice a week from bad dreams. His mother noticed that he turned on the light for a brief period and then returned to sleep without calling her. In the morning he reported that he had been frightened and had had a bad dream.

Timmy's development had progressed quite normally until his father left. He was well liked by teachers and other children; his mother, with whom he had always had a deeply affectionate relationship, described him as a spirited, independent, and rather stubborn child. Except for occasional bedwetting, he had no other psychological or physical problems. He had never before had a sleep disturbance.

The child had always been close to his father, and they had enjoyed roughhousing and playing football together. After the father left for Vietnam, Timmy repeatedly asked his mother if his father were being shot at. She denied the danger and assured the boy that father was trained to protect himself. However, the mother herself was anxious, unable to sleep at night because of her worry and longing. Timmy prolonged their tender good nights and she, on her part, had difficulty limiting them. Several weeks before the mother sought treatment for Timmy, he began to fear that he was beginning to forget his father's face, and she showed him a picture to remind him. The mother herself was away much of the day, completing a college course, and left the patient and his sister, who was sixteen months older, with a baby-sitter.

Timmy was a sturdy, earnest, intelligent boy, who related easily to the doctor. Soon, he told him of the letters and presents he was receiving from his father and of his concern for his safety. He told of how he was helping his mother more in his absence and declared his love for her. At first, he claimed only to be having good dreams and attributed bad dreams to grown-ups who watch TV. Then in one family scene, played out with small dolls, he attributed a scary dream to his father. "The father" dreamed of a great gorilla and fell into the gorilla's lap, whereupon it took its great claws and killed him and ate him. Soon, however, Timmy confessed a series of his own scary dreams. In one, a man was about to parachute from an airplane; the parachute became tangled, and he fell. Timmy had awoken in fear. Continuing, he said, "One time I dreamt I went out alone, and my mommy was gone and had left me. I went to a restaurant, but I had no money. I couldn't get any food." The doctor agreed that it was frightening to think of not having anyone to take care of you. Then Timmy told of still another dream in which the baby-sitter hurt his mother with her long fingers.

After telling of the dreams, he spoke proudly of the big hat, camera, long sword, and high shoes his father had sent him from Japan, the shoes being especially valuable to protect him "high up." Then he told of a little boy, who soon became himself, who liked to dress up in horrifying halloween costumes, climb into his parents' bed, and then play affectionate tricks with his mother. Then he took out a jet plane and made it crash violently. Clearly distressed, he repeated the flight several times, with a safe landing achieved by a more competent pilot. Following this, he drew a large bowl of soup with great columns of steam rising from it. The boy liked to smell it and longed to reach out and touch it, but that was forbidden. Finally, his mother gave him permission to drink it.

Over the next weeks of treatment Timmy revealed further, in his talk and play, the greatly intensified burden of erotic and aggressive feeling that his father's departure had brought about in him. The anxiety he experienced over the pleasure he felt when his mother hugged and kissed him was so intense that he changed the subject whenever he found himself disclosing his great love for her. However, it was the associated hostility toward his absent father, whose place he wished to appropriate permanently, that particularly frightened him. This aggression was conveyed above all in his concern for his father's safety. He assured his doctor of his father's skill as a parachutist; nevertheless, in his drawings he could never make the cords coming from the parachute canopy reach the outstretched hands of the man making the jump. Thus, to Timmy's distress the parachutist, whom he usually labeled directly as his father, crashed to his death or was in danger of so doing. In other play, his intense aggressive rivalry with his father was unmistakable. One time a boy and a father puppet battled furiously over the privilege of telling the lady puppet the secret love each had for her. In association with this aggression, Timmy repeatedly expressed concern for his own safety. He said that he never wanted to grow up, because when you grow up you die, and that's sad. He would play out repetitively the themes of death, loss, and restitution. A jet carrying him or his father climbed "way up to heaven." Then, said Timmy, "When you die you can come back as a man. You come back bigger. You die and come back. You die and come back."

It would have been burden enough for this little boy if he had had to contend only with the realistic worry and danger threatening his father, but sadly this was not the case. He was at the peak of his oedipal conflicts; although his father's absence was the result of unavoidable necessity and not the result of Timmy's wishes, the child was forced to contend with his own aggressive feelings, as well. His anxiety was heightened further by the fact that his father was not only absent, but in continuous actual danger—his mother's reassurances did not convince him fully—from guns, airplanes, and bad men, the very elements that he had already learned to employ to represent his own aggressive fantasies even before his father left. He was thrown closer to his mother by his father's departure; his heightened and externally less limited erotic and romantic relationship with her served only to intensify his hostile wishes toward his father as he longed to sustain this intimacy.

Timmy was not a neurotic child, and his nightmares served, under the circumstances, useful defensive and adaptive functions. Although terrifying, they gave harmless expression in fantasy to his aggressive impulses. In the dreams, he projected the aggression onto other persons, animals, and forces that seemed to be attacking from without. In one instance, Timmy even attributed the dream itself to the father who was the object of his aggression. In another dream the man fell to his death, not because of Timmy's hostility, but because his parachute became tangled. The nightmare can be regarded only as a failure of ego mechanisms from the standpoint of the dream's function in protecting sleep. However, this is too limited a viewpoint, for the dreams served Timmy well insofar as they may have helped to confine the expression of his conflicts to the nighttime and to prevent their intrusion into his daytime functioning; thus, they protected his actual relationships and other areas of ego functioning. Indeed, he was even able to master the frightening nighttime experiences by himself, without calling his mother, through turning on the light briefly to chase away the demons. A greater danger for Timmy's development was the regression of the relationship with his mother that was brought about through a combination of factors that included his father's actual absence, Timmy's increased intimacy with her, and her anxiety and temptation to infantilize the child out of her own need. Earlier terrors, related to fears of separation from the mother, were also revived and given expression in the dream in which Timmy was all alone, abandoned by his mother and with no one to take care of him.

A CRISIS OF CONSCIENCE IN A NINE-YEAR-OLD GIRL.   In the period from six through ten, the demands and strictures of the child's conscience, whose operation is often unconscious, become increasingly severe. Nowhere does this tyranny of conscience manifest itself more vividly than in the prohibition of aggressive impulses directed against loved persons; perhaps no psychological phenomenon of childhood can display this struggle more dramatically than a nightmare.

Carol was just nine when a critical dream occurred. She had been in treatment for a year and a half, having been brought initially for a school-learning problem. She was a sensitive, passionate, and attractive child, who related easily to the doctor. From infancy, Carol and her mother had struggled with one another. As a baby Carol was a poor eater, was cranky, and cried a great deal, giving her mother the feeling that she would not allow her to take care of her.

From her second year Carol directed frequent tantrums against her mother; to these the latter often responded with great anger. Carol's parents separated frequently from the time she was one, but were always reunited. There were long periods when she did not see her father, particularly between ages one and three; however, when they were together, their relationship was intimate. With her sister, Lorraine, two years older than herself, she maintained a hostile rivalry, especially for the father's affections. Another sister was born fourteen months before the dream occurred. From the time she was five, Carol had occasional nightmares or night terror attacks. Characteristically, she awoke during the night in terror, with her eyes wide open. She jumped about like a terrified animal or cowered in a corner. When her mother or father reached out to her, she cried out alternately, "I love you, I want you," or "Go away, don't touch me." When she was taken to her parents' bed, she might remain disoriented and be difficult to calm.

The nightmare to be described occurred in mid-October. During July and August, Carol had been away to camp and had left with the understanding that her parents were again separated, probably permanently; upon her return from camp, however, she found her parents living together again. To her mother's surprise, she responded to this discovery by becoming angry and irritable, refusing to eat, and asserting that she must die and would do so by not eating. To her doctor, she declared that she preferred to have her father living alone, for then she could visit him without having to share him with her mother; her mother's descriptions of Carol's rages at her, confirmed this statement. She stormed angrily about the house, announcing her hate for everyone, particularly her mother. At other times she confessed that she was glad that her parents were together and worried lest they separate once more. At times she was afraid to have her mother leave the house for fear that robbers might break in. Soon her parents argued once again and talked of separation.

The mother herself had suffered since early childhood from not infrequent nightmares (see example in Chapter 2, page 43). She awoke from these, terribly frightened with her heart pounding, sometimes screaming out. Several weeks before the patient's nightmare, the mother, whose own mother had recently died, had a severe nightmare in which her mother appeared to her and threatened her with death.

With her parents' reunion, Carol revealed a renewed preoccupation with the facts of sexuality; she asked many questions of her mother, such as how long it would be, now that she and her father were together, before her mother would have a baby. Two days before her attack, Carol's sadistic provocations had led her father to give her a ferocious spanking. During the days before the dream, Carol revealed her preoccupation with death, asking whether, when a person dies and is placed in a box underground— her maternal grandmother having recently died—he remained alive in the ground. Her questions to her parents and her behavior on the night of the dream revealed her association of death and sexuality. She asked eagerly what happens in marriage, how babies are made, about the "planting of the seeds," and specifically about the insertion of the penis in the vagina. She crushed a cigarette in a dish and then, as if she were trying to solve a problem, announced, "Okay, it's broken, the butt is a dead one." The full-sized cigarette, she declared emphatically, was a live one. On another occasion, she used two "dead butts" to represent the seeds in sexual union, making them join and grow to make a whole baby. That night she insisted on sleeping in her older sister Lorraine's bed, as she sometimes did when she was anxious at night.

Carol provided her own background information for the dream. She entered the office in a tense, quite excited state and said that her mother had told her to tell the doctor about the bad scary dream she had had the night before. The nightmare had been filled with characters from the TV show, the Addams Family, which she had watched most recently four nights before; this was a comic-horror program in which members of a family, led by a beautiful witch-mother, delighted in inflicting sadism upon one another and upon innocent intruders. In her dream, the cast took on sinister, distorted proportions that the characters in the banal TV show did not possess. For the mother she drew, instead of a beautiful dark-haired woman, a round-faced, "real scary," witchlike creature with the mouth turned down, spots on her face, and hair in wild disarray. The little girl, called Wednesday, had her braids and facial features replaced by X's, which were somehow terrifying. The other characters were similarly distorted in the dream. In the TV program, a giant butler named Lurch came on stage only when a bell cord was pulled. In stereotyped fashion, he then entered and said, "You rang" in deep sonorous tones. In the dream this ordinarily ominous face was made still more black and terrifying.

After the preamble Carol continued, "In the dream I'm older than Lorraine. Lorraine is a baby in a crib. Lorraine's sleeping in it. Then Lurch comes in with a stick in his hand and hits Lorraine, and Lorraine cries. Then I come in (she drew herself as a frightened innocent young girl). I don't draw myself very good. I have a sad face. Then Lurch (she became more anxious and excited) grabs a stick, and I keep pulling the string, and Lurch keeps saying, 'You rang.' Every time I pull the string Lurch says, 'You rang.' That's so Lorraine will be okay." She explained that, by pulling the string over and over again, to which Lurch must respond with "You rang," Lurch's stick was kept raised and did not descend upon Lorraine. "It's like suppose I kept saying to you I love you so that you would stop and wouldn't come in and hurt me. Well, Lurch is stopped when I keep pulling the string, and he has to say, 'You rang,' so Lorraine gets a chance to get out. Then there's a razor blade on the couch, and Lurch hits me with it. I have something special about me so I won't get hurt. It's like a paper bag. I grab the razor blade. While me and Lurch are doing it, Lurch and the grandfather are fighting. Then my father comes in through the door, and he's dripping with blood."

After awaking, Carol continued to reality-test the experience of the dream, but was still frightened, called for her mother, and asked to sleep between her father and mother in their bed. According to the mother's account, Carol called out for her, but the father got out of bed and met the child half-way to their room. Once in the parents' bed, her fears did not end. She imagined that noises in the house were the wind, then an animal, and finally a robber who had come to hurt her and her sisters. "I was afraid the man would come in and choke me because he would be strong, and I am weak. My father was the one who picked me up and brought me to his bed. He's strong. My mother's not so strong. Finally, I went to sleep."

In the interview, she continued to struggle to master the dream experience. "It's like a story," she observed. "You know, 'once upon a time I had a dream.'" She suggested to her doctor that they draw the scariest parts (see illustration). Particularly frightening was Cousin It, a bodyless swatch of yellow hair with black glasses who had "been there," but took no active part in the dream. She drew Lorraine as a buglike baby atop a great brown crib with the giant, long-legged Lurch standing beside her with a large arm holding the big stick over the baby. The pretty but frightened little Carol struggled to fend off Lurch by calling to him and now also through pulling the string itself, which was connected directly to his swordlike stick. In the drawing, she added to the bottom of the crib a black "cork" that could be pulled out to allow Lorraine to come out of the bottom to safety. She also added at the bottom a tiny little bed or couch, on which was the razor. Carol associated the dream with other scary dreams she had had in the past and said that, when she had these, she got into bed with her mother and father. They seemed to occur more frequently at times of argument when her parents were living together than during their separations.

The work of the next eight months of treatment could be regarded as a further investigation and exposition of the conflicts and themes introduced in the content of this nightmare. Carol's fear of her parents' separation soon gave way to sadness as they parted in reality once more within two weeks of the dream. The additional burden this placed on the child's already strained ego resources was poignantly conveyed in her play and in further dreams.

Once her parents were separated again, Carol proposed to her mother that she live with her father so that he would not be lonely. Carol offered to sleep in his bed with him or invited him to sleep "on top" of her, and she asked to be allowed to prepare his meals. She spoke to her doctor of her wish to marry her father and to have a baby, but worried because she was so small and he was so big. She feared going to the hospital and the "operation" of delivery lest the baby suffocate. She had another nightmare in which a great creature, a man with three heads, appeared. He had "a hand so big that one finger was as big as me, and it picked me up." The father did his part to keep Carol's fantasies alive, sleeping in the same room with her on weekend trips and appearing in his underwear before her until he was advised to give up these practices. When he found another woman, Carol was outraged and open in her hostility toward the rival. She protested bitterly, "He loves me best, but he sees her more." In her play, she shot this woman dead with great satisfaction.

The father's new girl friend and her sisters were convenient objects of displacement for the deeper rage Carol felt toward her mother. In one dramatic play sequence, a "little witch" was furious with her "mother witch" for having sent the father away out of her jealousy of the little witch's intimacy with him. The little witch battled with her hated mother and sneaked out at night to visit her father, who was always happy to see her. She feared the retribution of the mother witch if she found out. At

Carol's Nightmare

home, Carol was openly aggressive toward her mother, but this rivalry for her father's exclusive love had its counterpart, as shown in her possessiveness of her mother and her intolerance of her mother's interest in other men.

Carol revealed that her intense rage toward her mother, and to a lesser extent toward her sisters and father, was accompanied by a great weight of guilt. Her mother reported that she found endless ways of provoking punishments and seemed to smile with enjoyment when she received a spanking or other punishment. She believed that her wishes had driven her parents apart, that it was her fault, and expected to be punished by not being allowed to see her beloved father. She imposed an assault with a syringe upon the abdomen and head of a little girl whose naughtiness she declared warranted such an operation. She experienced her own agony of conscience through stomach pains, headaches, and other physical complaints that brought about painful, though negative, diagnostic procedures. On one occasion, in the midst of a series of provocations of increasing intensity, she declared to her mother flatly, "I will die, you will kill me." In addition to her efforts to displace her guilt onto various alter egos in her play, she sought to propitiate her conscience by various bits of generosity and through acts of self-sacrifice. These reached their ultimate expression in her wish to work as a teacher or a nurse in an orphanage helping children *whose parents had died.* Despite these efforts at sublimation, at other times she seemed virtually helpless in the face of her burden of anxiety, thwarted love, rage, and guilt.

Carol at nine was unable to resolve her oedipal conflicts or to renounce her oedipal wishes. On the contrary, her parents' repeated separations and reunions, together with her father's seductions, had kept her childish desires and fears alive with an intensity that impeded her learning and slowed her social development. Her parents' unexpected reunion several weeks before the dream reactivated her sexual wishes and inquiries, and she revealed in her questions at home her interest in their sexual relations and the processes of conception and the expectation that mother would have another baby. Her questions and the cigarette play before the dream unmistakably disclosed her equation of the ideas of sexuality and death. She wished to take her mother's place in the parental bed with her father and identified herself with the woman who received the father's penis and bore his child. Nevertheless, she knew that she was a little girl and that her father was large, with a penis that seemed huge—"I am weak, he's strong." Furthermore, she had a sadistic and destructive concept of sexual intercourse, partly on the basis of her misunderstanding of what she had observed of her parents' activities —who, in fact, argued a great deal at night—and partly because she had endowed the act with sadistic meaning on the basis of her own aggressive impulses. Furthermore, her superego was exacting in its demands for punishment of her forbidden sadomasochistic wishes. She had in fact provoked a severe spanking by her father two nights before the dream.

It was under these circumstances and in this context that the nightmare occurred. Although it was a highly elaborate and complex piece of "desperate creativity," rich in symbolism and in the store of psychological mechanisms it disclosed, its central theme was the conflict of the little girl struggling to stave off an attack on the part of a giant, monstrous man. Frantically she strove to ward off the descent of Lurch's menacing "raised" (erect) stick-penis that threatened the infant who clearly represented, in addition to her sisters, herself in her helplessness and vulnerability. Later in the dream the distortion fell away, and the father became involved directly in the sadistic encounter and was bloodied from tangling with a sadistic woman.

The danger of destruction, the potential for wanton aggression, imbued the dream with an ominous and nightmarish quality. The infant Lorraine—a condensation of both sisters—was in mortal jeopardy, and Carol was terrified lest she fail to protect her. Why must she protect her sister from attack? Precisely because her own wishes to destroy her rival sisters were forbidden both by her mother in reality and her own well-developed and exacting conscience. Direct hostility toward the mother was not expressed in the manifest dream, although the witch-mother was the central character of the Addams Family. In her preamble, Carol had drawn vividly the distorted, terrifying mother of the dream, but declared that she remained in the background and did not participate directly in the action. Nevertheless, in her associated play over the next few months the hostile impulses toward the mother and her surrogates were revealed to be the most important source of her anxiety. Deeply linked with early residues of the lifelong struggle with mother, this hostility retained the all-or-nothing, kill-or-be-killed quality that may be associated with the preoedipal relationship to the mother. Separation, abandonment, and loss of love were some of the dreadful consequences that the child feared might result from hostility toward the mother, and this atmosphere of infantile terror pervaded the dream. Death, with its composite meanings of masochistic surrender and destruction, annihilation, suffocation, and abandonment was revealed as an outstanding preoccupation before the dream.

All these conflicts had become largely internal ones for Carol.

The superego, whose demands and admonitions were experienced as guilt and a need for punishment in waking life, was personified in the dream through multiple threatening or punishing agents from which the child tried to protect herself through magic—"Nothing could hurt me." Like some villain of a Shakespearean drama whose sleep is disturbed by dreams that betray a conscience that will not be silent, so little Carol could not escape the assaults of her own uncompromising superego, the intensity of whose punishments was in proportion to the strength of the hostile or sadistic impulses that it forbade. For the latency-age child, the nightmare may reflect the burden of aggression more through the superego and its cruel demands than through the danger of the direct impulses toward the love objects.

The creative quality of the dream should not go unnoticed. Based on a story, it is itself full of invention. The raw material of the child's instinctually based conflict was molded through an imaginative variety of displacements, distorted characterizations, and substitutions into a high-geared, tension-filled drama. After waking, Carol wished in her doctor's presence to approach the dream further as a "story," to draw parts of it and embellish it. One may well ask what relevance dreams of this sort have in the origin of certain creative processes as they reflect the ego's struggle with the resolution of conflict (see Chapter 3). Also evident in the dream are a variety of protective ego defenses, notably displacement, projection, substitution, reaction-formation, and denial, all of which we have come to associate with conflicts over aggression.

The full depth of such conflicts over aggression and guilt may be revealed similarly in the nightmares of adults with a clarity and vividness that suggest their childhood origin. The case of the sixty-four-year-old female office worker, described in detail in Chapter 2, illustrates this problem. Despite the more than half a century by which Carol and this patient were separated in age, their nightmares resembled each other strikingly, and investigation revealed that similar forces were at work.

Theoretical Considerations

NIGHTMARES, AGGRESSION, AND THE DEVELOPMENT OF OBJECT
RELATIONS.   The particular conflicts that aroused hostility in our
case examples have varied, depending upon the developmental
phase, but in each instance the aggression was of great danger for
the individual and evoked an intense anxiety that found its most
vivid expression in nightmares. Whether, as in Sam's case, it was
the fear of retaliation for destructive wishes against the mother
provoked by her limitations of anal freedom and other restrictions or whether, as in Carol's case, the struggle was largely an
internal crisis of conscience, in all of the examples hostility toward loved persons created a great danger for the subject.

Murderous impulses in a two-year-old that would destroy any
person who thwarts his pleasures or in a five-year-old who would
wish the death of a father whose return home challenged the
child's claim to exclusive possession of the mother are equally
dangerous. It is perhaps the universality of the threat the child
experiences from such aggression toward loved persons that accounts for a certain uniformity in the nightmares of children and
adults. They follow a pattern. Inevitably the dreamer, whether
child or adult, is about to become the victim of a murderous or
devouring attack or is threatened with death by a destructive
creature. In only one instance, the case of the thirty-one-year-old
executive secretary, did the dreamer allow herself direct expression of violent impulses in a nightmare. In this example, it was
the intensity of her naked aggression and hatred that made the
dream so terrifying. Depending upon the developmental level
and psychological sophistication, the implements of death-
dealing or assault may vary, the cast of characters may be more or
less complex, and the dramas in which the dreamer is engaged
may be more or less richly imaginative; however, the fundamen
tal themes and the basic quality of anxiety do not vary. In part,
this is caused by the regressive reevocation of the conflicts and
dangers of earlier developmental phases in the dream situation
[32], but it is also the result of a certain unchanging quality in-
herent in destructive impulses, a monotony in the character of
destructive wishes. Libidinal aims vary according to the level of

development, but murder seems always to be murder, and retaliation may be anticipated whether the dreamer is a small child or an adult.

One may ask how we know that nightmares reflect conflict over the person's own destructive impulses. Is not the dreamer himself usually the victim of another's assault and not the attacker? Our answer to this question must be given with some humility, for we are dependent upon indirect evidence, upon associated facts and material. Even in the two-year-old child, however, the manifest dream cannot be taken at face value. In Sam's case, for example, we must look to his daily preoccupation with violence and his hour-to-hour absorption with his own destructiveness throughout the waking day in ordinary activity, symbolic play, and speech if we are to be convinced that his aggression is at the root of his terror. Similarly, the associated material of Andy's analysis demonstrates convincingly that his murderous hatred of his father is a fundamental root of his anxiety. In Carol's case, her subsequent treatment interviews revealed that her sadistic and destructive concept of the sexual relationship between a man and a woman and her murderous hatred of her mother were at the basis of the nightmare terror in which she and another helpless little girl were both victims.

However, we should not, as has often been the case in the past, overlook the role of outside aggression in the production of these terrifying dreams. The fact that the child's own aggressive wishes and simultaneous helplessness are of fundamental importance in these dreams does not mean that aggression and hostility experienced from without play a minor role. In Sam's case, for example, his terrifying dreams occurred after he had been shouted at and punished by his mother and physically assaulted repeatedly by his brothers. Regularly, one may find in dreams the symbolic representations of parents or other important persons who have *in reality* been expressing anger or aggressive threats toward the child. It is true, of course, that these attacks by another may come in response to the child's own expressions of hostility, but this fact serves to emphasize only what we already suspect to be the case: that the child's own hostile fantasies and wishes become inseparably linked in his mind with the aggression that he has experienced from without. That he also may disavow his own hostility and project it onto others does not argue against the importance of the actual hostility he has experienced from outside. Children who are in fact the objects of much parental hostility or hatred or repeated destructive threats seem to be particularly prone to suffer from nightmares.

NIGHTMARES, AGGRESSION, AND EGO VULNERABILITY. The sense of helplessness in nightmares in the face of violent destructiveness accounts for the intensity of terror that the dreamer experiences. Some children will look back upon certain nightmares as major events in their lives, especially if they occurred at an age, usually before five, when they were unable to test reality after waking, to know that the threat of being eaten up, for example, was only a dream.

Stern has argued that the overwhelming terror of *pavor nocturnus* is attributable to the inability of the sexually stimulated child to achieve orgastic discharge [33]. The role of genital excitement, frustration, and castration anxiety in our examples has been evident, particularly in children of oedipal age, but the occurrence of nightmares or night terrors at all ages and developmental stages from late in the first year of life into adulthood argues against applying this explanation too broadly. On the other hand, destructive aggressiveness toward the love object is equally dangerous, though in differing ways, at each phase of development, including adult life. Early in the second year, destruction of the object means loss of what that person can give, of food, warmth, affection, and protection. In the second and the third years, the child comes to fear the other person's retaliation and loss of the object's love. The hostile rivalries of the oedipal phase have their own familiar dangers of retaliation, castration, and annihilation; in the latency period, this struggle is carried on internally between the ego and a punitive agency of the mind or superego. Furthermore, unresolved conflicts involving hostility and hatred from earlier phases of development represent burdensome stresses upon the ego's resources that may be carried forward into each successive phase and will later contribute to the production of nightmares in adulthood.

The harboring of hostility toward important love objects is poorly tolerated, and considerable psychological effort may go into ensuring that these impulses are not acted upon or even experienced as coming from the subject himself. Radical defenses must be employed to nullify the potential danger of this aggression. Certain defensive measures, such as the introjection of the qualities of outside aggressors in order to incorporate their strength—identification with the aggressor—further burden the ego by setting up within it hostile attitudes and voices that additionally threaten the individual and contribute to his feeling of helplessness. In nightmares, the operation of these hostile internalized object representations becomes further imbued with the dreamer's own aggression, which, when turned against himself, contributes to the feeling of menace.

The desperate need of small children for love, comfort, and reality assurance when they awaken from a nightmare gives eloquent testimony to the power of these negative forces and the child's helplessness before their onslaught. The love of the parents seems almost to operate as a specific antidote to the hostile forces with which the child must contend helplessly and alone in his sleep. Sometimes a child learns to represent a loving parent or aspect of the parent within the dream itself, offsetting its nightmarish aspect and "downgrading" it to a nontraumatic dream. For example, a four-year-old boy was troubled with frequent nightmares in which an enormous brown giant, who resembled a gingerbread man, smelled like feces, and spoke in his father's angry voice, came to his bedside in the dark and threatened him with death if he dallied too long on the way to the bathroom. In his analysis, it was shown that these dreams occurred at times when two sets of forbidden impulses were at work: to enter the parents' bedroom and to soil his bed. From his father, who was the object of his hostility, he expected angry retaliation. His actual experience with the parents during the night was that they comforted him when he awoke with terror; his father's voice took on a kinder and more protective tone in subsequent dreams, menacing him only if the boy did not follow his dictates. A similar progression from nightmares to nontraumatic dreams can be observed in the course of psychoanalysis or psychotherapy, as the internalization of positive qualities of the therapist alters the negative impact of the dreamer's hostile impulses and introjects (see example in Chapter 5, page 177).

NIGHTMARES AND THE MASTERY OF AGGRESSION. We have repeatedly seen in case examples how the dreamer disowned his destructive impulses, attributing them to some other attacker. This projection, together with the variety of displacements of affect that occur in the dream's formation, represents, as discussed in the case of Sam, a thorough disavowal. The nightmares of oedipal and latency-phase children are distinguished from those of the two-year-old not only by the use of more mature defense mechanisms to ward off aggression or by a lesser use of disavowal. In addition, they reflect a libidinization of the aggression, an admixture with sexuality so that killing, as in Carol's dream, assumes a powerful sadomasochistic coloration and is linked with her concept of the sexual act. The projection and displacement of the aggression by the older child, however, are similar to those that occur in the case of the two-year-old.

In the discussion of Sam's case, we have seen how the dreamer may make use of the externalization that is part of the dreaming process to disown responsibility for aggression. The dreamer does not, however, successfully protect himself thereby. Some part of himself remains invested in or identified, not only with the witnessing self, but with each character, animal, or person in the dream. The secretary herself experiences terror as she smashes the men's hands. In Carol's dream it is the tiny Lorraine, not herself, who falls victim to Lurch's stick, yet she cannot avoid feeling terrified and awakens in fear to preserve her own life.

Earlier in this chapter we saw how the nightmare sufferer might paradoxically make himself the victim in order to preserve the object. Macnish tells of instances in which the nightmare failed in this purpose and individuals committed murder "under the panic of a frightful vision. They awake from such a dream— they see some person standing in the room, whom they mistake for an assassin, or dreadful apparition: driven to desperation by terror, they seize the first weapon that occurs, and inflict a fatal wound upon the object of their alarm" [34]. Similarly, the role of nightmares in protecting psychotic patients from their violent aggressive impulses has been noted by psychiatrists working in state hospitals. John Mackenzie has told the author of instances in which inexperienced residents have reassured schizophrenic patients that their nightmares were "just dreams" and that they did not need to fear the violence of which they fantasied themselves to be the victims [35]. When this reassurance had removed the restraint provided by the dream and delivered the patients of its threat, on occasion they assaulted the deliverer. The sacrifice of the nightmare victim in order to preserve the object could have some connection with the manifestly irrational process of human sacrifice in primitive cultures. Nightmares perhaps function as a kind of symbolic sacrifice in which the helpless subject offers himself for destruction in order to preserve the object or to protect himself from the wrath of its retaliation.

A more general explanation of the victimization of nightmares can be provided by considering the danger of aggressive impulses toward other persons at various periods of development rather than by thinking in terms of superego activity or a need for punishment. Such an explanation can, for example, account for the widespread occurrence of nightmares in very small children in whom a superego has hardly begun to form. Small children fifteen to thirty-six months of age are, however, able to experience the danger to their existence that is contained in their destructive hostility toward loved persons upon whom they are dependent. They dream and can make use of the dream process, although not by conscious design, to redirect their aggression away from the object and toward themselves.

One may ask how the advances in psychological structure that occur in later development, including the formation of a relatively independent functioning superego, affect the processes of dealing with aggression in the nightmare and during waking life. The threat of aggression, most often expressed in the oral-destructive imagery associated with the very early incorporative mode; the ego's sense of helplessness and vulnerability; the overwhelming character of the terror—all are present in the dreams of each phase. The differences lie in the complexity of the distortions, in the increased use of creative imagination and personifications within the dream, and above all in the ego's reality-testing and self-comforting activities after waking.

But what of the superego? Its activity seems to be obscured in the onslaught of the dream's annihilatory anxiety, although analysis of the dream may reveal its role. In Carol's case, for example, her guilt over her sexual wishes toward her father and her murderous rivalry with her mother played a fundamental role in the instigation of her nightmare. The seeming obliteration or reduction of the superego has to do with the regressive aspect of nightmares. The superego may play a role in the threat of annihilation in a nightmare. However, in these dreams this agency becomes infused with the early perceptions of the parents as aggressive and retaliative. This view has usually become combined later in childhood with more loving and realistic images of the parents. As a result of the regression that occurs in the nightmare, the loving aspect of the parents is temporarily abandoned, and the multiple aggressive attitudes, perceptions, and voices internalized in the course of the child's development are revived once more. In addition, the dreamer projects his own aggression onto those images that confront the ego in the nightmare from "outside," as they did once before in early childhood. Naturally, these internalized qualities of objects have not remained unchanged since early childhood, for the interaction of the individual with his environment in the course of development is continuously modifying these object representations. Nevertheless, it is striking how similar in many of its essential qualities the nine-year-old's dream is to that of a two-year-old, how much the brutal attacker in adult nightmares reminds us of the wolves and other devouring creatures of the child's night terror.

References and Notes

1. Hinde, R. A. The nature of aggression. *New Society* 9:302–304, 1967.
2. Tinbergen, N. On war and peace in animals and man. *Science* 160: 1411–1418, 1968.
3. Ibid. P. 1412.

4. Freud, S.   Beyond the Pleasure Principle (1920). In *The Standard Edition of the Complete Psychological Works of Sigmund Freud*, tr. and ed. by J. Strachey with others. London: Hogarth and the Institute of Psycho-Analysis, 1955. Vol. XVIII, pp. 7–64.

5. Freud, S.   New Introductory Lectures on Psychoanalysis (1933 [1932]). *Standard Edition*. 1964. Vol. XXII, pp. 5–182.

6. Waelder, R.   *Basic Theory of Psychoanalysis*. New York: International Universities Press, 1960.

7. "Fear," observed William James, "is a reaction aroused by the same objects that arouse ferocity. The antagonism of the two is an interesting study in instinctive dynamics. We both fear and wish to kill anything that may kill us." *The Principles of Psychology*. New York: Holt, 1890. Vol. II, p. 415.

8. Hartmann, H., Kris, E., and Loewenstein, R.   Notes on the theory of aggression. *Psychoanal. Stud. Child.* 3–4:9–36, 1949.

9. Spitz, R.   Aggression: Its role in the establishment of object relations. In Loewenstein, R. M. (Ed.), *Drives, Affects and Behavior*. New York: International Universities Press, 1953. Pp. 126–138.

10. Wolff, P. H.   The causes, controls and organization of behavior in the neonate. *Psychol. Issues*, Vol. V, No. 1, Monograph 17:92, 1966.

11. Hartmann, H., Kris, E., and Loewenstein, R.   Notes on the theory of aggression. *Psychoanal. Stud. Child.* 3–4:21, 1940.

12. Berkowitz, L.   *Aggression: A Social Psychological Analysis*. New York: McGraw-Hill, 1962.

13. Buss, A. H.   *The Psychology of Aggression*. New York: Wiley, 1961.

14. Scott, J. P.   *Aggression*. Chicago: University of Chicago Press, 1958.

15. As Tinbergen has recently written, "All species manage as a rule to settle their disputes without killing one another; in fact, even bloodshed is rare. Man is the only species that is a mass murderer, the only misfit in his own society." Tinbergen, N.   On war and peace in animals and man. *Science* 160:1412, 1968. Copyright 1968 by the American Association for the Advancement of Science.

16. Ibid. P. 1416.

17. Dollard, J., Miller, N. E., Doob, L. W., Mowrer, O. H., and Sears, R. E.   *Frustration and Aggression*. New Haven: Yale University Press, 1939.

18. Mowrer, O. H.   *Learning Theory and Behavior*. New York: Wiley, 1960.

19. Sears, R. R., Whiting, J. W. M., Nowlis, V., and Sears, P. S.   Some child-rearing antecedents of aggression and dependency in young children. *Genet. Psychol. Monogr.* 47:135–234, 1953.

20. Robey, J.   Personal communication, May 1969.

21. Joffe, W. G., and Sandler, J.   Notes on pain, depression and individuation. *Psychoanal. Stud. Child.* 20:394–424, 1965.

22. Jones, E.   Psychoanalysis and the Instincts (1935). In *Papers on Psychoanalysis*. London: Bailliere, Tindall and Cox, 1950. P. 169.

23. von Bertalanffy, L.   Comments on aggression. *Bull. Menninger Clin.* 22:50–57, 1958.

24. Rolde, E. J., and Goethals, G. W. Adolescent Aggression and Dependence. Unpublished manuscript. P. 11.
25. Freud, S. Papers on Metapsychology (1915). *Standard Edition.* 1957. Vol. XIV, p. 138.
26. Greenacre, P. Infant Reactions to Restraint: Problems in the Fate of Infantile Aggression. In *Trauma, Growth and Personality.* New York: Norton, 1952. Pp. 83–105.
27. Freud, A. Certain Types and Stages of Social Maladjustment. In Eissler, K. (Ed.), *Searchlights on Delinquency.* New York: International Universities Press, 1949. Pp. 193–204.
28. Freud, A. Aggression in relation to emotional development: Normal and pathological. *Psychoanal. Stud. Child.* 3–4:37–42, 1949.
29. Freud, A. *The Ego and the Mechanisms of Defense* (1936). New York: International Universities Press, 1953.
30. Congreve, W. *Love for Love,* III: 8. London: J. Bell, 1791.
31. Hall, J. W. The analysis of a case of night terror. *Psychoanal. Stud. Child.* 11:189–227, 1946.
32. The issue of the regressive revival in nightmares of conflicts from earlier phases of development is discussed more fully in a previous study. Mack, J. E. Nightmares, conflict and ego development in childhood, *Int. J. Psychoanal.* 46:403–428, 1965.
33. Stern, M. *Pavor nocturnus. Int. J. Psychoanal.* 32:302–309, 1951.
34. Macnish, R. *The Philosophy of Sleep.* New York: Appleton, 1834. P. 70.
35. Mackenzie, J. Personal communication, March 1966.

5

Nightmares and Psychoses

IN THIS CHAPTER we will consider the relationship that appears to exist between one type of dream, the nightmare, and one form of psychosis, the acute schizophrenic episode or turmoil state.* Although the old adage that a psychosis is but a waking dream or nightmare cannot be supported by careful examination of the two phenomena, my purpose in this chapter is to demonstrate that the relationship is more than one merely of analogy. Fundamental affective, cognitive, structural, and interpersonal relationships between nightmares and psychosis, as well as important differences, will be shown to exist. This relationship may be approached in several ways. First, *descriptive* resemblances may be noted, that is, manifest similarities between the ideational content and emotional reactions that occur in the two phenomena. Next, *dynamic* relationships can be documented: the connections that can be observed, especially in the same adult patient, between the nightmare and an acute psychosis. I have in mind here such matters as the expression of the same emotional conflicts in the two phenomena; the use of similar psychological defenses; the "progression" of a nightmare into the

---

* The American Psychiatric Association *Diagnostic Manual*, revised in 1968, defines the acute schizophrenic episode as follows: "This condition is distinguished by the acute onset of schizophrenic symptoms, often associated with confusion, perplexity, ideas of reference, emotional turmoil, dream-like dissociation, and excitement, depression, or fear" [1].

psychosis it seems to presage; or a reciprocity between the two conditions such that they alternate or are mutually exclusive, at least from the patient's point of view. Finally, between the child's nightmare and the later psychosis there are *developmental* relationships, whereby the forces and conflicts expressed in the nightmare in childhood erupt later in a more pervasive form in the adult's psychosis. It does not follow, because such *psychological* similarities or relationships seem to exist, that the eventual discovery of important *physiological* resemblances between the two conditions can also be expected. The most fundamental difference between the nightmare and the acute psychosis is the capacity of the ego to *limit* the eruption in the former instance to sleep and to a brief period following arousal, while in the later condition terror and belief in the actuality of frightening ideas or images persists during the waking hours. Some of the factors that may account for this difference will be explored.

Historical Considerations

DREAMS AND INSANITY. Similarities between dreams and certain forms of insanity have long been observed. Henry More, an English theologian and philosopher, noted in 1656 a "Melancholy Symptome, which Physitians call Extasie," caused by natural sleep and the effect of which is "the deliration of the party after he awakes; for he takes his dreams for true Histories and real Transactions"[2]. Immanuel Kant believed that the mad person was a dreamer awake [3]. The subject seems particularly to have fascinated nineteenth-century writers. Hughlings Jackson, for example, called dreams "the physiological insanity" and compared the "normal" regression or "dissolution" of sleep with the pathological "dissolution" of insanity [4]. The famous nineteenth-century German psychiatrist, William Griesinger, in particular regarded insanity as "analogous" to dreaming, "especially to dreams in the half-waking state." He observed that children "especially when under slight disease . . . while sleeping, still speak: For example, they understand the mother, they answer her, but nevertheless they dream on, and in particular they cannot withdraw themselves from uneasy dreamy ideas" [5]. Griesinger also pointed out many other resemblances between dreams and insane conditions as, for example, the lack of a sense of time in both states, the externalization in hallucinations of "sentiments which stand opposed to the I," the hallucinatory gratification of wishes, and the partial or complete dissociation of affect from mental content.

Although Freud held it likely that efforts "to throw some light on the mystery of dreams" would provide the explanation of the psychoses, there have been few systematic studies of the relationship between specific forms of mental illness and particular types of dreams [6]. Freud himself approached the problem in his paper, A *Metapsychological Supplement to the Theory of Dreams* [7]. In this essay he remarked upon the resemblance of projection as it occurs in dreams to paranoid projection. Freud noted that the hallucinations in dreams and the hallucinatory phase of schizophrenia resemble one another in representing wishful restitutions of the ideas of objects. The important distinction lies in whether the hallucinatory wish is believed or in the capacity for reality-testing, which Freud placed "among the major institutions of the ego." Thereafter, Freud made only a few limited efforts to bring together the fields of dreams and psychopathology. In one of his last papers, Freud referred to the dream as "a mental disorder occurring during sleep, which is transient and harmless and which, indeed, performs a useful function." He still held to his belief that the dream would provide a "key to the understanding of the mental diseases which are permanent and injurious to life" [8].

The chief difficulty in approaching the relationship between dream and mental illness seems to have been the failure to reduce the scope of the problem, to study it piece by piece, or to separate distinct aspects of the problem for investigation. Comparison has often been made, for example, between dreams in general and mental illness in general, rather than juxtaposition of a particular type of dream with a type of mental disorder, or comparison of a dream phenomenon or aspect of dreaming with an element of psychopathology. For instance, Katan compared "normal examples" of dreams with psychoses and found that the differences outweighed the similarities [9]. Despite similarities in content, according to Katan, the underlying conflicts and the structure of the dream differ from a psychosis in which severe ego regression has occurred. Furthermore, he states that the withdrawal of cathexes from reality is temporary and reversible in the dream in contrast to the psychosis, in which conflict brings about a more profound and lasting severance of the ties with reality. In addition, the regression is more profound, the narcissism is more absolute, and the projection is based on more unrealistic thinking in psychosis than in dreams. Katan has to some extent set up a straw man, which obligingly topples before the force of his argument. He has chosen to compare psychoses with normal examples, by which I assume that he means dreams without intensely painful affect or overwhelming of the ego in the sleeping state, following which the full return to reality is effected without difficulty. Had he compared, for example, certain acute psychoses with dreams in which the subject is overwhelmingly terrified, he might have come to different conclusions. He does observe, for example, that certain dreams may function to prevent the outbreak of a psychosis and that "the wish in the dream was the last barricade which the ego could erect against the oncoming pschosis" [10].

Lewin is one of the few psychoanalysts to attempt a systematic comparison of specific types of dreams with particular forms of psychopathology [11, 12]. He first noted similarities in the structure and underlying conflicts of many phobias and infantile anxiety dreams. "In both anxiety dream and phobia," Lewin writes, "the true disturber, that is the repressed impulse, breaks through as a displacement or projection. Waking up, itself, has the character of a flight from the object upon which the anxiety was displaced. We could without much difficulty formulate the simple anxiety dreams of childhood in the same terms as the childhood phobias" [13]. In a later paper, Lewin related the eroticized "blank dream," which he believes represents a symbolic memory trace of the breast in the nursing situation, with states of ecstacy, hypomania, and depression. These dreams he regards as psychoses that originate in the wish to sleep. According to Lewin, ecstacy is equivalent to a blank dream in which the reliving of the blissful nursing situation is undisturbed. In hypomania a similar regression is effected, but the gratification is unconscious and is covered by denial, displacement, and action. In depression the wish for oral gratification is also distorted, but by superimposed manifest painful affects and impressions. Whether or not one supports Lewin's thesis, he is one of the few analysts to approach comprehensively the relationship between specific aspects of dreams and psychopathological regression. A summary of current psychoanalytic thinking on the relationship between dreams and psychosis is provided in the report by the author of a recent panel discussion of this subject held by the American Psychoanalytic Association in May, 1968 [14].

NIGHTMARES AND PSYCHOSES. Schizophrenic psychoses have sometimes been compared with severe anxiety dreams or nightmares. Sullivan recognized the relationship of schizophrenic psychoses to nightmares and called schizophrenia a "continued dream-state" akin to nightmare and night terror [15]. The difference, he felt, lay in the healing or reintegrating process. In contrast to schizophrenia, one recovered from the "failing dissociation" of the nightmare by "some adjustment of interpersonal relations." In particular, Sullivan believed that the relationship of night terror states to catatonic schizophrenia was fundamental. In his words, "The content of the night terror is never conceptual or perceptual. . . . Just such nonconceptual, nonperceptual, ultrainfantile content is the analogue in dream of the content expressed in typical catatonic schizophrenia" [16]. Rosen has also remarked upon the similarity of such dreams and schizophrenia. "Psychoses and dreams, or perhaps more correctly, psychoses and nightmares, have much in common," he writes. "In the excited catatonic, we deal with a continuous nightmare from which there is no waking up, inasmuch as the conscious ego, which would have come to the rescue, consists of remnants or shadows of the normal ego and perforce must fail the sufferer" [17]. More recently, Arsenian and Semrad referred again to schizophrenia as "like a nightmare in which the patient struggles to regain reality" [18]. Fisher et al., in their recent physiological studies of nightmares, suggest that the Stage 4 (non-REM) nightmare especially may resemble a brief but reversible psychotic episode [19].

Although not usually approached from this point of view, one of the best illustrations we have of the relationship of children's nightmares to later psychosis occurs in Freud's case of an infantile neurosis [20]. The wolf nightmare of the frightened little boy just before his fourth birthday, following a period of premature sexual seduction and traumatization, is very well known. Less well appreciated is the intimate connection between this cannibalistic dream of menacing wolves and his later paranoid psychosis. Six years after the completion of his analysis with Freud, the "Wolf-Man" resumed his treatment with Brunswick because of a paranoid psychosis with delusions of persecution [21]. Both the content and structure of this psychosis were related to the childhood nightmare. In this second analysis, his psychosis seemed to have been brought about by an unresolved passive-homosexual transference to Freud. In the adult psychosis, as a result of the intensity of this unresolved transference, conflicts similar to those that were encapsulated and limited in the childhood dream pervaded the patient's consciousness and undermined his capacity for reality-testing. From a structural, dynamic, or genetic point of view, the wolf man's childhood nightmare contained the essential elements of his adult psychosis, but without the regression in the waking state that occurred in the psychosis. Remaining consistent with the original title of the case study, the nightmare might well be regarded as an "infantile psychosis" [22].

Although he employed a somewhat different developmental theory, Sullivan has been one of the few writers to recognize the profound resemblance of *childhood* nightmares to later psychotic states. He stated his conviction in firm language as follows: "There are phenomena occasionally to be observed in infancy which have a certain relationship to schizophrenia. The night terror and terror dreams of childhood are so closely related to schizophrenic panic states that it does violence to scientific method to arbitrarily separate the two groups. . . . These eruptions of fear during sleep are important omens of future mental disorder" [23]. Sullivan did not distinguish between nightmares or night terrors as isolated or episodic phenomena occurring normally in the course of child development from those instances where the occurrence of frequent nightmares indicates more profound ego regression. Thus, he regarded a history of "*pavor nocturnus*, nightmares, and the like" as of grave prognostic significance, demonstrating a very poor adaptation to reality and indicating such a poor "dream-handling of the child's life problems" that severe regressive phenomena were apt to occur later in life. This may in certain instances be so, but it is an important problem for study to learn how to distinguish those nightmares that are sporadic and are followed by appropriate resolution of phase-specific conflicts from those that do, indeed, represent the childhood nucleus of a later psychosis.

Descriptive Similarities Between Nightmares and Acute Psychoses

An examination of the manifest features of a nightmare of an adult or a child and of an acute schizophrenic psychosis or turmoil state readily yields several significant points of similarity. If we observe the individual as he wakes from a nightmare or in an acute schizophrenic episode, we notice in both instances the state of terror and the frightened, panicky behavior that suggest an awful danger, real or imagined, that the individual seems to be confronting. In the psychosis we may see disorganization of the patient's behavior in the face of his overwhelming terror. He may, for example, assault others on the ward whom he confuses with imaginary attackers. Similarly, upon waking from a night terror attack the dreamer, especially if he is a child, may remain in an irrational state, apparently unable to distinguish internal from external perceptions, running about as if to escape from imaginary assailants. Adults, too, may continue briefly in such a condition of disorganized terror after a severe nightmare, during which time they are in a state virtually indistinguishable from an acute hallucinatory psychosis. An illustration is provided by a thirty-three-year-old woman who was hospitalized because of nightmares and hallucinations. Several days before her hospitalization she had a dream in which an enormous man without a face and wearing a pointed hat and brown cape tried to destroy her. She woke up screaming in terror, but the image persisted for her in the corner of the room for many minutes. Her husband had to comfort her and to take her to the spot where she hallucinated the man before the image could be made to recede.

From the point of view of the dreamer or of the psychotic, the overwhelming character of the terror in the two states is very similar. In each instance, the individual feels himself to be weak, helpless, and profoundly vulnerable in the face of powerful external forces or beings that he believes will attack or destroy him. One difference lies in the tendency of the hallucinated danger in the nightmare to bear more distinctly the marks of the world of typical childhood fears and dangers. Snakes, insects, monsters, beings that bite, choke, or suffocate, and creatures of children's stories or of radio and television abound in the nightmares of adults, as well as those of children. In the psychosis by contrast, the persecuting figures are more likely to be persons familiar in adult life—personal enemies of the patient or recent assassins made notorious by newspaper accounts—or to reflect the influence of contemporary technology or current events: influencing machines or, currently, atomic radiations. The adult psychotic's persecutors may become elaborated into a system or community ("fixed delusions"), but the persecutors in nightmares, especially in latency-age children, may also operate in an intricate and equally elaborate web. Adult sexual fears—for example, "homosexual panic"—seem more likely to be expressed directly by the psychotic, whereas in the nightmare childish sadistic notions of sexual relations are more evident. The relationship of the helpless dreamer or psychotic to a usually violent attacker is similar in both instances, however, and destruction of the individual is the threatened result. Judgment, grasp of reality, or insight are lost equally in the case of the nightmare victim during the dream and for a short time thereafter and for the psychotic throughout his acute episode. In the case of the dreamer, of course, these functions are usually restored after waking. Finally, in both the psychosis and the nightmare, especially in children, the comforting, protective presence of another person is of vital importance in restoring equilibrium to the personality.

One recalls the example from Chapter 2, page 78 of the nightmare of the thirty-year-old woman who awoke in horror screaming, "It's not real—I've never been seduced by a woman." Except for the patient's good fortune in being able to wake up, her terrified, helpless, and persecuted state in the dream would have resembled that of a patient in an acute homosexual panic. Indeed, its further analysis revealed underlying conflicts and ego defenses—including the use of projection—similar in certain respects to those found in an acute paranoid psychosis. Of course, the most fundamental difference, to which we shall turn later, lies in the capacity of the better-integrated individual to limit the panic or turmoil state to the dream and the immediate waking moments. There are, however, psychoses that begin with a nightmare or seem literally to be nightmares from which the patient fails to wake.

It would appear at this point that we cannot advance purely descriptive observations of the similarity or differences between nightmare and psychosis much further. It is necessary, therefore, that we depart from a purely descriptive approach and consider the problem from other points of view.

Dynamic Relationships Between Nightmares and Psychoses

In the foregoing chapters we have examined the multiple determinants of nightmares and the psychodynamic processes that operate in relation to them. We have discussed in detail the significance of environmental threats and danger situations, memories of traumatic events, the revival of early childhood anxieties and conflicts, the disruption of human relationships, and the role of ego regression and helplessness in the production of nightmares. In particular, conflicts related to violent aggression, both originating within the individual and directed toward the individual from the outside world, and anxieties concerning ego disintegration and annihilation, loss of identity, and abandonment, have been shown to be of great importance.

The same psychodynamic processes operate in acute psychoses and account for the resemblance of nightmares to these. However, in the nightmare the effects of these processes are usually reversed shortly after waking. Later in the chapter we shall discuss the problem of what accounts for this reversibility, for the capacity to reestablish a firm reality sense with respect to the dream's content. The loss of this ability in adulthood distinguishes the patient who merely continues to have bad dreams from the one who becomes psychotic.

This problem is illustrated by the case of a twenty-four-year-old single woman who was in the hospital because of an acute psychotic episode involving *déjà vu* phenomena characterized by delusional fears that she would be attacked while she was asleep, by auditory and visual hallucinations, and by thoughts that people were talking about her. The patient reported having numerous terrifying dreams in the hospital. These were concerned with homosexual and heterosexual attacks, with beatings and traumatic injections, with loss of control and "going crazy," and with the world suddenly exploding. Upon awaking after these dreams, she often felt confused and unable to distinguish between real events and those that occurred in dreams. Although she had reestablished contact with reality and recognized that she had had a dream, in an interview she quickly became confused if she was asked to relate her nightmares. As she began to recount a dream, she paused and seemed lost in her thoughts; her expression was distracted, her manner was distant, her voice assumed an odd, childlike tone, and she sometimes gestured oddly. When she resumed her narrative, one could no longer be certain whether she was relating a dream or events she believed had really occurred. On one occasion she talked rationally and with appropriate feeling, maintaining good contact with the interviewer and her surroundings until she came to discuss her nightmares. She was then asked whether she ever felt that her frightening dreams seemed so real that, upon awakening, she would be concerned that they might be or become a reality. At this point she became confused, frightened, in more tenuous contact with reality, and odd in her facial expression and manner. It was necessary to change the subject completely in order to resume contact and continue the interview.

Since she was a day patient who went home each night and on weekends, she continued to live with her parents. Her father was suffering from a severe leg injury; as her mother was away a great deal in the evening, the patient was required to change his dressings and give him an injection, a task that both excited and terrified her. According to her account, her father had beaten her and her brother as children, and now she feared his anger and his painful screaming when she changed his dressings. She feared, too, her own murderous rage, precipitated by a sense of his ingratitude. She feared that she might lose control and actually kill him or that he might retaliate physically. She was afraid to turn to her mother to tell her of this fear, as the possibility of the parents' separation occasioned by the mother's intolerance of the father's behavior had always seemed a still greater threat. It was in this context of actual danger and threat that the patient had had many of the described severe nightmares in which the father himself or his symbolic substitutes attacked her. The conflict over killing and being killed that filled her dreams characterized her persecutory experience of the household reality, as well. On certain nights after a particularly traumatic time with her father, she awakened and believed that she had had a nightmare. With some difficulty she came to realize that she did not recall any dreams and that what she regarded as a dream had actually occurred earlier in the evening before she went to sleep.

This patient's case illustrates the vital importance of the capacity to distinguish dream from reality in maintaining sanity. Stated differently, when this function is impaired, an important barrier to psychosis is lost. The confusion may operate in two directions. The patient may be unsure as to whether a dream has actually occurred or he may have difficulty establishing that an actual traumatic situation has not been a dream. The dreams under consideration in this patient and in others in a similar plight are frequently nightmares. This is true for a number of reasons. For example, the concern with violent attack that characterizes nightmares is an acute problem for patients threatened with or undergoing a schizophrenic regression. Infantile fears of annihilation and destruction and the dread of abandonment characterize both states. Furthermore, the daytime experiences with other persons that furnish the day residues for dreams in actuality are often unusually traumatic for psychotic patients; dream figures and images that represent these persons become persecutors in the nightmares—and in delusions, as well.

Later in this chapter we shall consider the factors that may account for the ability of some individuals and the inability of others to limit their overwhelming terror to the sleep-dream situation, that is, why some people have only nightmares while others become psychotic.

Developmental Relationships Between Childhood Nightmares and Adult Psychoses

The profound relationship that may exist in the same individual between certain childhood nightmares and the later eruption of an acute psychosis can be demonstrated repeatedly in case studies. In the novel, *I Never Promised You a Rose Garden*, an extraordinarily vivid and moving account of the author's schizophrenic psychosis and psychotherapy, Hannah Green demonstrates the intimate relationship between childhood nightmares and an adolescent psychosis [24]. At age five she was hospitalized for the removal of a cyst in the genital region. She was lied to with bland assurances, misled about the nature of the procedure, and not prepared for the penetration of her body with needles and other instruments that, despite anesthesia, were intensely painful. The night after the operation she had had nightmares "about being broken into like a locked room, torn apart, scrubbed clean with scouring powder, and reassembled, dead but now acceptable." This dream was followed by another "about a broken flowerpot whose blossom seemed to be her own ruined strength" [25]. In her psychosis at sixteen, she lived in this nightmare world continuously. Her reality became, as she phrased it, "a walking nightmare." This was for her no mere analogy. The terror, the vulnerability and helplessness, the destructiveness and persecution by demonic creatures and forces, the world without confidence, trust, or protection—all of these carried over from her nightmares into the daytime state. Once, for example, one of the creatures in her delusional world took her to a region called "the fear bog" in order "to see the monsters and corpses of her nightmares accumulating there from year after year of terrifying dreams" [26]. In the elaboration of the details of her psychotic system, through the use of magic and fantasy invention she gained some mastery over the feeling of helplessness and the imminence of total destruction that was unrelenting in the nightmares.

The following example illustrates in detail this relationship between childhood nightmare and traumatic experiences, deception by parents, and subsequent psychosis.

A professionally successful thirty-five-year-old father of six children was admitted to the hospital in an acute psychotic state after his wife found him crouching in the corner of a room, fending off imaginary attackers with a knife. Five days prior to this he had been awakened by an intruder who had entered his bedroom while he and his wife were sleeping. Although there was evidence that a burglar had in fact entered his house, the patient's account of the incident was distorted as a result of his conflicts. The patient reported that he had been awakened at dawn by a sensation of a sheet being drawn over his thighs and genitals. At first he thought it was his wife and then that it had been a nightmare. He became convinced of the reality of the experience when he saw the man jump back and run out after the patient yelled at him and threatened him with a gun.

Over the next five days the patient was plagued by the fear that the man would return to attack him. He obtained new locks, set up a burglar alarm, bought a police dog, and kept a loaded gun handy. On the day of admission he related the experience to his father, who commented that it could not have happened and that he must have dreamt it. The patient responded to this with fury; reviewing the evidence in his mind, he began to doubt the validity of his own perceptions and decided that he must be insane. In a panic, he sent his wife away with the children; she returned several hours later to find him in the state described above.

The patient, the oldest of several children, was stricken at age four by a neurological disease that left his legs paralyzed. This disorder, together with the severely restrictive procedures involved in its treatment, contributed greatly to the patient's view of himself as weak, helpless, defective, and vulnerable. He recalled that, when he was about seven years old, his mother attempted a "mercy killing" by trying to smother him with a pillow as his grandmother, aged ninety, encouraged her. In his treatment, he recalled that the grandmother, seemingly in a rage, approached him with a pillow as he lay literally paralyzed in his bed. He remembered his grandmother saying, "I'll do it" and his mother saying, "No, I will." He screamed, "Don't do it." After the pillow descended upon his head, he feigned death by holding his breath. Then he suddenly grabbed the pillow and put it under his stomach, and the two women desisted.

When the child told his father about this attack, he seemed to believe him, but the patient later learned that his mother had made his father promise to deny that the incident had ever occurred. The father told him it was "just a dream." Thereafter, the child developed an acute disturbance in which the boundary between nightmare and waking reality broke down completely. In his nightmare-fantasy-delusions he was a white newt, the ruler over a band of black ants that later rose in rebellion and became raging, biting destroyers who threw him in the brig. Because they were black, he could not see them in the dark and was helpless before their fury.

According to the patient, from the time he was seven until eleven or twelve, his mother took his younger brothers into bed with her to protect her from the father's drunken assaults. Because of his deformity, she did not regard the patient as qualified for this protective function, and he was excepted. At the end of this period of his childhood he had a recurrent nightmare in which a threatening character that looked like the Joker in the old Batman comic books would "on come" from the dark and stand by his bed. Its face was maniacal and grimacing, angry and menacing, and seemed to enjoy the fear and pain it inspired. Characteristically, the boy awoke in terror and feared to open his eyes. He remembered thinking at the time that the figure represented madness to him and that, should he ever awaken and find him still standing there, then he would be mad, for "the on coming would have reached its final point" and have become a "continuing fact in time." In his treatment he associated the figure's face with his father's "insane rages," as well as with his own projected hatred.

The patient described his mother as a large, powerful woman, severely religious and fiercely strict in sexual matters. As a young person she had carried a gun and learned jujitsu. The patient felt that she hated him, and he feared her. When he was eighteen, she developed a malignant illness, from which she died in several months. When he learned of her illness, he obtained a rifle out of fear that her hatred toward him would be released by her sickness and that she would kill him. In the terminal stages of her illness, she would wander into his room to stand at the foot of his bed and stare. He felt that she wished to sit and talk and to tell him that she loved him; fearing to express his own buried love lest the intensity of his thwarted need drive him insane, he was able only to sit up and clutch his loaded gun. When his mother died shortly afterward, he felt that he had murdered her by his withdrawal of love. Aspects of this conflict were rearoused shortly before his acute illness when, after the birth of their fifth child, his wife began to practice birth control, which to the patient meant murder. In retaliation, he had forced his wife to perform fellatio and feared the break-up of his cherished marriage. He considered the possibility that the "intruder" was the product of his guilt, created by himself to come between him and his wife and destroy his marriage. Shortly before the episode occurred, his seven-year-old son experienced nightmares of his father's dying, and he resented the fact that his wife had taken the boy into bed with her.

A striking theme in this account is the repetitive specter of an intruder who threatens the patient with destruction or with violent sexual attack, an image based in each instance upon a traumatic nucleus of reality to which the patient applied the impulses and affects that he could not bear. In early childhood the intruder was the mother or grandmother who tried to destroy him. Later it was the father who threatened to attack the mother, with whom the patient was identified, in her bedroom. When he was eleven, this figure appeared as a menacing joker in nightmares, and at eighteen it was the dying mother who stalked his bedside. Finally, in adult life, dream and actuality, fantasy and reality became fused in the form of a menacing burglar-intruder whose frightening image overflowed the boundary of dream and reality and became, as in childhood the boy once feared it would, "a continuing fact in time." The adult situation of the patient's marriage, and particularly of the children who were coming between himself and his wife, had already reproduced a number of the conditions of childhood that provoked the nightmare. The burglar-intruder served to complete the traumatic situations of the father's earlier invasions and the mother's and grandmother's attack upon him.

The undermining of the patient's capacity to distinguish nightmare, fantasy, and reality had occurred earlier at age seven when his father told him that the mother's and grandmother's assault, which under any circumstances would be difficult for a seven-year-old to understand, was "just a dream." He had responded then, as might be expected, by losing the capacity not only to determine whether what had really happened to him was a dream, but also by becoming unable to know that his nightmares were not real. When, as an adult, his father told him once more that a traumatic, real experience "must have been a dream," he again lost the ability to distinguish fantasy from reality, real danger from nightmare. He developed an acute psychosis, as he had before as a child.

The child's nightmare, or, more accurately, the conflicts that underlie it, may undergo a different fate than to emerge in adulthood as an acute paranoid psychosis. They may be put to work, mastered, or transformed into a useful and even creative activity or occupation, as discussed in earlier chapters. For example, a father of a nineteen-year-old boy recently told me of the nightmares his son experienced at ages five and six. Many nights during that period the child awakened his parents by screaming about wires, circuits, and machines that were persecuting him. He insisted that the clock in his room was a time bomb and that they throw it out the window. The parents were proud to learn that at seventeen he was teaching a course on computers at M.I.T. and had obtained patents on several circuits he had devised. The only vestige of his childhood nightmare-paranoia was his unwillingness to plug in the computers he created; he insisted that his mother do it for him.

Theoretical Questions

DEVELOPMENTAL CONSIDERATIONS.   In considering the relationship between nightmares and acute psychoses, one is faced with two fundamental, though related, problems. First, why are some individuals able to confine their efforts to deal with ongoing conflicts to nightmares while others develop acute schizophrenic episodes? Second, what is the relationship between the nightmares from which an individual suffered as a child and the acute schizophrenic psychosis he develops as an adolescent or adult? A developmental approach to both of these problems seems to be the most useful one; it can also demonstrate how closely linked the two questions really are.

The adult's nightmare and the acute psychosis may both be regarded as responses to a threatening or painful experience in the outside world, a current reality that has had a profound internal psychological impact. This reality is most often an actual assault or a threat of attack, an intense thwarting of libidinal or object need such as a disappointment in a love relationship or the loss of an important person upon whom the individual is dependent. These precipitating factors are made painful not merely because of any intrinsically traumatic qualities that they possess. They have the potential for provoking a regressive response because of their association with persistent internal conflicts and traumatic experiences and situations in the individual's past, especially those of childhood. The ego reacts with anxiety and with various efforts to integrate the traumatic reality. Somatizing reactions and other neurotic symptoms may have occurred as an initial effort to master an increased amount of anxiety. In both the nightmare and the acute psychosis, the ego has been unable to limit the intensity of the anxiety, and it has become overwhelming, with the result that primitive projective and distortion mechanisms have come to predominate, and reality-testing has been severely impaired. The difference lies in the fact that in the nightmare only the ego in sleep, a state of regression under any circumstance, is affected. In the acute psychosis, overwhelming anxiety, the reliance upon projection and distortion, and the sacrificing of reality-testing persist into the daytime, as well.

For the nightmare victim and the psychosis-prone individual, the immediate precipitating factors have reevoked painful memories of abandonment by infantile love objects and conflicts over annihilation, oral incorporation, and destructiveness. Both the nightmare and the acute psychosis reflect the ego's efforts to deal with these early anxieties and conflicts through the construction of a primitive symbolic structure whose content is derived from the interweaving of the residues of daytime experience and regressively revived early memories. This regressive reevoking of fantasies of violent attack is of particular importance in the traumatic intensification of anxiety that occurs in both nightmares and acute psychoses.

What developmental considerations might be important in attempting to account for this difference, for the vulnerability to psychosis? In a study with Dr. Lester Grinspoon of the dreaming of acute schizophrenic patients hospitalized on a research ward, we were impressed, not only with how often these patients recalled frequent nightmares as children—for nightmares in childhood are commonplace if not inevitable—but that they were left to their own resources in dealing with the nighttime terror experience. Although it is possible that such memories can be distorted by the psychotic process, it was striking how rarely the patients remembered anyone coming to pick them up or tell them that they had been dreaming; many patients recalled periods of perceptual confusion in which they were immersed in a frightening world in which boundaries between reality, fantasy, illusion, and hallucination were lost. By age six to eight, a child has usually internalized corrective parental attitudes and achieved sufficient cognitive development to make the distinction between dream and reality for himself. In the psychosis-prone person, whose object relationships have always been unstable and filled with violence and hatred, as in the case of the young woman described on page 166, it is possible that this process of nighttime assurance and comforting has not occurred normally from infancy; the capacity to distinguish dream, fantasy, and reality has always remained to some degree fragile or incomplete. Since this capacity normally develops relatively late in childhood, it may quite readily become lost in the course of a regressive process. When, as in the case of the man described earlier in this chapter, the parent actively undermines the child's efforts to establish the distinction between his nightmares and actual frightening experiences, the individual may be particularly prone to the occurrence in adult life of a psychosis resulting directly from the breakdown of this differentiation. Although the regression of the capacity to distinguish dream and reality may not in itself define or account for the psychosis, which involves the loss of other ego functions as well, it often seems to provide the disorder with its most characteristic clinical features, namely, the intrusion into the waking state of images and fears, with accompanying distortions, that properly belong to the dream life.

The nightmares and night terrors of childhood may be a precursor of later acute schizophrenic psychosis. They contain many of the elements of later madness. The struggles over passivity warded off through violent action, over helplessness and vulnerability, over a hunger for love accompanied by a terror of annihilation should love be repulsed or met with hate, the capacity for projection—all of these exist in any child, as well as in the adult. Both nightmares and acute psychoses give expression to profound anxieties regarding intense dependent oral longings and wishes for fusion with the parent in association with violent and destructive hatred that is projected onto a menacing attacker. In both the child's nightmare and the acute psychosis a loss of ego identity and integrity is threatened, but in the case of the child's dream, in contrast to the adult psychosis, reality-testing can be restored, and madness becomes reversible. The way in which the parents deal with the nightmare experience—whether or not they comfort the child in the night, turn on the lights, or support his growing capacity to know after waking he has been dreaming —bears on the development of reality-testing in relation to the dream and also upon the later capacity to confine the boundaries of the nightmare to sleep and the immediate arousal period.

Since, as we have seen, threatening realities foster the occurrence of nightmares, a child whose life is filled with traumatic experiences may have many nightmares and will confront those who take care of him at night with many opportunities to intervene in his frightening dreams. However, if the parents themselves are in reality destructive figures for the child, it is unlikely that they will offer much in the way of clarification or comfort when he has nightmares. Conversely, when parents, in their shame over the attacks to which they subject the child, attempt to take advantage of the child's weak ability to distinguish dream and reality and, as in the previous case, trick him into thinking that assaults he has actually perceived and felt are "but a dream," then the damage to the development of the capacity for reality-testing may be even more severe. He may always retain some difficulty in convincing himself that his nightmares are not real or that traumatic realities are not dreams.

In the event that a comforting person is not available to the child to assure him that his monsters of the night are not real or to help him learn that his terrifying journeys after dark are something called "dreams," he will be forced to rely on his own stabilizing capacities. Very often these themselves operate at the expense of reality. Several acute psychotic patients interviewed by the author have relied heavily since early childhood upon magical devices to offset the threatening power of frightening dream images; these patients have grown up believing in the prophetic power of dreams, in their actuality, or in their capacity to influence events. In psychotic regression, these mechanisms may dominate the clinical picture. Furthermore, if the patient's childhood experience with other persons has been predominantly negative, which is likely to be the case in the psychosis-prone individual, in the regression that follows upon the initial stress these internalized representations of figures from the past will reemerge as hostile or threatening percepts, not only during sleep in a nightmare, but during the waking hours, as well. As the psychotic regression takes place, the power of hatred and of the force of internalized hostile qualities of persons revived from the past can overwhelm the ego during sleep to the point that a nightmare may itself seem to continue into the daytime as an acute psychosis. The relationship that such *developmental* difficulties in reality-testing have to the *vulnerability* to later psychosis is a subject that requires further investigation.

LEVELS OF EGO INTEGRATION.   The nightmare and the acute psychosis may be thought of as representing different levels of ego integration, or varying responses on the part of the ego to a threatening external reality that has become associated with early infantile anxieties and conflicts. One might conceive of a continuum between normal affective dreaming and acute psychosis, with the nightmare seen as an intermediate state. The concept of levels of ego integration might be applied also to the fact that a nightmare may usher in an acute psychosis or progress to a psychosis or that nightmares may alternate or occur in conjunction with acute psychotic states. Such an association of nightmares and acute psychoses in the same individual is illustrated by the case of a fifteen-year-old boy who killed his mother several months before his hospitalization. His struggle to ward off the overwhelming psychological reality of his deed had passed through a gamut of "neurotic" defenses that included paralysis of his limbs and various somatic symptoms. As his anxiety mounted, he had a severe nightmare in which his mother appeared as a haggard specter advancing threateningly toward him with outstretched clawlike hands. The following night he reported, instead of a dream, that he had actually seen his mother, who told him of her suffering and threatened him with death. The patient's experience of believing in his mother's actual return was brief, and reality-testing was soon established. The nightmares then occurred once again.

A nightmare may be the only indication of the ego's struggle to integrate an overwhelming reality experience. A thirteen-year-old boy was the only witness to the older sister's shooting their mother to death. He never discussed what he had seen with anyone. Except for a generally subdued and morose manner, he gave little evidence of the continuing impact of this experience. Three years later he was brought to the hospital because of severe nightmares from which he partially awakened, pounded his fist on the bed, and cried out in terror, "She is dead, she is dead. She was shot. Leave her alone, leave her alone." The burden of integrating the overwhelming reality of what he had witnessed could not be borne by his usual characterological defenses. The traumatic experience was reactivated in the encapsulated nightmare-psychosis.

The personality reintegration that occurs following an acute psychosis can sometimes be traced in the dream-life itself, with less frightening dreams replacing nightmares as the patient recovers. The patient described on page 164 had lost briefly the capacity to reality-test the images of the nightmare that led to her hospitalization. As her psychotherapy progressed, she had a dream quite similar to the original nightmare, but the menacing and destructive figure of the man in the first dream was modified and made less terrifying by becoming fused with the protective image of the patient's doctor.

Summary and Conclusions

In this chapter we have examined the possible relationships between one type of dream, the nightmare, and one form of psychosis, the acute schizophrenic episode or turmoil state. I have described manifest similarities between the two conditions: the terror of overwhelming intensity, the perception of external danger, the elements of violence, the use of projection and distortion mechanisms, and the ego state of helplessness and vulnerability. I have also discussed the interrelation of an environmental reality, perceived as threatening, with internal conflicts and anxieties concerning infantile dependent longings, earlier traumatic experiences, abandonment, primitive destructive rage, and mutual annihilation in producing both conditions. Important relationships that may exist between severe or repeated childhood nightmares in the same individual and later acute psychosis have been demonstrated.

Although nightmares may "progress" to an acute psychosis, coexist with psychotic states, or alternate with them, the fundamental difference has been noted to lie in the reversibility of the former, in the capacity to reestablish reality-testing or contact. This difference has been approached in terms of the concept of levels of ego integration, in which the nightmare may be regarded as an encapsulated or delimited state, intermediate between normal dreaming and acute psychosis.

The later incapacity in the psychosis-prone individual to confine the regressive reaction to a nightmare, or, conversely, the ability to maintain the "nightmare level" of integration without further regression appears to depend on three interrelated factors, all bearing on the development of reality sense and reality-testing in childhood. These are:

1. The relative intensity of latent violent or destructive impulses in the individual. As intense aggressiveness is in part a function of early object relations, a child who is the object of hatred for persons in the environment is likely to incorporate such aggressive attitudes into his own personality. Later representations of these persons projected onto imaginary attackers may emerge in nightmares or acute psychotic episodes. Furthermore, as destructive impulses are themselves threatening to the child when directed toward persons upon whom he is dependent, he will rely on the defensive use of projection, which has the result of causing the outside world to seem excessively destructive and threatening, all at the expense of a more realistic view.

2. The availability or absence in childhood of the comforting and reassuring presence of the parent figures when frightening dreams or other anxiety-laden experiences occur at night. The incorporation of the qualities and realistic attitudes of such comforting persons probably plays a vital role in establishing the capacity to maintain dream-reality differentiations. On the other hand, in the absence of such comforting, the child may be forced to rely upon his own magical devices to offset the dream's threat at the expense of reality, thus contributing to later psychosis vulnerability.

3. The specific role of the parents in helping or undermining the child's developing capacity to differentiate between nightmares and terrifying "real" experiences that threaten him, a distinction that is more difficult for the immature ego to consolidate than is generally appreciated. Gross deception of the child by the parents in relation to the distinction between dream and reality, especially during the years when this is a fragile and developing capacity, may leave the child prone to later breakdown

of this distinction in adolescence or adult life and thus perhaps make him vulnerable to acute schizophrenic psychosis, as well.

References

1. *Diagnostic and Statistical Manual of Mental Disorders.* 2d. Ed. Washington, D.C.: American Psychiatric Assoc., 1968.
2. More, Henry. In Hunter, R., and Macalpine, I. (Eds.), *Three Hundred Years of Psychiatry, 1535–1860* (1656). London: Oxford University Press, 1953. P. 153.
3. Kant, I. In Weischedel, W. (Ed.), *Werke.* Darmstadt: Wissenschaftliche Buchgesellschaft, 1966. Vol. I, p. 893.
4. Jackson, J. H. In Taylor, J. (Ed.), *Selected Writings of John Hughlings Jackson* (1881). London: Hodder and Stoughton, 1931.
5. Griesinger, W. *Mental Pathology and Therapeutics* (1867). New York: Hafner, 1965. P. 107.
6. Freud, S. The Interpretation of Dreams (1900). In *The Standard Edition of the Complete Psychological Works of Sigmund Freud*, tr. and ed. by J. Strachey with others. London: Hogarth and the Institute of Psycho-Analysis, 1953. Vol. IV, pp. 88–92.
7. Freud, S. A Metapsychological Supplement to the Theory of Dreams (1917 [1915]). *Standard Edition.* 1957. Vol. XIV, pp. 222–235.
8. Freud, S. An Outline of Psychoanalysis (1940 [1938]). *Standard Edition.* 1964. Vol. XXIII, p. 195.
9. Katan, M. Dream and psychosis: their relationship to hallucinatory processes. *Int. J. Psychoanal.* 41:341–351, 1960.
10. Ibid. P. 349.
11. Lewin, B. Phobic symptoms and dream interpretation. *Psychoanal. Quart.* 21:295–322, 1952.
12. Lewin, B. Sleep, narcissistic neurosis and the analytic situation. *Psychoanal. Quart.* 23:487–510, 1954.
13. Lewin, B. Phobic symptoms and dream interpretation. *Psychoanal. Quart.* 21.302, 1952.
14. Mack, J. E. Dreams and psychosis. *J. Amer. Psychoanal. Assoc.* 17: 206–221, 1969.
15. Sullivan, H. S. *Schizophrenia as a Human Process.* New York: Norton, 1962.
16. Ibid. P. 19.
17. Rosen, J. *Direct Analysis.* New York: Crune & Stratton, 1953. P. 40.
18. Arsenian, J., and Semrad, E. V. Schizophrenia and language. *Psychiat. Quart.* 40:449–458, 1966.
19. Fisher, C., Byrne, J., Edwards, A., and Kahn, E. A Psychophysiological Study of Nightmares. Freud anniversary lecture, April 8, 1969.
20. Freud, S. From the History of an Infantile Neurosis (1918 [1914]). *Standard Edition.* 1955. Vol. XVII, pp. 7–122.
21. Brunswick, R. M. A supplement to Freud's *History of an Infantile Neurosis. Int. J. Psychoanal.* 9:439–476, 1928.

22. Weinshel, E. M. Severe regressive states during analysis. *J. Amer. Psychoanal. Ass.* 14:538–568, 1966.
23. Sullivan, H. S. *Schizophrenia as a Human Process.* New York: Norton, 1962. P. 161.
24. Green, H. *I Never Promised You a Rose Garden.* New York: Holt, Rinehart & Winston, 1964.
25. Ibid. P. 53.
26. Ibid. P. 98.

6

Nightmares and the New Biology of Dreaming

DISCOVERIES BEGINNING in the mid-1950s by Aserinsky, Kleitman, Dement, and other research workers established the fact that distinct, repetitively demonstrable biological events are regularly associated with dreaming. Considerable progress has been made in relating the psychological phenomenon of dreaming to observable physiological processes. Since many excellent recent résumés of this work are available [1–6], a detailed re view would not be appropriate to the present study. However, it has a number of implications that need to be considered here. Although such research may not make clearer the meaning of particular dreams, for the first time it makes it possible to establish important psychophysiological correlations in the dream field, and it may help us to formulate a general theory of dreaming.

The finding that has perhaps brought about the most dramatic shift of emphasis in our thinking about dreams is the discovery that we dream, not fleetingly or under special circumstances, but regularly and nightly for large portions of sleep; or, more accurately, the observable physiological events that are correlated with dreaming span this period. Dreaming sleep—or sleep that is associated with rapid conjugate eye movements (REMS) [7], a low-voltage desynchronized electroencephalogram [8] from which awakening produces dream reports in a high percentage of instances—occupies 20 to 25 percent of the time that young adults sleep. Furthermore, in the newborn infant the sleep phase that later comes to be associated with dreaming occupies from one-third to one-half of its existence; until a child reaches the age of four or five, the percentage of sleep time he spends in REM (rapid eye movement) or dreaming sleep exceeds that of the adult [4, 9, 10].

This distinct phase or stage of sleep, variously called the REM phase or Stage 1 REM or D state [11], has been shown to be a period of intense cellular activity in the cortex and in other parts of the nervous system, accompanied by a 30 to 50 percent higher blood flow through the brain than in non-REM periods [12–14]. Cardiorespiratory irregularities, penile erections [15–17], and other evidences of autonomic activity also indicate that, contrary to traditional views of sleep as a time of central nervous system (CNS) dormancy, the REM periods are times of intense activity and even "turmoil" in the brain. During REM sleep, as Roffwarg has phrased it, the brain appears to be "in business for itself." Another finding, of special significance for the present study, is that motor pathways to the periphery appear to be blocked during REM sleep. The studies of dream deprivation [1, 18, 19] or, more accurately, of repeated interruption of the REM phase, have shown that prevention of REM sleep can lead to a variety of psychological and psychophysiological changes including hunger, tension, anxiety, motor irritability, increased aggressive behavior, disturbed relationship with reality, paranoid themes, and susceptibility to hallucinations that are not found if the awakenings occur during non-REM periods. Although recent studies have shown differing responses to D state deprivation, this work suggests that dreaming, or, more properly, the D state, may serve important functions in maintaining the well-being of the human organism.

The elucidation of somatic correlates of dreaming with the demonstration of the adverse effect of repeated interruption of REM sleep has resulted in a shift of emphasis away from the study of the meaning of particular dreams and toward the consideration of the possible functions of dreaming itself. Trosman [20], Fisher [1], and other writers have suggested that dreams may be necessary as a mode of discharging tensions, conflicts, and anxieties that arise in waking life; this could play a role over and above their relationship to sleep. Similarly, Ullman [21, 22] has stressed the fact that dreams serve to integrate disturbing environmental events with past experiences and function in the service of vigilance, transforming threatening stimuli symbolically while evaluating the need for arousal. Recent theoretical discussions that attempt to formulate a general theory of dreaming emphasize the function of the REM or D state in maintaining personality integration [23, 24]. Meissner has made a far-reaching effort to correlate the fundamental neurophysiological findings of recent sleep and dream research with psychoanalytic theory. He regards the D state as functioning to regulate the discharge of unconscious energy during sleep "in a manner which is neither psychologically overwhelming nor neurophysiologically disruptive" [25].

This emphasis upon adaptive or biological functions of dreaming has raised the question whether dreams are in any way concerned with wish-fulfillment, disguise, or repression. However, it may be that separate dimensions of a problem that can be approached at different levels or from different points of view have become confused. The problem of determining the phylogenetic origins or evolutionary functions of the central nervous structures involved in dreaming is, for example, a valid subject of inquiry, but one that is quite distinct from, even if related to, the ontogeny of these structures in a given individual. Similarly, the physiological functioning of the D state in the sleep cycle is a discrete problem, difficult at best to correlate with the psychological function of dreaming. Finally, an inquiry into the adaptive functions of dreaming in psychological terms raises many questions not related to an understanding of the relevant intrapsychic dynamics in any given dream report; such an understanding depends essentially upon eliciting mental content from different levels of consciousness. For example, a particular child's terror dream of a ghastly monster coming to eat him may have been instigated by a hostile wish toward his parents. The understanding of the dream's meaning achieved by an analysis of symbols and an exploration of the mechanisms of defense may uncover murderous wishes toward the parents. However, the *function* of the dream may be understood quite differently. The dream may, for example, be regarded as serving to alert the child to danger, to force waking, or to integrate external threats with instinctual forces occurring from within. The dream could have an essentially self-preservative or adaptive function.

In reviewing studies that interpret the findings of research in dream physiology, one finds considerable blurring of the distinction between the psychological functions of dreams and the biological functions of REM sleep. That the D state has no essential or inevitable relationship to dreaming is dramatically borne out by its high percentage of occurrence in newborn infants [4, 9, 10] and by animal experiments that demonstrate that its basic physiological features are maintained despite complete decortication [26]. The most plausible view seems to be that, as the central nervous system matures, dreaming occurs as a psychic phenomenon employing pathways that, from a neurophysiological standpoint, may have quite different discrete functions and that, in turn, may not be the same for the mature organism as in early development [4].

If, as Dement asserts, "the rapid eye movement period, during which dreaming is presumed to occur, is an entirely unique and independent state of being with a separate and specialized neuroanatomical mechanism" [27], we would look for broad and possibly essential biological functions of this state. In this regard Snyder, after tracing the phylogeny of the REM state, which has been observed in all mammals studied, has offered his "sentinel hypothesis" [28]. According to this theory, the REM mechanism, which is accompanied by a state of heightened inward arousal, serves a sentinel or vigilance function, and contributes to the survival of the animal. REM periods tend to be followed by brief periodic arousals during which the environment could be scouted for danger. The preparatory activation of the organism during the REM periods would prepare it for appropriate fight or flight responses. Thus, the REM state could, according to Snyder, serve during sleep to protect the organism from potential external danger; the prolonged sleep and REM periods of higher mammals might reflect their relative safety or invulnerability to attack that permits prolonged and uninterrupted sleep. This view is consistent with the high percentage of REM time, the restlessness, and the more frequent awakenings of infants, who are more helpless, vulnerable, and more easily threatened or endangered. However, arguing against this theory is the fact that, since the organism is particularly difficult to arouse during REM sleep, the D state would not offer much real protection. Broughton's observations that phenomena such as sleepwalking, nightmares, and night terrors are disturbances of an arousal mechanism [29] is more consistent with a theory of adaptation or protection during sleep. However, these phenomena occur during both the non-REM and REM sleep periods.

Nightmares and the Psychophysiology of Dreaming

The utilization of a biological process for psychological purposes, such as has occurred in the REM-dream situation, does not *necessarily* mean that the biological purpose initially had anything to do with the psychological intent. However, a theory such as Snyder's that relates dreaming to the alerting or warning functions of the nervous system is consistent with what we understand regarding the psychology of nightmares. Snyder has, for example, noted that "the extent of awakening following each REM period is somehow modulated to accord with latest estimates of expected danger" [30]. Furthermore, he points out that preparatory cerebral activation should take the form of an hallucinated reality, "such as the animal might be in danger of encountering at the time of awakening." In human nightmares, especially in those of small children, the hallucinated threat universally appears as an attacking animal or other common environmental threat; this suggests that older phylogenetic linkages in human nervous system activity may be aroused in the regressive experience of dreaming. Sackett's experiments [31] with monkeys reared in social isolation have shown that the frightened response to a threatening stimulus may be innate, requiring only the appropriate environmental stimulus for its release (see Chapter 2, p. 42). Similarly, Chance has observed highly ritualized innate retreat or "cut-off" behavior on the part of rats and certain species of birds confronted by a threatening member of their own species, for which they simultaneously show evidence of attraction [32]. This behavior cuts off the other animal from view and effectively reduces in both the level of excitement and aggression, thus permitting the animals to remain close to one another. These observations suggest the possibility that the stereotyped threat-retreat content that is so common in nightmares may be related to highly ritualized, innately patterned behaviors that have proved to be adaptive in the course of species evolution. Furthermore, nightmares, which frequently lead to awakening, seem to occur at times of vividly heightened danger for the individual; because of the greater complexity of human mental life, this danger is a product, not only of actual external threat, but of the meaning given to such threats on the basis of internal forces and conflicts.

The discovery of the high percentage of sleep time, or of each twenty-four hours, that is spent in the REM state in infants and small children and the relatively high degree of CNS activity associated with this state have possible implications for our thinking about the relationship of children's dreams to their psychological and emotional development. Since the intense CNS activity that occurs in the REM state is present at or before birth and appears to be relatively independent of external stimuli, it must to a large extent be an internally generated mechanism. This does not, of course, imply that external or environmental factors cannot influence REM activity or that dreaming does not serve a function in relation to the integration of experience in the outside world.

Because of the large amount of time that infants and small children spend in REM or activated sleep and because of the fact that this diminishes with age, Roffwarg [4] and his coworkers have proposed that the vigorous stimulation of the immature portions of the brain by lower centers that mature earlier, as occurs during the REM state, may assist neuronal differentiation and the maturization and myelinization of higher centers. According to this theory, structural building in the nervous system, especially in the visual-sensory system toward which impulses

flow during REM activity, would occur in response to this endogenous CNS stimulation. There is evidence that premature infants spend an even higher percentage of time in the REM state
[9]. This finding suggests that endogenous stimulation *in utero*
from REM state activity, at a period in development when exogenous sources of stimulation are minimal, is particularly intense;
it lends further support to the view that the REM state plays a
role in CNS maturation. The hypothesis that the intense CNS
activity that occurs during the REM state plays an important
part in central nervous system maturation is consistent with
knowledge from a variety of fields regarding the growth and development of the nervous system. Roffwarg and his coworkers
reviewed an extensive literature from the fields of neuroanatomy,
neuropathology, and neuroembryology that supports the view
that chemical and neural stimulation, including that which arises
within the nervous system itself, is essential for the development,
differentiation, and maintenance of structures in the nervous system.

One of the most intriguing aspects of theories such as those of
Roffwarg, Broughton, or Snyder is the correlations they suggest
with psychoanalytic theories of childhood psychological development, anxiety, and ego functioning as they pertain to dreaming.
Anyone who has observed small children during the night, who
has tended them when they awake in terror, or who has chosen
to be attentive to their reports of monsters, witches, harrowing
chases, or enchanted voyages reported in the morning will readily
acknowledge that children rarely sleep like "logs." The sleep of
very young children, probably to a greater degree than that of
normal adults, is filled with dream activity. Parmelee has even
designated a specific "active sleep state" in infants, characterized
by irregular respiration, eye movements, and intermittent small
limb movements [33, 34]. External sources of stimulation from
daytime activities seem not to be readily assimilated by small
children and tend to be carried over into sleeping nervous system
activity, including dreaming. Children's dreams often have for
them a compelling and lasting quality, and their affective and
perceptual content may carry over into a whole variety of emerging daytime activities and developing ego functions. Further-

more, the development of specific ego functions that contribute greatly to the formation of psychic structure seems to be intimately associated with dream processes. The mastery, control, and transformation of aggressive impulses and the development of the capacity to distinguish perceptions that arise from internal sources from those of external origin are two such ego functions that seem to be connected with dreaming. As the REM state seems to function in relation to central nervous system development and differentiation, so, concomitantly, dreaming may be intimately associated with developing psychological functioning in childhood.

From the adaptive standpoint, a psychophysiological arousal mechanism that would enable the organism to move quickly from sleep to a state of alert preparedness could be highly protective. Nightmares, as Broughton's recent observations have shown, may be thought of as arousal phenomena, since they occur at a moment of transition between sleeping and waking. Such an arousal mechanism would not, however, be intimately associated, as in Snyder's theory, with the D state, since nightmares may occur in any stage of sleep, the most severe ones tending to occur during non-REM sleep. A neurophysiological arousal mechanism, operating during sleep and manifested in certain instances by nightmares, would be consistent with the psychoanalytic theory of anxiety.

This theory proposes that small quantities of anxiety serve a signal function, alerting the ego to possible danger and calling forth the mobilization of psychological defense mechanisms. If the threat that mobilizes the anxiety is too severe, these ego defenses will prove inadequate, and a traumatic state, accompanied by overwhelming anxiety, will result. This overwhelming of the ego's defensive capabilities by the resulting terror state is likely to occur particularly in situations of ego helplessness such as sleep, when the individual is deprived of external sources of comfort and of reality-testing. This is the situation in nightmares. These dreams, which may themselves become severely traumatic for a small child, reflect in their content and in the child's associated efforts to deal with them the emerging ego defensive capabilities of the individual. It is in these dreams, for example, that we first find the child struggling to tell himself, "It is only a dream."

Snyder writes only of external threat to the organism, whereas psychoanalytic studies have compelled us to take into account the interplay of environmental dangers with internal drives, forces, wishes, and defenses. Nevertheless, it is striking that in nightmares the child almost invariably apprehends only an external danger and perceives this threat so regularly in the form of attacking creatures that we cannot help thinking that perhaps his long-standing membership in the phylogenetic community of mammals has been reactivated in the regression of the nightmare. This externalization of danger in dreams has previously been discussed in relation to the development of the psychological mechanism of projection (see Chapters 4 and 5). The psychological complexities with which nightmares are associated in human beings could thus be seen to rest on a psychophysiological core, a neurophysiological hyperalert mechanism shared by lower animals in which hallucinations of an attacker, "such as the animal might be in danger of encountering at the time of awakening," serve a protective function for the organism. In the course of evolution, this mechanism could have become adapted by human beings to the requirements of psychic conflict wherein anxiety and fear become the resultant of a complicated interplay of external and internal threats and tensions. In human dreams, particularly in nightmares, the links with the phylogenetically older mechanisms are thus maintained. Nightmares are especially common in children, and awakening from them frequently occurs. This is consistent with the small child's greater helplessness, the immaturity of his ego, and his relative incapacity to deal with external and internal sources of threat or danger.

When Nightmares Occur in the Sleep Cycle

Any attempt to establish the time at which nightmares are most likely to occur in the sleep cycle meets familiar difficulties of definition and of the interpretations of findings. Furthermore, to confound the matter further, there is little agreement between laboratories about some stages of sleep.

Gastaut and Broughton, in one study of paroxysmal events in sleep that included five children and two adults, found that "nocturnal anxiety attacks," "nocturnal terrors," and "night-

mares" occurred during slow-wave sleep [35]. In a later report of
six subjects (five adults and one adolescent), the same authors
again found that nightmares occurred during slow-wave (non-
REM) or Stage 4 sleep and were associated with extremely intense awakening reactions [36]. The typical sequence was a
burst of delta-wave activity in the EEG, succeeded in turn by an
ample alpha rhythm, several ocular movements, blinking, very
significant tachycardia, hyperpnea, polypnea, and movement followed by intense global muscular contraction. Complete apnea
up to five seconds was sometimes recorded. The motor and autonomic components reached a peak after five to twenty seconds
and then started to subside, associated at first with a return of
respiration, a guttural cry, and further body movement. In this
report seven "night terror" attacks in seven children occurred in
Stage 4.

An aspect of uncertainty in evaluating these reports is added
by the fact that these writers do not regard nightmares as terrifying dreams, but see the intense anxiety as a secondary response to
certain physiological events such as polypnea, apnea, and palpitation rather than the reverse—a somatic terror reaction that occurs
in response to, or in conjunction with, a terrifying idea. According to these writers, mental content is generally *not* associated
with either the nightmare or night terror attack; when it
does occur, it serves to "rationalize" the terror experienced.
Nevertheless, studies by Hobson et al., for example, have shown
a definite correlation between high and variable respiratory rates
and emotionally laden dream content and also between apnea
and such fearful "respiratory" content in dreams as choking
[37]. Since most clinical workers in the dream field accept the
idea that nightmares are a type of terrifying dream—although
night terrors are sometimes distinguished from nightmares by
the relative absence of reported content—from a clinical standpoint it is not clear what phenomena are here under consideration.

In an earlier paper, Gastaut and his coworkers reported on an
intensive study of a psychoneurotic man with both night and day
terror attacks [38]. They reported that the night attack began
during slow-wave sleep; as it progressed, there occurred a shift to

a wakinglike EEG with rapid eye movements, that is, the attack occurred at a point of transition from slow-wave to rapid or REM sleep. However, Broughton reports that reinterpretation of these data shows that the subject was being aroused from slow-wave sleep into wakefulness [39].

Dement's several statements on this question similarly leave doubt as to when in sleep these events occur [40, 41]. He states that children's night terror attacks occur chiefly in Stage 4 (slow-wave, non-REM) sleep [27, 40]. Similarly, an experimental subject has been observed several times to awaken abruptly out of Stage 4 sleep with a blood-curdling scream [2]. He was found sitting up in a state of fright, but with no memory of the dream or other occurrence. Still more recently, the same author has written, "Nightmares. These of course occur during REM sleep" [42].

Two papers demonstrate an intimate relationship between nightmares and the eruption of delirium tremens or other alcoholic terror states with hallucinations [43, 44]. Alcoholics, for example, frequently suffer from periods of intensely disturbing nightmares for several months prior to the onset of the acute psychosis; not infrequently the episode of hallucinosis or delirium tremens will begin as a continuation of a nightmare from which the patient has awoken abruptly. In several such patients monitored with the electroencephalogram, the nightmares occurred during Stage 1 REM sleep. One of Greenberg's patients woke up from a vivid nightmare following a night in which his sleep record showed 100 percent Stage 1 REM.

In their recent papers on REM and non-REM nightmares, Fisher et al. conclude that the most severe night terrors of adults, as in the traumatic neuroses and the true *pavor nocturnus* of children, arise out of slow-wave sleep. In the adult subjects they studied, 70 percent of the attacks occurred in the first non-REM period, i.e., the first one to one and a half hours of sleep [45, 46]. However, these authors observe that severe anxiety dreams with less intense terror, but which the subject calls a "nightmare," do occur during the REM period of sleep.

There is some evidence that an unusually high percentage of REM sleep time may be associated with nightmares under other

circumstances. In addition to withdrawal from alcohol, the withdrawal of drugs such as amphetamines and barbiturates, for example, which may suppress REM sleep time during chronic use,
is followed by an increased percentage of REM sleep and nightmares [47]. It is not known what relationship exists between the
nightmares and the high percentage of REM sleep time.

Fisher et al. note that most examples of what are called nightmares are severe REM anxiety dreams; only six of the thirty-
seven subjects who responded to their advertisement soliciting
people who had frequent nightmares actually had non-REM
nightmares. In subjects who had both non-REM and REM nightmares in a single night, the thematic content of the different
dreams was often similar or interrelated.

If one were to summarize these somewhat disparate observations and remarks, it would probably be correct to say that terrifying episodes can interrupt both REM and non-REM sleep.
Night terror attacks, which tend to be distinguished *psychologically* from nightmares by the overwhelming character of the
terror and the lesser amount of readily obtainable mental content, are likely to be distinguished from them *physiologically* by
their tendency to occur in non-REM rather than REM sleep.
Conversely, of the terrifying episodes that awaken us in the
night, those that are richer in hallucinatory dream *content* seem
more likely to occur during REM sleep. As Fisher et al. have
noted, it is as if "the REM dream has a mechanism for temper-
ing and modulating anxiety" and for "abolishing or diminishing
the physiological concomitants" [46].

It is interesting to speculate why ordinary dreaming seems to
occur to a greater extent during REM periods, whereas night terrors or severe nightmares with relatively little mental content
seem more likely to erupt during non-REM or slow-wave sleep.
Perhaps the differences reported in the nature of the mental content recovered from REM period and non-REM awakenings are
relevant to this question. Various authors have found that non-
REM awakenings tend to yield reports that are less bizarre, less
affective, more like ordinary thought—or secondary-process
thinking, in psychoanalytic terminology—and more concerned
with the contemporary lives of the subjects. Rechtshaffen et al.

have shown that non-REM mentation often may resemble ordinary background thinking [48, 49]. If, as has been repeatedly suggested, dreams reflect an effort to resolve conflict and to integrate present experiences with earlier memories and conflicts, the availability of active primary process mechanisms during REM periods could be useful toward this end. Conversely, in non-REM sleep periods, directly disturbing daytime experiences or day residues that have revived early traumatic events could not be as extensively modified or transformed by the regressive, symbolic mechanisms of dreaming. The situation in non-REM periods would thus be less flexible, less fluid, less capable of modulating tension levels, and the sleeper would perhaps be more prone to sudden or massive eruptions of repressed fears, hostility, or other disturbing wishes or ideas. Even in the REM nightmare the dreamer seems better able to "deal with" the anxiety and to mute it as compared to the explosive, cataclysmic non-REM nightmare.

Nightmares and the Paralysis Issue

Hawkins has offered us the following graphic description of the onset of a REM period: "As one spends a night in the dream laboratory one cannot help being impressed as one watches the various polygraphic instruments just before a REM period that there are instinctual forces impelling the subject toward action. Everything seems to be becoming activated. Then at the last moment it is as if a switch is thrown, and instead of waking and acting the subject goes into a different phase of sleep and plays out the action on a screen in the mind" [50]. With Dement we too may "wonder what it is that holds the organism to its resting place in the face of this inner turmoil" [51]. The answer seems to be that, with the onset of REM sleep, the pathways of motor discharge become largely blocked as a result of descending inhibitory impulses originating in the brain stem that reduce the activity of the motor neurons [52–54], while centers in the sensory portions of the nervous system show increased activity [12, 55]. These findings provide physiological support for Freud's concept that in dreams we are paralyzed and that impulses whose motor expression is blocked could flow toward the perceptual end of the system [56].

Over thirty-five years ago, in an analysis of an adult patient with attacks of *pavor nocturnus*, Deutsch called attention to the "throttled motor discharge tendency" that occurred during her patient's episodes [57]. During the terrifying dream he was unable to move or scream and continued in this state for a short while after waking, clutching his erect penis. Deutsch interpreted this patient's motor paralysis psychologically in terms of his compulsion to inhibit forbidden sexual impulses associated with childhood masturbation. The subjective experience of paralysis has long been recognized as a frequent feature of nightmares and *pavor nocturnus* [58, 59]. Therefore, it is clear that, in the concurrence of the physiological motor inhibition or paralysis during the D state and the psychological experience of inability to move in nightmares that occur during REM periods, we have come upon an interesting area of possible psychophysiological correlation.

Another dimension of this problem is contributed by the finding that the cataplexy and sleep paralysis components of the narcoleptic sleep attack appear to be states in which the motor inhibitory aspect has become dissociated from other aspects of the REM state [60]. In these conditions, motor paralysis occurs suddenly without loss of consciousness or persists after consciousness has been recovered. The hypnagogic hallucinatory state that accompanies sleep paralysis may represent the perceptual component of the D state occurring in the presence of motor inhibition, but without the other physiological features of sleep, that is, dreaming while partially awake. It is particularly intriguing, therefore, that the hallucinatory fantasies reported by these narcoleptic patients as occurring in their "paralyzed" hypnagogic states were of menacing intruders entering the house and other nightmarish experiences in which attack seemed imminent, but escape was impossible because the limbs would not move [60, 61].

Liddon has recently discussed further this relationship between nightmare, sleep paralysis, and hypnagogic hallucinations [62]. He has stressed the fact that motor paralysis, severe anxiety, a tendency to suffocation, and a frightening hallucinatory experience seem to be regular features of both nightmares and sleep paralysis, and he has suggested that the two phenomena are closely related. In Liddon's view, "obligatory" physiological processes that occur in the REM cycle are employed by the individual in dreams for the expression and solution of mental conflicts. The "obligatory" occurrence of penile erections during the REM cycle [15, 16] could well facilitate the expression of sexual conflict in nightmares or other dreams even though these erections had no direct sexual function. From the standpoint of ego functioning, the correlation of motor paralysis with subjective dread in the dreaming individual or in the person undergoing hypnagogic or hypnopompic hallucinatory experiences is of considerable interest. If one considers the relative helplessness of the sleeping or just awakened individual, under any circumstances the sense of passivity and vulnerability that would be expected to accompany actual physiological paralysis could be most intense.

It has been observed frequently that children between two and five suffer from frightening or other disturbing dreams with particular frequency and that such dreams predominate over other types at this age. It is possible that a contributing factor in the frequency of such dreams during this period is the child's experience during REM sleep of peripheral motor blocking while vivid sensory images first taking clear shape in his consciousness impel him to action. Perhaps the frequent dreams of being chased but unable to move that begin at this time are related to this phenomenon. A number of years ago Aserinsky and Kleitman found that in infants, unlike adults, eye movements may parallel body movements [63]. In infants, non-REM periods have little muscular activity, but during REM periods there are almost continuous muscular contractions, grimaces, facial mimicry of emotions, whimpers, smiles, twitches and shifts of limb position, all suggesting aborted actions [4]. In the period from two to five this activity has already become reduced, that is, the motor outflow blocking mechanism has become increased [10]. In adults, with full development of the spinal inhibitory mechanism, these actions during REM periods have become reduced to occasional twitches [2], although Wolpert found that, even during the dreams of adults, small abortive movements accompanied by increased electromyographic potentials sometimes occurred in the extremity involved in a particular dream's action [64].

We thus have a situation in which small children, who tend ordinarily to rely very heavily on play execution and other action for warding off anxiety and discharging tension, are besieged during sleep with intensified perceptual and hallucinatory experiences and possibly by increased upper motor neuron discharges impelling movement, but are incapable of responding with definitive action. This neurophysiological circumstance, operating in association with the intense psychological conflicts that small children regularly confront, could well contribute to the high frequency of disturbing dreams in this period.

A word of caution is in order at this point lest we begin to be too entranced with our speculations. We are trying essentially to correlate subjective psychological phenomena with certain physiological observations. We do not know, for example, that this subjective sense of being unable to move in nightmares is caused by or even related to peripheral motor blocking during REM sleep; neither do we know that the dread that narcoleptics experience during their hypnagogic hallucinations is related to motor paralysis. Terror can occur in dreams where paralysis is not part of the content; during REM periods in which motor blocking is present, many dreams elicit no conscious anxiety. Furthermore, as previously discussed, the most severe terror states emerge from non-REM sleep periods in which the peripheral blocking mechanism is not in effect, and motility is restored. We are probably on the surest ground if we think in terms of specific psychological conflicts and the physiological mechanisms discussed above working together, or operating simultaneously, in the production of certain though not all terrifying dream states.

Nightmares and Psychoses: What Physiological Evidence Is There of a Relationship?

Clinical relationships between nightmares or night terrors and certain acute psychotic states have long been observed; in Chapter 5 we have presented clinical evidence pointing to various similarities and differences between the two sets of phenomena. It would be satisfying, therefore, if physiological studies could also adduce evidence demonstrating psychophysiological correlations and similarities. Indeed, Snyder, an outstanding worker in the field of dream physiology, has stated, "the phenomenon of night terrors in children would seem to represent an intermediate condition between dreaming during sleep and psychotic hallucination while awake" [65]. However, with the exception of the acute alcoholic psychosis, no convincing physiological evidence has so far been presented to show that an etiological relationship between nightmares or other dreams and psychosis exists or that psychoses occur as a result of physiological disturbances of the sleep-dream cycle [5].

Although the mechanism is poorly understood, Gross et al. and Greenberg and Pearlman have presented evidence that acute alcoholic psychoses, such as delirium tremens and acute alcoholic hallucinosis, not only resemble terrifying dreams psychologically, but in some if not all instances are a continuation into the waking state of nightmares that have begun during REM sleep [43, 44]. In each of four patients studied by Gross et al., direct observations and EEG monitoring confirmed the patients' reports that their terrifying dreams continued into waking hallucinations. Characteristically, a period of several weeks or months of disturbed sleep and insomnia with frequent nightmares preceded the onset of the acute psychosis. Certain patients reported a transitional phase in which they were uncertain as to "whether he is asleep and having a nightmare or awake and hallucinating" [66]. The full-blown hallucinatory episode in each instance studied began at night and either continued from a specific nightmare or evolved out of a series of such dreams. Similarly, Greenberg and Pearlman have shown an intimate association between high percentages of REM sleep, nightmares, and the onset of delirium tremens.

In functional psychoses or those in which no organic causation has been demonstrated, clear physiological relationships between nightmares or other dreams and the pathological disorder have been more difficult to demonstrate. Numerous sleep studies [67–74] have shown that acute schizophrenic patients tend to have a greater variability in the phases of the sleep cycle. They may, for example, have a shorter REM latency, that is, a decrease in the time between the onset of sleep and the start of the first REM period [73]. This finding suggests a "need for REM" in acute schizophrenic patients. Such a need could arise on the basis of partial REM deprivation occurring as the result of frequent awakenings caused by intense anxiety or other stresses that characterize the disorder. The available evidence, though not consistent or conclusive, suggests that schizophrenic patients are particularly sensitive to REM deprivation [75] and that such deprivation will intensify the psychotic process or aggravate schizophrenic disorganization [76]. Hartmann has provided a useful review of the work that attempts to relate the phases of the sleep-dream cycle and mental illness [5].

Greenberg has recently observed an inverse relationship between nightmares and depressive and paranoid symptoms in patients on a psychiatric ward [77]. In a study of five insomniac patients, he found that the sleep interruption occurred in order to avoid intolerable nightmares and contributed to the intensification of the psychotic symptomatology during the daytime. Treatment of the insomnia with tranquilizers resulted in recurrence of nightmares and longer periods of dreaming, with reduction of psychotic symptoms. A recent review of the effect of tranquilizers upon dreams and dreaming in schizophrenic patients by Ornstein et al. has failed to demonstrate any consistent significant alteration in the D state as a result of administration of these drugs, despite the fact that these agents effectively reduce schizophrenic symptomatology [78].

Conclusions

Studies of the physiology of sleep and dreaming may paradoxically lead us back to the psychology of dreams. The efforts to deprive subjects of dreaming, for example, by repeated interruptions of REM sleep have failed to produce consistent physiological changes other than a more rapid onset of REM sleep and a greater tendency to dream when the experiment is halted. Similarly, no physiological explanation has so far become available to account for the overwhelming anxiety that occurs in nightmares. Gastaut and Broughton attribute the nightmare to the "still emerging consciousness of the biological components of an intense awakening reaction" [79], but acknowledge that this fails to explain why only subjects with nightmares note the awakening reaction or suffer from it. They suggest the possibility of "some sort of unconscious tension" or the "sudden expression of that marginal mental life already envisaged as being continuous during sleep" and bring us by the road of physiology once more to the gates of the unconscious and to the complexities of mental conflict. Physiological research in relation to nightmares has demonstrated, not surprisingly, that they are linked with fundamental biological processes and has provided some information regarding the correlations between the psychological experience in these frightening dreams and the physiological states and processes that accompany them. Such research has not, however, contributed greatly to an understanding of the factors that determine the occurrence of a nightmare in any given instance or the significance and meaning that particular terrifying dreams of this nature possess for the dreamer.

Fisher has suggested that a greater pressure of drives toward discharge might result in a qualitative change in the dream, such as the development of nightmares [1]. This, however, would be only one of a number of factors. The occurrence of nightmares, or dreams in which anxiety becomes overwhelming, can probably be understood only by careful attention to a multiplicity of factors that include the physiological condition of the person; the state of the ego; the interplay of environmental threats that are specifically meaningful to the individual with drives arising from within; the psychological links between these environmental elements and past threats, memories, and conflicts; and finally the nature and availability of supporting figures in the sleeper's environment. A conflict theory seems indispensable to the understanding of nightmares; without the inclusion of all of the above dimensions of conflict, the nightmare's shock will seem, not only unexpected, but unintelligible.

It has been argued that a nightmare is a dream that has failed; if we require of dreaming that it ensure tranquil sleep, this may be so. This would be a static approach, however, failing to take into account the task set before the mind of the sleeping individual. A great variety of integrative efforts is often apparent in severe anxiety dreams; from the dreamer's viewpoint, his awakening with a fearful scream may halt his sleep while it appears to protect him from the far greater misfortune that he apprehends in the nightmare. It is possible that in the nightmare the dream does not serve to preserve sleep, but is linked with a phylogenetically older mechanism that functions to preserve the organism itself. From this point of view, the nightmare hardly appears to be a failure. The sleeper's failure would lie in overestimating the actual danger, in mistakenly equating a hallucinated danger with an actual threat in the outside world. Sleep would have been sacrificed in an effort to save the sleeping animal.

References

1. Fisher, C. Psychoanalytic implications of recent research on sleep and dreaming. *J. Amer. Psychoanal. Ass.* 13:197–303, 1965.
2. Dement, W. An Essay on Dreams. In Newcomb, T. (Ed.), *New Directions in Psychology*. New York: Holt, Rinehart & Winston, 1965. Vol. II, pp. 135–257.
3. Snyder, F. The Organismic State Associated with Dreaming. In Greenfield, N. S., and Lewis, W. C. (Eds.), *Psychoanalysis and Current Biological Thought*. University of Wisconsin Press, 1965. Pp. 275–315.
4. Roffwarg, H. P., Muzio, J. N., and Dement, W. C. Ontogenetic development of the human sleep-dream cycle. *Science* 152:604–619, 1966.
5. Hartmann, E. *The Biology of Dreaming*. Springfield, Ill.: Thomas, 1967.
6. Luce, G., and Segal, J. *Sleep*. New York: Coward-McCann, 1966.
7. Aserinsky, E., and Kleitman, N. Regularly occurring periods of eye motility and concomitant phenomena during sleep. *Science* 118:273–274, 1953.
8. Dement, W., and Kleitman, N. Cyclic variations in EEG during sleep and their relation to eye movements, body motility and dreaming. *Electroenceph. Clin. Neurophysiol.* 9:673–690, 1957.
9. Parmelee, A., Akiyama, Y., Monod, N., and Flescher, J. EEG patterns in sleep of full term and premature newborn infants. *Electroenceph. Clin. Neurophysiol.* 17:455–456, 1964.
10. Roffwarg, H. P., Dement, W. C., and Fisher, C. Preliminary Observations of the Sleep-dream Pattern in Neonates, Infants, Children,

and Adults. In Harms, E. (Ed.), *Problems of Sleep and Dreams in Children.* New York: Pergamon, 1964. Pp. 60–72.

11. Hartmann, E.   The D-state: A review and discussion of studies on the physiologic state concomitant with dreaming. *New Eng. J. Med.* 273:30–35; 87–92, 1965.

12. Evarts, E. V.   Activity of neurons in the visual cortex of the cat during sleep with low voltage fast EEG activity. *J. Neurophysiol.* 25:812–816, 1962.

13. Evarts, E. V.   Activity of Individual Cerebral Neurons During Sleep and Arousal. In Kety, S., Evarts, E. V., and Williams, H. W. (Eds.), *Sleep and Altered States of Consciousness.* Baltimore: Williams & Wilkins, 1967.

14. Kanzow, E., Krause, D., and Kuehnel, H.   Die vasomotorik der hirnrinde in den phasen desynchronisierter EEG—activitat im natürlichen Schlaf der Kätze. *Pflueger Arch. Ges. Physiol.* 274:593–607, 1962.

15. Fisher, C.   Dreaming and Sexuality. In Loewenstein, R. M., Newman, L. M., Schur, M., and Solnit, A. (Eds.), *Psychoanalysis: A General Psychology.* New York: International Universities Press, 1966. Pp. 537–569.

16. Fisher, C., Gorss, J., and Zuch, J.   Cycle of penile erection synchronous with dreaming (REM) sleep. *Arch. Gen. Psychiat.* (Chicago) 12:29 45, 1965.

17. Snyder, F.   Autonomic Nervous System Manifestations During Sleep and Dreaming. In Kety, S., Evarts, E. V., and Williams, H. L. (Eds.), *Sleep and Altered States of Consciousness.* Baltimore: Williams & Wilkins, 1967. Pp. 469–487.

18. Dement, W., and Fisher, C.   Experimental interference with the sleep cycle. *Canad. Psychiat. Ass. J.* 8:400–405, 1963.

19. Sampson, H.   Psychological effects of deprivation of dreaming sleep. *J. Nerv. Ment. Dis.* 143:305–317, 1966.

20. Trosman, H.   Dream research and the psychoanalytic theory of dreams. *Arch. Gen. Psychiat.* (Chicago) 9:9–18, 1963.

21. Ullman, M.   The adaptive significance of the dream. *J. Nerv. Ment. Dis.* 129:144–149, 1959.

22. Ullman, M.   Dreaming, altered states of consciousness and the problem of vigilance. *J. Nerv. Ment. Dis.* 133:529–535, 1961.

23. Breger, L.   Function of dreams. *J. Abnorm. Psychol.* Monograph 72:5, No. 641, 1967. Pp. 1–28.

24. Meissner, W. W.   Dreaming as process. *Int. J. Psychoanal.* 49:63–79, 1968.

25. Ibid. P. 77.

26. Jouvet, M.   Telencephalic and Rhombencephalic Sleep in the Cat. In Wolstenholme, G. E. W., and O'Connor, M. (Eds.), *The Nature of Sleep.* Boston: Little, Brown, 1961. Pp. 188–208.

27. Dement, W.   Experimental Dream Studies. In Masserman, J. (Ed.), *Science and Psychoanalysis.* New York: Grune & Stratton, 1964. Vol. VII, pp. 129–162.

28. Snyder, F.   Toward an evolutionary theory of dreaming. *Amer. J. Psychiat.* 123:121–142, 1966.
29. Broughton, R.   Sleep disorders: Disorders of arousal? *Science* 159: 1070–1078, 1968.
30. Snyder, F.   Toward an evolutionary theory of dreaming. *Amer. J. Psychiat.* 123:134, 1966.
31. Sackett, G. P.   Monkeys reared in isolation with pictures as visual input: Evidence for an innate releasing mechanism. *Science* 154: 1468–1473, 1966.
32. Chance, M. R. A.   An Interpretation of Some Agonistic Postures: The Role of "Cut-off" Acts and Postures. *Zoological Society of London Symposia* 8:71–89, 1962.
33. Parmelee, A. H., Schultz, M. A., Akiyama, Y., Wenner, W. H., and Stern, E.   A fundamental periodicity in sleep in infants. Los Angeles: Assn. for the Psychophysiological Study of Sleep, 1967.
34. Parmelee, A. H., Akiyama, Y., Wenner, W. H., Schultz, M. A., and Stern, E.   Sleep cycle characteristics in infants. Los Angeles: Assn. for the Psychophysiological Study of Sleep, 1967.
35. Gastaut, H., and Broughton, R.   Paroxysmal psychological events and certain phases of sleep. *Percept. Motor Skills* 17:362, 1963.
36. Gastaut, H., and Broughton, R.   A Clinical and Polygraphic Study of Episodic Phenomena During Sleep. In Wortis, J. (Ed.), *Recent Advances in Biological Psychiatry.* New York: Plenum, 1965. Vol. VII, pp. 197–223.
37. Hobson, J. A., Goldfrank, F., and Snyder, F.   Respiration and mental activity in sleep. *J. Psychiat. Res.* 3:79–90, 1965.
38. Gastaut, H., Dongier, M., Batini, C., and Rhodes, J.   Étude électro-clinique des terreurs nocturnes et diurnes concomitantes d'un rêve ou d'une idée obsedante chez un névrose. *Rev. Neurol.* 107:277–279, 1962.
39. Broughton, R.   Personal communication, Oct. 18, 1967.
40. Dement, W.   The Psychophysiology of Sleep and Dreams. In Arieti, S. (Ed.), *American Handbook of Psychiatry.* New York: Basic Books, 1966. Vol. III, pp. 290–332.
41. Dement, W.   Sleep and Dreams. In Friedman, A., and Kaplan, H. (Eds.), *Comprehensive Textbook of Psychiatry.* Baltimore: Williams & Wilkins, 1967.
42. Ibid. P. 87.
43. Greenberg, R., and Pearlman, C.   Delirium tremens and dreaming. *Amer. J. Psychiat.* 124:133–142, 1967.
44. Gross, M., Goodenough, D., Tobin, M., Halpert, E., Lepore, D., Perlstein, A., Sirota, M., Dibianco, J., Fuller, R., and Kishner, I. Sleep disturbances and hallucinations in the acute alcoholic psychoses. *J. Nerv. Ment. Dis.* 142:493–512, 1966.
45. Fisher, C., Byrne, J., and Edwards, A.   REM and NREM Nightmares and Their Interrelationship. Lecture delivered to the Department of Psychiatry, Mt. Sinai Hospital, New York, Apr. 10, 1968.
46. Fisher, C., Byrne, J., Edwards, A., and Kahn, E.   A Psychophysiological Study of Nightmares. Freud anniversary lecture, April 8, 1969.

47. Kales, A. Drug dependency: Investigations of stimulants and depressants. *Ann. Intern. Med.* 70:591–614, 1969.
48. Rechtschaffen, A., Vogel, G., and Shaikun, G. Interrelatedness of mental activity during sleep. *Arch. Gen. Psychiat.* (Chicago) 9:536–547, 1963.
49. Foulkes, W. D. Dream reports from different states of sleep. *J. Abnorm. Soc. Psychol.* 65:14–25, 1962.
50. Hawkins, D. R. A review of psychoanalytic dream theory in the light of recent psychophysiological studies of sleep and dreaming. *Brit. J. Med. Psychol.* 39:85–104, 1966.
51. Dement, W. An Essay on Dreams. In Newcomb, T. (Ed.), *New Directions in Psychology*. New York: Holt, Rinehart & Winston, 1965. Vol. II, p. 165.
52. Giaquinto, S., Pompeiano, O., and Somogyi, J. Descending inhibitory influences on spinal reflexes during natural sleep. *Arch. Ital. Biol.* 102:282–307, 1964.
53. Hodes, R., and Dement, W. Depression of electrically induced reflexes ("H-reflexes") in man during low voltage EEG "sleep." *Electroenceph. Clin. Neurophysiol.* 17:617–629, 1964.
54. Pompeiano, O. The Neurophysiological Mechanisms of the Postural and Motor Events During Desynchronized Sleep. In Kety, S., Evarts, E. V., and Williams, H. W. (Eds.), *Sleep and Altered States of Consciousness*. Baltimore: Williams & Wilkins, 1967. Pp. 351–423.
55. Bizzi, E. Discharge patterns of lateral geniculate neurons during paradoxical sleep. Washington, D.C.: Assn. for the Psychophysiological Study of Sleep, 1965.
56. Freud, S. The Interpretation of Dreams (1900). In *The Standard Edition of the Complete Psychological Works of Sigmund Freud*, tr. and ed. by J. Strachey with others. London: Hogarth and the Institute of Psycho-Analysis, 1953. Vol. V, pp. 533–549.
57. Deutsch, H. Hysterical Conversion Symptoms: *Pavor Nocturnus*, Bedwetting, Impotence. In *Neuroses and Character Types*. New York: International Universities Press, 1965. Chap. 3, pp. 29–56.
58. Macnish, R. *The Philosophy of Sleep*. New York: Appleton, 1834.
59. Jones, E. *On the Nightmare*. London: Hogarth, 1931.
60. Dement, W., Rechtschaffen, A., and Gulevich, G. The nature of the narcoleptic sleep attack. *Neurology* 16:18–33, 1966.
61. Rechtschaffen, A., and Dement, W. Studies on the Relation of Narcolepsy, Cataplexy and Sleep with Low Voltage Random EEG Activity. In Kety, S., Evarts, E. V., and Williams, H. W. (Eds.), *Sleep and Altered States of Consciousness*. Baltimore: Williams & Wilkins, 1967. Pp. 488–505.
62. Liddon, S. C. Sleep paralysis and hypnagogic hallucinations: Their relationship to the nightmare. *Arch. Gen. Psychiat.* (Chicago) 17:88–96, 1967.
63. Aserinsky, E., and Kleitman, N. A motility cycle in sleeping infants as manifested by ocular and gross bodily activity. *J. Appl. Physiol.* 8:11–18, 1955.
64. Wolpert, E. Studies in psychophysiology of dreams: An electromyo-

graphic study of dreaming. *Arch. Gen. Psychiat.* (Chicago) 2:231–241, 1960.

65. Snyder, F.   The new biology of dreaming. *Arch. Gen. Psychiat.* (Chicago) 8:381–391, 1963.

66. Gross, M., Goodenough, D., Tobin, M., Halpert, E., Lepore, D., Perlstein, A., Sirota, M., Dibianco, J., Fuller, R., and Kishner, I. Sleep disturbances and hallucinations in the acute alcoholic psychoses. *J. Nerv. Ment. Dis.* 142:494, 1966.

67. Fisher, C., and Dement, W.   Dreaming and psychosis: Observations on the dream-sleep cycle during the course of an acute paranoic psychosis. *Bull. Phila. Ass. Psychoanal.* 11:130–132, 1961.

68. Koresko, R. L., Snyder, F., and Feinberg, I.   "Dream time" in hallucinating and nonhallucinating schizophrenic patients. *Nature* 199: 1118–1119, 1963.

69. Feinberg, I., Koresko, R. L., Gottlieb, F., and Wender, P. H.   Sleep electroencephalographic and eye-movement patterns in schizophrenic patients. *Compr. Psychiat.* 5:44–53, 1964.

70. Feinberg, I., Koresko, R. L., and Gottlieb, F.   Further observations on electrophysiological sleep pattern in schizophrenia. *Compr. Psychiat.* 6:21–24, 1965.

71. Gulevich, G. D., Dement, W. C., and Zarcone, V. P.   All-night sleep recordings of chronic schizophrenics in remission. *Compr. Psychiat.* 8:141–149, 1967.

72. Vogel, G., and Traub, A.   REM deprivation of schizophrenics. Los Angeles: Assn. for the Psychophysiological Study of Sleep, 1967.

73. Stern, M., Fram, D., Wyatt, R., and Grinspoon, L.   The sleep-schizophrenia paradigm: I. All-night sleep studies of acute schizophrenics. Denver: Assn. for the Psychophysiological Study of Sleep, 1968.

74. Snyder, F.   Sleep Disturbance in Relation to Acute Psychosis. Paper presented at the Symposium on Physiology and Pathology of Sleep, U.C.L.A., May 22–23, 1968.

75. Zarcone, V. P., Gulevich, G. D., Pivik, T., and Dement, W. C. Partial REM phase deprivation and schizophrenia. *Arch. Gen. Psychiat.* (Chicago) 18:194–202, 1968.

76. Koranyi, E., and Lehmann, H.   Experimental sleep deprivation in schizophrenic patients. *Arch. Gen. Psychiat.* (Chicago) 2:534–544, 1960.

77. Greenberg, R.   Dream interruption insomnia. *J. Nerv. Ment. Dis.* 144:18–21, 1967.

78. Ornstein, P., Whitman, R., Kramer, M., and Baldridge, B. J.   Drugs and Dreams. IV. Tranquilizers and Their Effects Upon Dreams and Dreaming in Schizophrenic Patients. Paper presented before the Carl Neuberg Society for International Scientific Relations at the Symposium on Drugs and Dreams, May 1967.

79. Gastaut, H., and Broughton, R.   A Clinical and Polygraphic Study of Episodic Phenomena During Sleep. In Wortis, J. (Ed.), *Recent Advances in Biological Psychiatry*. New York: Plenum, 1965. Vol. VII, p. 219.

7   Toward a Theory of Nightmares

SEVERE ANXIETY DREAMS or nightmares contain in themselves, or are related to, so many fundamentally important clinical phenomena that they present a unique challenge and opportunity for the kind of investigation that can lead to the development of psychoanalytic and other psychological theories. The psychology and physiology of dreaming, the problem of anxiety, the adaptation to external threat or trauma, the relation of nightmare to psychosis, the development of early ego functions and mental structures, the psychic handling of aggression, the relationship between erotism and destruction, and the various forms of regression with which such dreams are associated—all are among the major topics that come under consideration when one attempts to achieve a comprehensive view of the nightmare.

Our review and analysis of nightmares up to this point has placed certain demands as well as restrictions upon any theory that might be proposed. Such a theory must, for example, take into account the fact that nightmares—or at least awakening from an apparently fearful hallucinatory experience—can occur in children of about one year of age in whom the development of psychic structure has advanced very little. Also, it must explain how such severely disturbing dreams can take place, not only in emotionally disturbed individuals, but also in persons who otherwise appear to function well or give little or no evidence of being anxious, troubled, or especially "neurotic" during waking life. The theory must be consistent with the widespread occurrence of nightmares and therefore be applicable to persons of other cultures, including primitive societies, who seem to have no immunity from such disturbing dreams. We need also to consider the fact that, unlike other dreams or mental phenomena that occur during sleep, the most severe nightmares seem to take place in non-REM periods rather than during REM periods, of which dreaming is regarded as more characteristic. Finally, our explanations must account for the fundamental clinical characteristics shared by nightmares at any age: the feelings of helplessness and powerlessness, the perception of severe danger, the overwhelming or life-and-death quality of anxiety and, finally, the threat or actual presence in the dream of violence and destructiveness.

The Situation of the Dreamer

Before trying to approach the particular experience of the nightmare further, it may be useful to look once again at the situation of the dreamer. To begin with, he is usually alone and in the dark. If anyone doubts that such a situation can cause concern for small children, he has only to recall the vigorous efforts with which they resist the inevitable nighttime separation, complain about being left alone in their rooms, seek out the parents repeatedly before finally allowing themselves to be retired for the night, and fortify themselves for the hours ahead through presleep rituals and the gathering of bedtime companions, both real and imaginary. Many children have nightmares when they sleep alone; these usually cease when they have in the same room a sibling or any other person—it often matters little who it is. These fears of being separated and alone at night persist in varying degrees in persons of all ages. In addition, many children and adults struggle against the act of falling asleep, as if this helpless surrender were itself dangerous, apart from the anxieties that may be encountered during sleep. The danger associated with relinquishing reality and withdrawing from the outside world, especially from love objects, also contributes to this fear of surrendering to sleep. Total darkness makes the absence of the parents more complete, deprives the child of the familiarity of his surroundings and of external cues that could aid in reality judgment, and makes more difficult the realistic assessment of anxiety-provoking fantasies before the onset of sleep. These frightening fantasies may then contribute to the content of subsequent nightmares. For example, frightening illusions, that is, distorted perception of objects in the environment, are commonplace for children going to sleep in the dark; the biting monster the child creates from a familiar chair may also find its way into a nightmare. Furthermore, when a child—or an occasional adult, as well—awakens from a severe anxiety dream, the restoration of reality is usually more difficult than is the case in most dreams; conversely, the persecutory images of the dream persist much longer, especially in total darkness. Thus, the helplessness that accompanies separation and the sense of isolation and anxiety that accompany surrender to sleep may all contribute to the intensity of such feelings as occur in the nightmares themselves.

The anxiety associated with this surrender may relate also to the regression with which sleep is associated, especially the revival of infantile dependent longings and fears that replicate in many ways the conflicts that grow out of the early mother-infant relationship. The anxieties evoked by the regressive cloistral aspect of the sleep situation may also contribute to the revival in the dreams of early conflicts related to infantile dependent desires and fears.

In Chapter 2 we saw how many of the features that characterize dreaming and distinguish dreams from ordinary thinking may be considered in relation to the concept of regression. Topographical regression refers to the revival in dreaming of forms of thought that rely upon concrete imagery and the representation of ideas and wishes in visual and other concrete sensory modes. In addition, the traces of early thoughts and memories are revived. In dreams there also occurs a libidinal regression, accompanied by a return, not only to wishes for earlier forms of sensual gratification, but to the dependent and more helpless qualities of the small child's relationships with other persons, especially the parents. In these relationships he feels, and in dreams may appear, very small in relation to larger, more powerful creatures. The narcissistic regression of dreams also contributes to the abandonment of persons in the outside world as the dreamer becomes totally invested in his own feelings and mental productions.

Although certain ego functions continue to be active during sleep—as demonstrated, for example, in the capacity of some persons to monitor the time for their awakening or of sleeping mothers to discriminate faint sounds of the nursery from louder but more neutral noises—ego functioning also succumbs to the regression that accompanies sleep and dreaming. Primitive, childlike forms of thinking predominate, and dreams reflect the symbolization, distortion, displacement, and projection mechanisms that characterize the thinking of early childhood. Although many ego functions remain intact within dreams, the individual's capacity to judge the dream phenomena by the measures that he applies to reality during the waking hours suffers most. It is as though one portion of the ego has split off and can carry on in the dream as if it were dealing with life as usual, while another portion—the part that is ordinarily busy in the daytime deciding what is possible and what is real, discriminating what is a thought from what is happening in the outside world, and distinguishing a mere wish from an accomplished deed—is largely unavailable. Dostoevsky, in a passage in *The Idiot*, revealed his understanding of this split in the ego during dreaming, as well as the active part played by unconscious wishes and desires not revealed in the dream's manifest content [1]:

You remember first of all that your reason did not desert you throughout the dream; you remember even that you acted very cunningly and logically through all that long, long time, while you were surrounded by murderers who deceived you, hid their intentions, behaved amicably to you while they had a weapon in readiness, and were only waiting for some signal; you remember how cleverly you deceived them at last, hiding from them; then you guessed that they'd seen through your deception and were only pretending not to know where you were hidden; but you were sly then and deceived them again; all this you remember clearly. But how was it that you could at the same time reconcile your reason to the obvious absurdities and impossibilities with which your dream was overflowing? One of your murderers turned into a woman before your eyes, and the woman into a little, sly, loathsome dwarf—and you accepted it all at once as an accomplished fact, almost without the slightest surprise, at the very time when, on another side, your reason is at its highest tension and showed extraordinary power, cunning, sagacity and logic? And why, too, on waking up and fully returning to reality, do you feel almost every time, and sometimes with extraordinary intensity, that you have left something unexplained behind with the dream? You laugh at the absurdities of your dream, and at the same time you feel that interwoven with those absurdities some thought lies hidden, and a thought that is real, something belonging to your actual life, something that exists and has always existed in your heart.

In summary, our sleeping nightmare victim is likely to be alone in darkness, separated from those he loves and upon whom he may still be dependent; he may be in a regressive state and withdrawn from reality. We have only set the stage and described the situation of any dreamer. We have set forth some elements in his vulnerability to nightmares, but have said nothing that distinguishes the nightmare from an ordinary dream or the nightmare victim from any person asleep. We shall now turn to these considerations.

Nightmares and the Problem of Anxiety

I have defined the nightmare as a type of severe anxiety dream in which the level of anxiety reaches overwhelming proportions. The principal problem this definition raises is one that Freud posed in 1925. "Again," Freud wrote, "it is not to be expected that the explanation of anxiety dreams will be found in the theory of dreams. Anxiety is a problem rather of neurosis, and all that remains to be discussed is how it comes about that anxiety can arise under dream conditions" [2]. I would amend this statement of the problem and suggest that the explanation will not be found *solely* in the theory of dreams or in the theory of neurosis or anxiety. Rather, the problem belongs both to the theory of dreams and the theory of anxiety and, above all, involves the relationship between the two.

A number of authors have pointed out that the ego must undergo some development before true anxiety can develop in infancy [3–6]. Above all, there must be sufficient cognitive development to give structure to perceptions, to represent them internally, and to assign meaning to them. According to Spitz, the earliest anxiety occurs in the second half of the first year as stranger anxiety, the shock the infant experiences upon seeing some unfamiliar face, not his mother's. Benjamin has distinguished a second form, separation anxiety, from stranger anxiety, documenting its onset in the sixteen-to-eighteen-month period. According to Benjamin, separation fear, in contrast to stranger anxiety, requires a more complete mental representation of the mother and thus demands an appreciation of the significance and danger that attend her departure or absence. Fears occurring after onset of sleep are among the earliest clear manifestations of anxiety that parents note in their infants; some of the earliest nightmares that have been described occurred either in relation to confrontation with strangers, separation situations, or the child's fear of some destructive or "devouring" agency or a machine such as a vacuum cleaner [7, 8].

Two observations in Freud's later theory of anxiety are particularly relevant for the study of severe anxiety in dreams. First, Freud noted that each phase in the child's development had its characteristic danger situation and associated form of anxiety. Thus, according to Freud, the earliest danger, arising when the child is psychologically and biologically most immature, is fear of loss of the person who cares for him and, later, loss of that person's love. In later phases of development, fear of the loss of a valued part of the body—castration anxiety—takes precedence, and this is followed by fear of disapproval by an internal self-judging agency or superego. Anna Freud has added to this list fear of the intensity of one's instincts, the fear of being overwhelmed by uncontrollable forces from within [9], and Waelder has stressed the danger some individuals experience of masochistic surrender [10]. Each of the danger situations, Freud noted, could exist side by side, and the ego could react at a later period with anxiety that was originally appropriate to an earlier one. As we have seen, adulthood also has its characteristic danger situations, such as the possibility of failure or the various risks and dangers associated with commitment to the adult responsibilities of marriage and parenthood. The analysis of these adult fear situations often shows that they are intimately linked with unresolved childhood anxieties.

The second observation of Freud, particularly important for our understanding of nightmares, is that small amounts of anxiety under the control of the ego may act as a signal to prevent the development of a traumatic situation, in which there occurs anxiety of overwhelming proportions. In a recent attempt to amplify Freud's theory, Rangell has viewed anxiety of varying intensities as a kind of sampling of a traumatic state that has the function of preventing the occurrence of a more severe traumatic situation [11]. This signal or sample anxiety gives the ego the opportunity to avoid the danger situation or to bring into play judgment, reality-testing, and various psychological defenses that may help to prevent anxiety of overwhelming intensity from arising.

How can these two observations of Freud be applied to our understanding of the intense anxiety that occurs in nightmares? In our case examples, we have seen repeatedly that, in each phase of development, nightmares occur in association with the external danger situations that are characteristic of the period. The two-year-old Sam, for example (see Chapter 2), who faces the danger of loss of love because of his destructive impulses, has nightmares in which a lion threatens to bite him. Rachel at age four (Chapter 2) feared grabby monsters that might take her away or cause genital injury. Carol at nine (Chapter 4) was struggling with powerful feelings of love and hatred toward both her mother and father that caused her intense feelings of guilt. Her guilt precipitated a complex nightmare in which she engaged in a terror-filled struggle to ward off a blood bath brought about by monstrous figures that would destroy her and her sister. The young father (Chapter 2) who struggles with his ambivalent feelings toward his baby son has a nightmare about a threat to the infant and violent feelings toward those who would neglect it. Many other examples could be cited.

In each instance in which it has been possible to obtain detailed information regarding the dream and its associated material, we have seen that in the nightmare the anxiety related not only to the current danger situation that confronted the dreamer during his waking hours; in the regressive sleep-dream situation, the current danger became linked with earlier dangers, the current anxiety with earlier anxieties. Thus, in the nightmare of five-year-old Timmy, precipitated by his father's assignment to an overseas war zone, we find both fear of retaliation for his hostile wishes toward his father and fear, stemming from an earlier period of childhood, of being abandoned by his mother and separated from her with no one to take care of him. Similarly, the seduction nightmare of the thirty-year-old woman described in Chapter 2 was precipitated by the revival in analytic treatment of her conflicts over forbidden childhood sexual curiosity. The analysis of the determinants of the overwhelming anxiety of the nightmare revealed that it was linked with many childhood fears extending back to the early danger of loss of her mother's love at the time of her brother's birth when she was twenty months old. Thus, the intensity of anxiety in nightmares may occur in part as a result of the regressive linking or coalescence of current anxieties with those of earlier periods, especially in the second year of life when abandonment and loss of love are such critical dangers for the child. This regressive revival of early fears and wishes in nightmares may account for the frequency with which cannibalistic experiences of being bitten or devoured occur, not only in the nightmares of early childhood, but in those of older children and adults, as well.

Ego regression may also contribute to the intensity of anxiety in nightmares and especially to the quality of utter helplessness that is usually experienced in these dreams. It appears as if, in the nightmare, the ego state that once accompanied childhood fears is revived along with the fears themselves. Thus, even the adult nightmare victim confronts his nemesis, not as the competent person he may actually have become, but as the small and helpless child surrounded by a world of large people and dangerous forces that he perceives in much the same way as he did in the earlier period when they confronted him daily with his powerlessness. This factor of ego regression and helplessness seems also to contribute to a certain uniformity among nightmares in the various developmental phases.

The second factor that contributes to the occurrence of such overwhelming anxiety in dreams is the failure of the signal function to prevent the development of more intense anxiety. The ego in the dream situation is unable, if we may use Rangell's terminology, to "sample" a traumatic situation in the dream or to regulate effectively the amount of anxiety that is experienced. One factor that accounts for this inability has already been discussed, namely, the power of the regressive pull in the dream situation that leads to ego regression and the revival of earlier anxieties. In addition, however, as discussed earlier in this chapter, there are unavailable to the dreamer certain ego functions that ordinarily serve to limit the intensity of anxiety during the waking hours. Ego defenses such as repression and intellectualization do not function effectively in dreams; above all, the capacity to judge danger situations and avoid them, to evaluate reality, and to distinguish frightening thoughts from genuinely threatening situations, is impaired. Furthermore, during the dream other persons are unavailable to provide reassurance or love or even to aid in reality-testing, a service among human beings whose importance even in everyday waking life is often underestimated. Thus, in the dream all threatening objects or perceptions are regarded as if they were external or real, as if the danger were actual. The struggle to remedy this troublesome situation is demonstrated by the dreamer's effort to assure himself that what he is undergoing is "nothing but a dream." The ego regression within the nightmare compounds an already difficult situation for the dreamer, who is in any event little able to judge the status in reality of his dream images. Once massive anxiety has developed, the nightmare victim has only one available option: to wake up. In so doing, he reestablishes a sense of reality and judgment and regains his perspective. Adults can usually accomplish this task by using only their own ego functions. Small children, however, require reunion with the parental love object in order to receive help with these difficult tasks. As Kanzer has written, "nightmares pass directly into communication when the child cries for his mother, or reflect the paralyzing fear of being unable to establish such communications" [12]. If the individual is unable, soon after awakening, to reverse this appraisal of the dream dangers as actual, we are dealing not with a nightmare, but with a psychosis. The nightmare, as the patient described in Chapter 5 stated, would then have become "a continuing fact in time."

In addition to their occurrence in response to obvious danger situations, nightmares seem also to take place in association with developmental shifts or advances in childhood or critical periods in adult life. Learning to walk and explore, toilet training, the heightening of phallic interests, puberty, marriage, parenthood, and increased career responsibilities are a few such milestones that seem frequently to be associated with nightmares. One possible explanation has already been mentioned: that the assertiveness that produces the advance or shift is associated with destructive wishes or intentions. Another factor may be operating as well. Throughout this book we have stressed the fundamental importance in nightmares of feelings of helplessness, of the sense of vulnerability. The earliest helplessness, an attitude that seems to underlie the anxiety in nightmares at all ages, resembles that of the very small child who feels powerless to control the coming and going of the mothering person upon whom he is totally dependent. This feeling of powerlessness and the anxiety with which it is accompanied may recur each time a major new task is attempted, until skills that will lead to mastery and a reduction of anxiety are attained. Nightmares are often a sensitive indicator of the presence of anxiety and may reflect this feeling of helplessness that occurs when major new tasks are undertaken before the motor skills, cognitive capacities, defenses, or other ego functions necessary for such mastery have developed. The content of the dreams may be of the usual "raw-head-and-bloody-bones" variety, but the ego factor of powerlessness, which makes the dreamer feel subject to danger and attack, may be of greater importance than the instinctual elements that are suggested by the dream's content.

Nightmares and the Concept of Trauma

A nightmare can be traumatic in two senses. First, as will be discussed shortly, it is by definition a traumatic response to external or internal events or stimuli. Second, the frightening dream can produce a further traumatic effect through the persistence during the waking hours of its powerfully disturbing affects.

A recent book devoted to the subject of psychic trauma has demonstrated that it is easier to write about the clinical effects of traumatic events than to define trauma [13]. Freud used the term originally in relation to a hypothetical stimulus barrier that, under ordinary circumstances, protected the organism from psychic injury. Stimuli of too great intensity arising from outside or inside the organism could potentially overwhelm this barrier, leading to a state of helplessness and an accumulation of excitation with which the organism was incapable of dealing. In recent psychoanalytic literature, Freud's stimulus barrier has come to be regarded as a kind of precursor of ego defense functions; the concept of trauma has been approached in terms of the ego's capacity to deal with a variety of potentially noxious or injurious conditions [14].

The principal difficulty in the use of the term *trauma* has been the uncertainty as to whether to emphasize the events or threats that give rise to a disturbing state or to stress this traumatic state itself, the *response* of the individual. Nightmares can be helpful in clarifying the problem of trauma, since they dramatize the lack of correspondence between the objectively disturbing or dangerous quality of outside events and the intense response of the nightmare victim, which may be out of all proportion to these threats. The nightmare is a *traumatic response* inasmuch as the ego is overwhelmed with anxiety, and the dreamer experiences an acute feeling of helplessness, criteria cited in virtually all definitions of trauma. The nightmare gives evidence that the organism has been "traumatized." However, if the traumatic response is limited to the sleep situation in the form of a nightmare, does not invade waking consciousness, and is not accompanied by other symptoms, signs of ego regression, or developmental difficulties, it is reasonable to say either that this is a "successful" handling of the traumatic situation or that the traumatic experience has been well circumscribed. In my discussion, the term trauma will refer to this *response* of the individual.

The question then arises: a traumatic response to what? The

case examples make clear that this question can be approached only in terms of the interplay between external events and the internal meaning these have for the dreamer. Clearly, there is no direct relationship between the magnitude of an outside threat or potential danger and the intensity of a nightmare or other traumatic response. In the case of the traumatic war neuroses, in which repetitive nightmares are the most characteristic symptom, the external threat to the life of the soldier has often been constant and severe.* Similarly, children and adults have frequent night terrors and nightmares following or during a period of surgery. By contrast, often the event that precipitates a nightmare is manifestly anything but threatening and may even appear to be a source of gratification, as in the case of the young father described in Chapter 2 (page 53) who had a severe nightmare the night after he had proudly shown his eight-month-old son to his in-laws. Alternatively, as in the case of eight-year-old Laura's nightmare (see Chapter 2) soon after a trip to the planetarium, the traumatizing event may give no indication at the time of being disturbing; the reason it precipitated a nightmare will be unclear unless the specific meaning of the incident or series of events leading up to the dream is understood. In Laura's nightmare of the yellow monster, for example, it was important to know the relationship between the scientific demonstration at the planetarium (that the sun might collide with and consume the earth) and Laura's anxiety about being too close to her mother or being swallowed up in this troublesomely intimate relationship.

* G. W. Crile has given a vivid description of the battle nightmares of men in the trenches in World War I: "The dream is always the same, always of the enemy. It is never a pleasant pastoral dream, or a dream of home, but a dream of the charge, of the bursting shell, of the bayonet thrust! Again and again in camp and in hospital wards, in spite of the great desire to sleep, a desire so great that the dressing of a compound fracture would not be felt, men sprang up with a battle cry, and reached for their rifles, the dream outcry startling their comrades, whose thresholds were excessively low to the stimuli of attack.

"In the hospital wards, battle nightmares were common, and severely wounded men would often spring out of their beds. An unexpected analogy to this battle nightmare was found in anesthetic dreams. Precisely the same battle nightmare, that occurred in sleep, occurred when soldiers were going under or coming out of anesthesia, when they would often struggle valiantly,—for the anesthetic dream like the sleep dream related not to a home scene, not to some dominating activation of peaceful days, but always to the enemy, and usually to a surprise attack" [15].

The power of an event or series of events to bring about a traumatic response depends upon their confirmation of the fears that are currently active for the child or adult or the capacity of such events to revive the memories of incidents that were previously disturbing, often in association with the anxieties of earlier developmental phases. A child between one and two, for example, who fears being abandoned as a consequence of his aggression is likely to have nightmares following even brief separations from the parents because these departures confirm the possibility he fears most. Sara's frightening hallucination of a biting snake was precipitated by the conflicts surrounding her exaggeratedly erotic oedipal situation. However, the anxiety related to her destructive wishes toward her mother in the oedipal rivalry reevoked in the sleep situation the fears associated with multiple *actual* separations from the mother from the time she was one-and-a-half; these corresponded to what she most dreaded and possibly also revived a memory of having been frightened by a rat in her bed at age one. It was the coalescence of the current fears with anxieties from earlier developmental phases that gave the nightmare its overwhelming traumatic quality. Many similar examples have been provided. Freud may have had something similar in mind when he wrote, "Affective states have become incorporated in the mind as precipitates of primaeval traumatic experiences, and when a similar situation occurs they are revived like mnemic symbols" [16].

Although the overwhelming character of anxiety in nightmares and the sense of powerlessness and helplessness that characterize these dreams lead us to define them as traumatic, under ordinary circumstances this is a very limited sort of trauma. As Sandler has recently pointed out, early childhood is filled with traumatic situations, with many "silent traumas" [17]. The only "noise" these give off may be an occasional nightmare. To fall repeatedly while learning to walk, to give up the stool, to observe that living things can be destroyed—these are but a few of the many experiences whose threat to the child and whose traumatic impact may become evident only in a nightmare that can pass virtually unnoticed. Usually the dreamer awakens and, if he cannot restore reality by himself, calls the parents, who provide comfort and reassurance and turn on the light. Perhaps this is as it should be, for nightmares are a small price to pay for the achievement of important developmental strides. In the case of older children and adults, simply waking up is usually sufficient to restore reality and terminate in a short time the traumatic effects of a nightmare, although the tendency of nightmarish affect to persist for many hours after waking is well known.

However, there are several situations in which the traumatic effects of the nightmare are more extensive. The simplest of these is the case of the childhood nightmare or night terror, the frightening power of which pervades the waking hours, requiring further parental or even professional intervention. The child's immature ego is unable to offset or defend itself adequately against the powerful affects carried over from the dream or, as in the cases of several three- and four-year-old children described earlier, to distinguish persisting dream images from perceptions emanating from the outside world. When severe, such states can progress to a childhood hallucinatory psychosis. In these instances, the history often reveals that there have been repeated severe threats to the child's body or to his or her very existence preceding the nightmare. In older children or adults a nightmare may become more severely traumatic when it persists into the waking hours as, for example, in states of febrile delirium or when, as in the case of alcoholics, it erupts into delirium tremens. Even in normal adults, the emotions and disturbing scenes of a nightmare may carry over into the waking hours, sometimes affecting the individual's mood throughout the day. Acute schizophrenics may find their nightmares—even ordinary dreams—severely traumatic when they have lost the capacity to distinguish where dreams leave off and waking reality begins. Finally, by the very intensity of its terrifying content a nightmare may become traumatic, even for an adult, if the individual has difficulty integrating its disturbing content. This is illustrated by the case Levitan has described of a forty-five-year-old woman who reexperienced as a blinding flash of light in a nightmare the devastating impact of the news she had received earlier that day of the sudden death of her husband [18]. In this instance the nightmare was experienced as a kind of second traumatic event.

Repetitive nightmares are one of the principal indications of traumatization and one of the most prominent symptoms of traumatic neuroses. The nightmare represents, with varying amounts of symbolic distortion and condensation with earlier traumata, a repetition or reliving of the disturbing experience that precipitated the disorder. The war or battle neurosis is the best-known example of a traumatic neurosis; sufferers from these disorders very frequently experience repeated severe nightmares that may persist for many years after the individual is removed from the stressful situation [19]. Although war neuroses are the best described of such disorders, frequent nightmares can also occur following accidents, injuries, hospitalization or surgery, unusual cruelty, brutalization of children by parents, or loss of important persons upon whom the individual is dependent. The common feature in all of these situations is an external event that is perceived as threatening to the life or person of the individual and that cannot be integrated with the psychological resources available to him. Such a situation, as we have seen repeatedly in this book, is particularly common in early childhood when the ego is immature, when the threatening significance of environmental threats tends to be exaggerated, when reality-testing is fragile, and when dependency upon others is extreme.

The observation of the existence of these disorders caused Freud and his associates to revise their theory of the sexual etiology of neurotic disturbances [20, 21]. They did not abandon the role of sexuality, but recognized that symptoms could arise as a result of conflict within the ego itself on the basis of narcissism, that is, the investment of libido in the subject's own ego. In the traumatic disorders the ego experiences a threat to itself, a fear of annihilation. Such symptoms of the traumatic neurosis as anxiety dreams reflect the ego's struggle to guard itself, to "protect its investment," to survive. Thus, these disorders require a reconsideration of the role of self preservation in human motivation and the reintroduction of concepts closely allied to Freud's earlier concept of "ego instincts."

The repeated nightmares and other symptoms that occur in the traumatic disorders are not the result simply of a current reality experience. Rather, the current traumatic events become regressively linked with earlier traumatic situations, dating back to early childhood, the common feature of which is the ego's experience of helplessness in the face of overwhelming danger. For example, Lidz has shown that, even in the nightmares associated with combat neuroses, the men often had long histories of unstable relationships in which early terror and insecurity were common [19].

One view of repetitive nightmares, as well as of other phenomena that the individual seems compelled to repeat in a seemingly irrational fashion, is that they represent an effort to transform a traumatic experience, in which the individual was passive and painfully helpless, into one of active mastery. For example, Freud suggested that, in the traumatic neuroses, the frightening dreams are "endeavoring to master the stimulus retrospectively, by developing the anxiety whose omission was the cause of the traumatic neurosis" [22]. In fact, Simmel developed for these disorders a treatment in which he encouraged the nightmare victim to convert his terror of death into fierce outbursts of rage against his imaginary dream adversaries, who presumably represented the attacking enemy, or against the superiors who had put the soldier in such a helpless position, demonstrating once again the close association between nightmares and violent aggression [23].

Since Freud made his famous statement about mastering a stimulus retrospectively, debate has persisted as to whether such repeated nightmares actually represent an effort at mastery and adaptation or are merely the result of nightly regression in which, to use a later expression of Freud, the "upward pressure of traumatic fixation" is irresistible. In my own view, there is no contradiction as long as one does not limit mastery and adaptation to conscious or deliberate processes. The mind does turn back to the past in sleep; memories that can be kept out of awareness during the waking hours, when the individual is in contact with other people and has a full range of defenses available to him, inevitably force themselves upon the ego during sleep and dreaming. Recent and past memories of events that have had a traumatic effect are reevoked in sleep in what may be regarded as an obligatory regression. At the same time, however, through dream-formation and elaboration, the individual may struggle to limit and confine to the sleep situation the anxiety associated with memories of the traumatic situation; the experience does not therefore necessarily pervade the individual's waking consciousness and overwhelm the ego and its functions as it originally did.

Interestingly, Simmel felt that the symptoms of war neuroses served to protect soldiers against a more serious regression, that is, from psychosis. "The war neuroses," Simmel wrote, "are essentially interposed guarantees, the object of which is to protect the soldier against psychosis. Anyone who has examined a great number of patients for eighteen months with perception that has been analytically sharpened must recognize that the proportionately small number of war psychoses is only to be explained by the proportionately large number of war neuroses" [24]. Inasmuch as some psychoses begin at night in association with the regressive experiences of sleep and dreaming, it would be of particular interest to study further how the ego's defensive and adaptive mechanisms operate in sleep and dreaming and how, in a nightmare, they circumscribe a disorder that otherwise contains the ingredients or potentiality for becoming a psychosis. It should be stressed once more that these are not deliberate or conscious processes. Rather, we are concerned with fundamental early ego defenses and adaptations—and perhaps also with physiological homeostatic mechanisms—that function to maintain the equilibrium and integrity of the organism as a whole during sleep and waking.

Nightmares and Instinctual Drives

In psychoanalytic theory, sexuality and aggression are regarded as instinctual drives that are believed to underlie most conflicts. However, extensive research, including numerous studies of animal behavior, has failed to find evidence in either animals or man to support a view that either libido or aggression necessarily builds up or accumulates simply as a result of deprivation or the absence of opportunities for drive discharge or gratification [25].

On the contrary, the available evidence, reviewed recently by Holt, indicates that both sexual and aggressive drives arising from within the organism function in a continuous ongoing relationship with external forces that stimulate, arouse, provoke, frustrate, or otherwise act to call forth the expression of one drive or another [26].

Similarly, in the case of nightmares, which have traditionally been conceived of as a kind of massive discharge phenomenon for accumulated instinctual tensions [27, 28], there is little evidence to support the view that these terrifying dreams occur in association with a buildup of instinctual forces. Indeed, the work of Fisher et al. and of Broughton has demonstrated that the most severe nightmares can arouse the dreamer spontaneously from the state of non-REM sleep [29, 30], in which the physiological activity of the organism is generally less intense than during the REM periods with which dreaming is more regularly associated. Nevertheless, in our case examples we have seen repeatedly that nightmares do occur in situations in which the dreamer has been undergoing severe conflict over sexual and aggressive impulses or drives and that these dreams are filled with aggressive content (see Chapter 4).

There is really no contradiction in these observations if one is willing to abandon a physical energy-discharge model in conceiving of these dreams and to consider the possibility that the motives, desires, or wishes that have given rise to the conflicts reflected in nightmares are not active during sleep in the same way as they are in the daytime. Let us assume that the individual during his waking hours, including both the recent and distant past, has accumulated or "internalized" countless mental representations, stored in his mind as memories, of the possible consequences of particular wishes or intended actions. Let us assume also—as recent research in the sleep-dream field strongly suggests —that the mind is active during a large proportion of the sleeping hours, or at least that ideas occur in the mind, even though we cannot observe how this comes about or know the content of these thoughts. The danger for the child or adult from his impulses or wishes could then be represented in nightmares by thoughts without necessarily assuming the accumulation or discharge of drive energies during sleep.

Let us say, for example, that a four-year-old boy has had an intense interest before going to sleep in visiting his parents' room and climbing into bed with his mother. He has made such a nuisance of himself that his father has yelled at him angrily and even threatened punishment. Reluctantly, the boy dozes off to sleep, only to be awakened two hours later by a nightmare in which he is being chased by a horrid monster that threatens to eat him. How could the nightmare have come about? A possible answer is that it could have been precipitated by thoughts that arose in the sleep situation. Enraged by his father's authority, he has had thoughts of murdering him before going to sleep, and these may have continued to form in his mind once he is asleep. However, these thoughts are potentially very dangerous, not only because his father might retaliate if he tried to kill him, but also because he is likely to conceive of the deed as accomplished; his still fragile ability to distinguish the difference between thoughts and deeds may lead him to equate the wish or thought with the deed, and he does not want to lose his father. This conflict may then be carried over into sleep, with the murderous thoughts and their anticipated consequences finding representation in dreams or nightmares. Furthermore, the danger associated with the current situation becomes linked with the mental representations of earlier dangers, for example, the possibility of being left by the mother or of being eaten. The regression in thinking that occurs in dreams may also contribute to the form of the manifest dream thoughts, giving rise to images of devouring monsters and the like. Finally, as discussed previously, the terror is intensified by the dreamer's difficulty in applying a realistic judgment to the dream's content. Thus, the conflict over sexual and aggressive wishes may actively give rise to the dream and be represented in its symbolic content. This does not necessarily mean, however, that sexual and aggressive drives are directly active in the nightmare in the same sense that they may be when the child is engaged with objects during the waking hours.

The problem is complicated by the fact that, in dreams,

thoughts can give rise to a direct biological sexual response, as in a nocturnal emission. There is little evidence, however, that nightmares are related to eroticism in this direct sense. When it occurs in dreams, anxiety seems actually to inhibit eroticism [31]. In the case of aggression, there seems to be even less likelihood that physiologically active destructiveness gives rise to nightmares. All-night sleep recordings furnish no physiological evidence that accumulated signs of rage, for example, precede the onset of nightmares [29, 30, 32]. In the instances described in the literature in which nightmares were followed by actual murders, the killing occurred because the dreamer interpreted the nightmare images to mean that he was in mortal danger; in apparent self-defense, while only partially awake, he assaulted an anticipated assailant in the outside world whom he confused with his dream attacker [33].

In conclusion, conflicts over sexual and aggressive impulses probably lead to nightmares, not through the biological expression of these drives during sleep, but through the danger experienced in relation to the mental representations of the conflict as these confront the dreamer in more or less distorted form in the dream. This view is based on the assumption that the mental representations of the elements of conflict can give rise to anxiety apart from the biological activity of the drives that originally may have played a part in the conflict.

Nightmares, Conflict, and the Development of Psychic Structure

Nightmares occur in response to the characteristic danger situations that human beings confront in the course of development, beginning with the fear of strangers and the dread of abandonment in infancy and the fear of bodily injury in early childhood, and ending with the fears of failure, death, and loss of function in adulthood and old age. Frequently the anxiety that may accompany these dangers is not evident in the lives of healthy individuals during waking hours; it may emerge only during sleep in an anxiety dream at a time when the individual does not have available the psychological defenses he normally employs during the daytime. William James actually stated, evidently with confidence: "In civilized life, in particular, it has at last become possible for large numbers of people to pass from the cradle to the grave without ever having had a pang of genuine fear. Many of us need an attack of mental disease to teach us the meaning of the word" [34]. He might have added to "mental disease" the more frequent experience of a nightmare. Nightmares may become the prototypic expression of the anxieties that characterize each period of development.

From the neurophysiological standpoint, the apparatus essential for dreaming, or at least for the occurrence of the various sleep stages and the REM-non-REM sleep cycle that is associated with dreaming, exists at birth. However, if nightmares are to take place, the capacity to experience anxiety, for the ego to anticipate danger, must be present. The object of outside danger must be perceived, represented internally, and then feared, a mental operation requiring the formation of psychic structure. According to Benjamin, the development of this capacity coincides with the first clearly defined infantile anxiety, the fear of strangers, which develops in the second half of the first year. In Benjamin's view, this anxiety depends not only upon the infant's libidinal attachment to the mother: "To this must be added what is at the least a highly *contributory*, and possibly a *necessary condition* for these particular anxiety manifestations: the maturational organization of aggression as such into *object-directed* hostility and anger, with the resultant marked increase in fear of object loss" [35]. We have seen how this fear of the consequences of hostility directed at other persons continues to play an important role in the occurrence of nightmares at later stages of development, as well; it may be obvious in the dreams of adults, as well as those of children. The complexity and structure of nightmares advance greatly as development proceeds, but the fear of hostility toward other persons may usually be detected.

The increase in the complexity of nightmares seems to occur largely as a result of various identifications with parental objects and through the elaboration of symbolic structures. Internalization of the qualities of persons who threaten the child, "identification with the aggressor," is a prominent defense mechanism through which the individual seeks to avoid danger from another person's wrath or disapproval by merging with the object or by taking its threatening qualities into the self. However, this incorporation of aspects of other persons who are perceived as threatening or dangerous sets up in the ego potentially destructive elements that may emerge in nightmares as angry voices, noises, or threatening creatures that endanger the dreamer once again. A simple example is provided by a girl between three and four who had, after a great deal of screaming and resistance, reluctantly submitted to shots and other pediatric procedures and examinations. In her subsequent play she angrily identified with the doctor who gave shots, viciously sticking a toy needle into the chest and ears of a recalcitrant child, represented by a small doll. That night she awoke from a nightmare screaming, evidently suffering from hallucinations in which aspects of the menacing pediatric personnel had become associated with other threats. "Don't let them get my nose," she wailed.

After age four or five, through the extension of these and more positively acquired identifications, superego structures form; these regulate the child or adult's behavior from within. As discussed in detail in Chapter 2, the qualities of objects that were internalized in the course of development to form the superego and other stable psychic agencies or structures may become reseparated into discrete voices or visages in nightmares and confront the dreamer once more in the hostile form in which they appeared to the child in the earlier developmental period.

The distinction between punishment and anxiety dreams or nightmares may depend on the depth of regression involved, that is, upon the degree to which previously internalized aspects of objects become "separated out" and externalized in the dream in the destructive form they assumed for the child in an earlier period. In a simple punishment dream, for example, a critical voice or attitude of a teacher or parent figure may confront the dreamer, inspiring merely feelings of guilt and moderate anxiety. The deeper regression of a nightmare, however, may additionally include the emergence of more primitive superego precursors that are perceived in the dream, as they were by the child in an earlier time, as potentially annihilating or devouring. The processes of condensation, segregation, and displacement that occur in dream production result, of course, in the formation of *new* combinations of percepts and images from the present and from the recent and distant past; consequently, the manifest content of the dream tends to be unique or original, that is, not simply a reproduction of the qualities of the objects that have been internalized in the course of development.

An endlessly fascinating subject that remains unsettled is the degree to which anxiety promotes the development of psychic structure. In Kris' formulation, "comfort serves to build object relationships, discomfort stimulates the differentiation, i.e., structure formation in the psychic apparatus" [36]. We may well ask how much discomfort promotes differentiation as opposed, for example, to disintegration? When one studies the elaborate structure of some children's nightmares—for example, those of Laura (Chapter 2), Carl (Chapter 3), or Carol (Chapter 4)—one cannot help but be impressed by the dream's rich and creative unfolding and elaboration in response to the anxiety situation. Whereas some nightmares seem to have no content other than a menacing sight, sound, or voice, others resemble works of art, pieces of desperate creativity, remarkably rich in form and meaning that have occurred in response to the traumatic situation. This creative elaboration does not cease with the dream work, but proceeds during the telling of the dream in further imaginative embellishments, a process related to but extending beyond Freud's "secondary revision." Some writers (see Chapter 3) have put the creative elaboration associated with dreams and their subsequent embellishment into the service of their art, or at least have claimed to do so. More research is needed regarding the various relationships between anxiety, dream formation, creativity, mastery, and the development of psychic structure.

Nightmares, Hallucinations, and the Development of Reality-testing

There is a period in early childhood in which dreams are regarded as real and in which the events, transformations, gratifications, and threats of which they are composed are regarded by the child as if they were as much a part of his actual daily life as his daytime experiences. The capacity to establish and maintain clear distinctions between the life of dreams and life in the outside world is hard-won and requires several years to accomplish, not being completed even in normal children before ages eight to ten. Nightmares, because of their vividness and compelling affective intensity, are particularly difficult for the child to judge realistically; the various regressions of ego functioning that accompany them may also contribute to the child's problem in knowing that such dreams are not in fact real disaster or danger situations.

Four seems to be a critical age in the development of the capacity to reality-test dreams. Some four-year-olds treat their dreams, and their nightmares in particular, as they would any important part of their lives. We may recall how the four-year-old girl Rachel, described in Chapter 1, suffered from nightmares that were so troubling to her that only her mother's actual presence at night could comfort her. During the day, she continued to think about the dream's monsters and became increasingly anxious as night approached, for she knew that she was likely to encounter the monsters once more after falling asleep. Even after she awoke, the nightmare monsters seemed as real as any part of her life. Another four-year-old described elsewhere had begun to achieve a compromise in his judgment of his dream attackers, concluding that lobsters that bit his toes at night were not really in his room, but were images of lobsters transmitted from somewhere else by television [37].

The development of the capacity to reality-test the nightmare experience seems to depend on several factors. Among the most important of these is the attitude that the parents take toward the dream experiences as the child reports them. The very early role of the parents in helping the child to distinguish fantasy and reality in relation to nightmares and to master the anxiety contained in them is illustrated by the experience of a twenty-seven-month-old boy whose father took him to the zoo. Two weeks before this outing, the child had developed a viral infection with high fever lasting several days, after which the parents went away for four days. The boy endured the separation uneventfully, but for a week thereafter was unusually fearful. He was afraid to let his mother leave him during the day, had great difficulty sleeping at night, and refused to let his mother leave the room before he went to sleep at night. This was the situation when the trip to the zoo took place.

At the elephant house, the father reached out his hand toward one of the elephants, who obliged him by holding out his trunk to be petted. The child, who had been watching this somewhat apprehensively from a considerable distance, suddenly burst into tears, evidently fearful that something would happen to his father. He was inconsolable and had to be taken home. After this he began to awake each night from terrifying dreams in which he cried out, "Elephant scare you." His mother was forced to awaken him fully, assure him that he need not fear elephants, and show him that there were no elephants in his room. At first, the mother could not leave the child's room after he awoke from a nightmare until she had given him milk and rocked him to sleep. After several nights, he was sufficiently reassured if his parents called out to him from their room when he awoke from frightening dreams; they also provided him with a night light. The nightmares soon ceased altogether. Shortly thereafter, the child developed the habit of talking in his crib for several minutes before going to sleep, as if preparing himself for the night ahead. One night his mother listened outside his door and overheard him muttering, "Elephants scare me. Monkeys scare me." This was followed by a brief period of silence; then, in his mother's tone of voice and using her inflection, he declared, "Oh, come on. Elephants don't scare you." Then he was quiet and went to sleep.

This little boy was able to internalize his mother's reassuring voice and attitude and to make use of the clarification she provided in order to dispel the terror of his nightmares. The compassionate parental intervention enabled him to make these reassurances a part of his own ego functioning and thereby to master the anxiety he experienced in his dreams.

Not all parental intervention following nightmares is so compassionate, skillful, and constructive. A nursery school teacher who worked with disadvantaged children in a large city found that virtually all of her four- and five-year-old pupils reported obvious nightmare experiences as real; many of these children continued to be haunted by their nighttime attackers throughout the day, often requiring that she contend with these distortions during the class [38]. As she interviewed the parents of these children, she found that the child's conflicts corresponded with theirs; alternatively, the child's fear at night revived the parent's fears with such intensity that they themselves had difficulty offering comfort or reality-oriented corrections of the hallucinatory distortions reported by the child. The parent might even confirm the child's apprehensions by treating the nightmare content as a reality. Some parents were so uncomprehending or angered by the child's screaming that they chastised the child for making a disturbance. Other parents employed the hallucinated attackers described by their children to manipulate and control them, threatening that the monsters or ghosts would return in the night if they did not behave. This pathological handling of nightmare content by parents reminds us of the way in which members of primitive cultures treat the events and perceptions of dreams as real and manipulate the situation accordingly (see Chapter 1). However, in these cultures the implications for later development are not so severe because the distortion is a "shared delusion" in which the dreamer may participate in the other supports that the society provides. Furthermore, in these cultures the distorted handling of the dream experience does not reflect a disturbed relationship between the parent and the child. In our society, however, such handling of the dream experience has grave implications for the future ego development of a particular child. The parents have a vital role, not only in comforting the child at night and in allaying fear, but also in aiding the child's cognitive development with respect to dreaming and dream-reality distinctions. As discussed in Chapter 5, the failure to reality-test the nightmare experience, as well as the undermining by the parents of the child's early efforts to establish boundaries between dream and reality, may be of profound importance in predisposing the individual to the later development of psychosis.

The daily environmental realities with which the child must deal constitute another important element affecting the development of the capacity to reality-test or integrate the nightmare experience. If, for example, the child's actual experience is of a world filled with violence in which his parents attack each other or himself or in which he is subjected to frequent losses, abuses, and actual abandonments, the terrifying nightmare-hallucinations may be particularly difficult for the child to distinguish from the experience of his waking life. It may be true that the nightmare images are distorted as a result of the child's conflicts and by the dream process; he may never literally have encountered monsters such as those that populate his dreams; nevertheless, the ego state of helplessness in the dream and the terror experienced in the face of powerful external forces that threaten to destroy or overwhelm him may differ little qualitatively or even quantitatively from his waking experience of outside reality. Furthermore, since these daytime realities, including such violence or threats, constitute the day residues that the child attempts to integrate each night in his dreams, he is additionally burdened by their intensity and threatening qualities. Serious sleep disturbances are commonplace among children who live in a continuously threatening environment. They are awakened by frequent nightmares that overwhelm them, both as a result of the dream's intensity and because of their inability after waking to offset the disturbing quality of dream experiences through reality judgments and by obtaining external comfort. If one adds to all this the previous observation of how parents may foster deficiencies in reality-testing rather than its growth, then one can readily see how the combined effect of all these factors may seriously impede the development of these functions. Although a situation such as this is more common in lower-class families that live more continuously with violence and loss or in an atmosphere of jeopardy and danger affecting the whole family, these same circumstances arise in middle- or upper-class families, as well.

Nightmares: Symptom or Adaptation?

As Fisher et al. have recently pointed out, the nightmare may be regarded as a symptom, a compromise between instinctual wishes or forces and the demands of the ego or superego [29]. Looked at from this point of view, the nightmare becomes a pathological structure, disrupting sleep and terrorizing its helpless victim. Fisher et al. conclude that "if the function of the nightmare is to master traumatic anxiety it cannot be said that it is very efficient," and Fisher observed that several of their subjects had continuous repetitive nightmares for over twenty years. How, then, can the nightmare be regarded as adaptive or as aiding in the mastery of anxiety? Surely, the experience of such intensely disruptive anxiety must be considered a failure of ego functioning, a failure to master anxiety.

Success and failure with respect to ego functioning are not absolute concepts; if they have any value, they must be considered in relation to the task or challenges at hand and the maturity of the ego or in relation to other possible outcomes. Let us consider, for example, the five-year-old child Timmy described in Chapter 4 (page 136), who developed nightmares when his father went to an overseas war zone. Terrifying dreams in which his father was in grave danger interrupted his sleep about twice each week; if one judges his dreams from the standpoint of their function in preserving sleep—an early hypothesis of Freud that has been seriously questioned in recent years—the nightmares reflect failure. However, this boy was living in a situation of daily fear, which his mother was also experiencing, in which the possibility of the father's death and loss was a continuous threat. Although the boy suffered from nightmares, his functioning in school and in his relationships with others was unimpaired, and he had no unusual fears during the daytime. If the nightmares may be looked upon as limited, circumscribed expressions of intense anxiety occurring specifically under the regressive conditions of sleep, they could hardly be regarded as a "failure." Furthermore, by forcing the child to wake and cry out, they may enable a child to be reunited with his mother in order to allay the anxiety. This particular boy became able to manage the dream anxiety by turning on his own light, and after a time he did not need to call for his mother. In the case of a child whose nightmare becomes a severely disturbing experience or continues during the remainder of the day as a terrifying hallucination, or of an adult who becomes disorganized or psychotic following a nightmare, we are dealing with a different situation, one in which reality-testing and other ego functions continue to be overwhelmed even after waking from the dream. In these situations we find it more difficult to see the nightmare as serving an adaptive or integrative function. Surely, here we may say that the nightmare has "failed" to achieve any adaptive or integrative purpose. Nevertheless, even in these situations we need to ask, for example, what the situation of the dreamer was preceding the dream; how long he had had nightmares before becoming psychotic; what threats to life, losses, or separations he had undergone; what drugs he might have taken; and whether he had a fever. Here again the nightmare may have served as an "attempt" at psychological integration, not in a conscious or purposive way, but in the employment of fundamental mechanisms available to the organism during sleep for the handling of anxiety and conflict. The fact that hallucinosis or psychosis eventuates does not, therefore, necessarily mean that the nightmare did not function adaptively. The dream in this instance may reflect the individual's efforts to master anxiety and conflict and represent an intermediate handling of conflict that was unsuccessful and was therefore followed by a psychotic regression.

Freud repeatedly stated his view that the anxiety dream represented a failure of censorship, a threatened breakthrough of instinctual wishes in which the dream content has undergone little distortion. Although this view has been generally accepted by psychoanalysts, there is little real evidence to support it. There is actually great variation in the amount of disguise or distortion that occurs in anxiety dreams or nightmares; when distortion is absent, it seems more often to be the threatening force in the outside world that appears undisguised or that appears in combination with a projected impulse of the dreamer, rather than an instinctual wish. In other anxiety dreams there is marked distortion of content, with some nightmares containing bizarre transformations and elaborate disguises; in the case of small children, these dreams demonstrate some of the most precocious examples of symbolic representation. Because nightmares so frequently reflect conflict over primitive destructive impulses, the disguises that occur therein follow the mode of early ego defenses against aggression, especially projection, externalization, and displacement. As we have seen repeatedly in case examples, however, even in the case of violent aggression the subject's own wishes are rarely directly expressed as he falls victim in the nightmare to imaginary external creatures or forces. By definition, there is a failure to contain anxiety in nightmares, but direct expression of libidinal or aggressive wishes is uncommon.

The fact that an individual may have repetitive nightmares throughout his lifetime does not in itself mean that the nightmare fails to master anxiety, for we do not know what the alternative might be. In this situation, the nightmare could serve to compartmentalize a conflict related to highly disturbing unconscious memories, the disruptive potential of which might become evident only during sleep. For example, it is possible that, were it not for the nightmares, the individual might be even more burdened with anxiety during the daytime, perhaps even unable to function effectively. It should be pointed out, however, that stating the possibility that nightmares may serve an adaptive function does not constitute evidence that this is so. To obtain positive evidence that any kind of dream serves adaptation is very difficult, indeed, as will be discussed further.

From a psychological standpoint, it is perhaps more useful theoretically to look upon the nightmare as a kind of end product, reflecting a great variety of other forces, some of which foster adaptation and integration, while others tend to bring about disintegration or disorganization. For any child or adult, dangerous environmental threats, loss and separation, unstable object relations, ego immaturity or disturbances of function, inner hatred and aggression, unassimilable sexual stimulation, certain drugs or fever, and the store of traumatic memories from the past might all operate in the direction of disintegration. At the same time, the availability and stability of other human relationships, the ego defenses of the individual, including the capacity to limit and control the extent of regression, and internalized positive object representations may operate in the direction of integration. Nightmares, as we have seen, arise in the context of environmental threat, the revival of traumatic memories, or the thrust of developmental advance, but the *outcome* of the dream, whether or not it is followed by integration and mastery or disintegration and further regression, depends upon the complex interplay of *all* of the above forces as they interrelate uniquely in any given instance or individual situation. Such an approach does not greatly emphasize the adaptive or integrative potential of the dream itself, which may be a problem of neurophysiology as well as psychology; rather, it would see the dream or nightmare in relation to all of the forces that impinge upon the ego and act together to produce the dream and the changes that follow.

This complexity—the great number of determinants of nightmares—may account for the difficulty of anticipating on any given night whether a particular child or adult will have a nightmare or of explaining why some individuals seem to be especially prone to express conflict through nightmares. I have described situations such as loss, separation, certain spontaneous developmental changes, and hospitalization or surgery, which seem regularly to lead to nightmares in children; we have seen examples of characteristic danger situations, such as war, failure, professional advancement or disappointment, and loss of body function, which often precipitate nightmares in adults. However, to which kinds of external situations different individuals will respond is highly idiosyncratic and often difficult to predict. Furthermore, even if we suspect which external situations are likely to be especially threatening, it is difficult to ascertain the multitude of internal factors that must operate in relation to them in order to produce a nightmare. Furthermore, if a given combination seems to have led to a nightmare in one instance, we cannot be certain that the same coexistence of factors will do so in the next. Neither can we explain why similar conflicts may produce nightmares without neurotic symptoms in the daytime for one person, while another equally troubled individual may suffer from phobias or other fears without having nightmares.

"A dream, a nightmare, a madness"—Dostoevsky's phrase describes a hierarchy, possible levels of personality disorganization. In Chapter 5 I have noted how we may think of "ordinary dreaming," nightmares—we might insert here as another "level" repetitive, unusually severe, or disorganizing nightmares—and

acute psychoses as functioning on a continuum in the maintenance of personality integration. Perhaps the word "maintain" is
inappropriate, implying a more explicit or active functional role
for the nightmare than is actually the case. We are on surer
ground if we observe that these different levels of organization
exist and reserve judgment as to how they are maintained. Many
of the same mechanisms, such as distortion, symbolization, externalization, projection, and regression, operate in the dream,
nightmares, and psychoses. However, in nightmares ego defenses
against disorganizing anxiety begin to fail, projection is employed
intensively with respect to destructive aggression, and return to
reality after waking is more difficult. In the acute psychosis, externalization and projection continue during the daytime, object
relations are severely disturbed, and thinking may become chaotic or confused, while the establishment of reality contact and
judgments becomes impaired. The clinical sequence dream–nightmare–disorganizing nightmare–frank psychosis is often observed
and frequently occurs in reverse order during recovery.

Lesse studied 1,000 dreams of 130 adult patients with a variety
of clinical diagnoses [39]. He found that the degree of terror,
violence, and rage in nightmares was one of the best indicators of
the overall course of the patient's treatment and his general level
of anxiety. As anxiety in dreams mounted, other clinical symptoms appeared, and vice versa. In certain patients, greater
amounts of anxiety led to the disorganization of manifest dream
content and to the occurrence of hallucinations in the waking
state. Lesse regarded hallucinations and other psychotic symptoms as primitive structuring, "the last of a succession of secondary defense mechanisms to be called into play—the last line of
defense before the ego is completely overwhelmed and psychic
anarchy prevails" [40]. In Lesse's view, the primary function of
both dreams and hallucinations is as a "secondary defense mechanism against mounting anxiety," with the psychotic symptom
serving as a kind of last effort to maintain integration. My own
view has points in common with Lesse's, although I would see
the dream, the nightmare, and the psychosis more as basic psychic and physiological processes reflecting the state of the organ-

ism as a whole rather than as serving as such active instruments of adaptation.

Nightmares and the Problem of Survival

Our point of departure in this consideration of severe anxiety dreams or nightmares has been the quality, manifest in all such dreams, of danger or jeopardy, by reason of which the dreamer feels helpless and especially vulnerable in the face of powerful forces that threaten to destroy him. I have suggested that this quality of helplessness relates to the sense of powerlessness of the very young child, whose early perception of the precariousness of his existence—and the possibility that he, like the objects around him, might disappear or be destroyed—is incorporated into his earliest dreams and finds expression in nightmares. I have suggested also that this early ego state is regressively revived in the nightmares of older children and adults and accounts for the tendency of nightmares in individuals of various ages or periods of development to resemble one another, not only in the affective state of terror they possess, but in the threatening content of the dream images, as well. It is to this matter of danger and survival that I will devote the concluding paragraphs.

The neurophysiological findings of the past fifteen years in the fields of sleep and dreaming, especially the discovery that we probably dream for a considerable portion of the night, have shifted the attention of many workers in this field, including a number of psychoanalysts, away from the consideration of the meaning of individual dreams toward the study of the functions of dreaming itself or of the sleep phases with which it is associated. In addition to this discovery, several other findings have led to considerable theorizing regarding the importance of the REM periods, with which dreaming is particularly associated, in promoting central nervous system growth and development and of REM and non-REM periods in maintaining physiological and psychic integration. These include (1) the surprising activity of the central nervous system during REM periods in which limbic-hippocampal and other subcortical and cortical structures are undergoing a high degree of activation and excitability, (2) the discovery that infants spend a particularly high proportion of sleep in the REM state, and (3) the finding that REM deprivation can produce anxiety, irritability, illusions, hallucinations, and a variety of other symptoms or evidences of psychic disorganization.

These and related findings have inspired a number of useful theoretical papers concerned with the role of the various sleep phases and of dreaming in maintaining the integrity of the organism, not only during sleep, but throughout the twenty-four-hour sleep-waking cycle. Excellent papers by Breger, by Ephron and Carrington, by Hawkins, and by Meissner present the range of evidence and arguments that support these views [41–44].

The terms *integrity* and *integration* are used in several ways, and it is important to keep these various meanings clear before proceeding further. For example, integrity is used to designate intactness of ego function, especially the maintenance of psychic defenses. This is essentially a psychological or psychoanalytical usage. The term is also used in a physiological sense with a meaning close to that of homeostasis. Ephron and Carrington, for example, suggest that the REM period "serves a homeostatic function of periodically restoring 'cortical tonus,' thereby promoting cortical efficiency or a readiness for adaptive responses while sleep is permitted to continue" [45]. It may or may not be possible to correlate this theorizing on a physiological level with concepts derived from psychoanalytic ego psychology. When these same authors, for example, speak later of the "ego-reintegrative process in the dreams" that "mobilizes emotional responses and memories and integrates them into images of special meaning for the dreamer" [46], they are pursuing a discourse on an entirely different level. It is important to avoid the pitfalls of shifting too readily from the use of terms such as *adaptation* and *integrity* in their physiological sense to applying them in a psychoanalytic or metapsychological theoretical framework. For example, if the REM state promotes growth and development of cerebral structures in early childhood or maintains cortical activation during sleep when sensory input to CNS structures from outside sources is cut off or greatly reduced, it does not follow that dreams necessarily solve problems or maintain intact ego functioning. Either one of these possibilities or both or neither might be true, depending on additional evidence.

With these cautions in mind, we can turn to the possible functions of nightmares from these two points of view. From the physiological standpoint, the individual who is having a severe nightmare is reacting, like an animal in mortal danger, with bloodcurdling screaming, intense autonomic discharge, rapid heart rate, and rapid, irregular respiration, terminating in arousal [29, 30, 32]. The psychic content that accompanies both these and less severe nightmares is also related to intense and immediate dangers to the dreamer, often with the imminent threat of annihilation. As Broughton and Fisher et al. have pointed out, however, there is as yet no method available for determining whether the terrifying dream occurs in response to a spontaneous physiological arousal phenomenon or to a terrifying thought that has arisen during sleep. Although a primary physiological "arousal response"—one occurring without any particular relationship to preceding mental content—to which the subject then reacts by dream elaboration cannot be ruled out, the analysis of many examples of nightmares in this book has shown that they occur principally in relation to conflicts in the individual's life that he experiences as life-threatening or in which the memories of earlier conflicts involving the danger of annihilation were regressively revived in the sleep situation.

Although the most catastrophic nightmares or night terror attacks seem to occur during non-REM periods, especially the first one of the night, the more common, less severe nightmares usually seem to occur during REM periods. I have suggested earlier (see Chapter 6) that the lesser intensity of anxiety during REM periods may be related to the greater availability and flexibility of symbol formation, displacement, and other primary process mechanisms for transforming threatening dream content in accordance with the defensive requirements of the sleeping ego and for bringing such content into some degree of equilibrium with earlier memories and conflicts. Conversely, such modification or transformation of dream content seems to be less possible during non-REM periods, which tend to be limited to more literal, less symbolic forms of thinking; this is true, whether this content is a direct representation of an immediately threatening event in the individual's life, as in Levitan's case described on page 218, or is heavily influenced by earlier traumatic memories.

In both non-REM and REM nightmares, the dreamer experiences himself as being in situations of grave danger; waking and arousal occur from both states in order to avoid these perils. Thus, the nightmare is manifestly concerned with danger; in the case of most children and many adults following the experience, the reestablishment of contact with a protective person indicates that a critical function of awakening from the nightmare is to ensure survival and safety. I have tried to show that the deeper latent or unconscious content of nightmares is also involved with conflicts and fears concerning destructive aggression, sexuality that is linked with annihilation, devouring, and being devoured, and loss of the protecting or need-satisfying object, in all of which the survival of the individual himself is at stake. Although the immediate precipitating stress for a nightmare may relate to a problem at a more mature developmental level, the various forms of regression that accompany sleep result in the revival of these earlier infantile conflicts, accounting for the similarities of nightmares at various ages.

In the sleep situation the dreamer, cut off from reality and unable to distinguish between real and imaginary attackers, seems to revert to self-preservative mechanisms similar to those that would be brought to bear were the subject in an objective danger situation. Arousal, reestablishment of motility, action and even preparation for counterattack, flight, and turning to a mothering person for protection are among the self-preservative mechanisms that occur in association with nightmares.

In recent years interest has been growing in the possible functions of the various sleep phases in maintaining psychic vigilance during sleep, in alerting the organism to possible dangers in the environment, or in mobilizing orienting mechanisms or impulses that might enhance survival [42, 47, 48]. These mechanisms may be grounded in the phylogeny of mammalian species that must ensure some protection, even while asleep, from predators and other possible dangers in the environment. In nightmares, the dreamer reacts to dangers, the origin of which may be in large part internal or at least the result of the interplay of external and internal factors. However, he reacts entirely as if he were confronted with an external danger. Such a reaction may be influenced by phylogenetically transmitted mechanisms that originally had the function of alerting and protecting the organism from real external danger. In the nightmare such mechanisms may be exaggeratedly or even unnecessarily triggered by minimal environmental threats recalled in the sleep situation or by disturbing impulses arising internally; these may be mistaken for external threats, particularly when given visual, externalized representation through the processes that lead to the formation of dream images. In this way the nightmare may not only be made up of memories and other aspects of mental functioning that originated in early childhood, but may be linked with neurophysiological mechanisms subserving self-preservation and survival that are phylogenetically older than those that are the exclusive possession of the human species.

References

1. Dostoevsky, F. *The Idiot*. (Trans. by Constance Garnett.) New York: Bantam Books, 1963. Pp. 438–439.
2. Freud, S. Some Additional Notes on Dream-Interpretation as a Whole (1925). In *The Standard Edition of the Complete Psychological Works of Sigmund Freud*, tr. and ed. by J. Strachey with others. London: Hogarth and the Institute of Psycho-analysis, 1961. Vol. XIX, p. 135.
3. Benjamin, J. D. Some developmental observations relating to the theory of anxiety. *J. Amer. Psychoanal. Ass.* 9:652–668, 1961.
4. Brenner, C. An addendum to Freud's theory of anxiety. *Int. J. Psychoanal.* 34:18–24, 1953.
5. Schafer, R. Contributions of longitudinal studies to psychoanalytic theory. Panel report. *J. Amer. Psychoanal. Ass.* 13:605–618, 1965.
6. Spitz, R. Anxiety in infancy: A study of its manifestations in the first year of life. *Int. J. Psychoanal.* 31:138–143, 1950.
7. Fraiberg, S. *The Magic Years*. New York: Scribner, 1959.
8. Mack, J. E. Nightmares, conflict and ego development in childhood. *Int. J. Psychoanal.* 46:403–428, 1965.
9. Freud, A. *The Ego and the Mechanisms of Defense*. New York: International Universities Press, 1946.
10. Waelder, R. *Basic Theory of Psychoanalysis*. New York: International Universities Press, 1960.

11. Rangell, L.   A further attempt to resolve the "Problem of Anxiety." *J. Amer. Psychoanal. Ass.* 16:371–404, 1968.
12. Kanzer, M.   The communicative function of the dream. *Int. J. Psychoanal.* 36:260–266, 1955.
13. Furst, S. S.   *Psychic Trauma.* New York: Basic Books, 1967.
14. Greenacre, P.   The Influence of Infantile Trauma on Genetic Patterns. In Furst, S. S. (Ed.), *Psychic Trauma.* New York: Basic Books, 1967.
15. Crile, G. W.   *A Mechanistic View of War and Peace.* New York: Macmillan, 1915. P. 27.
16. Freud, S.   Inhibitions, Symptoms and Anxiety (1926 [1925]). *Standard Edition.* 1959. Vol. XX, p. 93.
17. Sandler, J.   Trauma Strain and Development. In Furst, S. S. (Ed.), *Psychic Trauma.* New York: Basic Books, 1967.
18. Levitan, H. L.   A traumatic dream. *Psychoanal. Quart.* 34:265–267, 1965.
19. Lidz, T.   Nightmares and the combat neuroses. *Psychiatry* 9:37–49, 1946.
20. Freud, S.   Introduction to Psychoanalysis and the War Neuroses (1919). *Standard Edition.* 1955. Vol. XVII, pp. 207–210.
21. Jones, E.   War Shock and Freud's Theory of the Neuroses. In Ferenczi, S., Abraham, K., Simmel, E., and Jones, E., *Psychoanalysis and the War Neuroses.* London: International Psychoanalytical Press, 1921. Pp. 44–59.
22. Freud, S.   Beyond the Pleasure Principle (1920). *Standard Edition.* 1955. Vol. XVIII, p. 32.
23. Simmel, E.   In Ferenczi, S., Abraham, K., Simmel, E., and Jones, E., *Psychoanalysis and the War Neuroses.* London: International Psychoanalytical Press, 1921. Pp. 30–43.
24. Ibid. P. 32.
25. Dahl, H.   Psychoanalytic theory of the instinctual drives in relation to recent developments. Panel report. *J. Amer. Psychoanal. Ass.* 16:613–637, 1968.
26. Holt, R. H.   On the Insufficiency of Drive as a Motivational Concept, in the Light of Evidence from Experimental Psychology. Paper presented at the meetings of the American Psychoanalytic Assn., Dec. 15, 1967.
27. Stern, M.   Pavor nocturnus. *Int. J. Psychoanal.* 32:302–309, 1951.
28. Hadfield, J. A.   *Dreams and Nightmares.* Baltimore, Md.: Penguin Books, 1954.
29. Fisher, C., Byrne, J., and Edwards, A.   REM and NREM Nightmares and their Inter-relationships. Lecture delivered to the Department of Psychiatry, The Mount Sinai Hospital, New York, April 10, 1968.
30. Broughton, R.   Sleep disorders: Disorders or Arousal? *Science* 159:1070–1078, 1968.
31. Karacan, I., Goodenough, D. R., Shapiro, A., and Starker, S.   Erection cycle during sleep in relation to dream anxiety. *Arch. Gen. Psychiat.* (Chicago) 15:183–189, 1966.

32. Gastaut, H., and Broughton, R. A Clinical and Polygraphic Study of Episodic Phenomena During Sleep. In Wortis, J. (Ed.), *Recent Advances in Biological Psychiatry*. New York: Plenum Press, 1965. Vol. VII, pp. 197–221.

33. Macnish, R. *The Philosophy of Sleep*. New York: Appleton, 1834.

34. James, W. *The Principles of Psychology*. New York: Holt, 1890. Vol. II, pp. 415–416.

35. Benjamin, J. O. Some developmental observations relating to the theory of anxiety. *J. Amer. Psychoanal. Assn.* 9:662, 1961.

36. Kris, E. Data in psychoanalytic perspective on the mother-child relationship. *Psychoanal. Stud. Child.* 17:175–215, 1962.

37. Mack, J. E. Nightmares, conflict and ego development in childhood. *Int. J. Psychoanal.* 46:425, 1965.

38. Berman, D. Personal communication, March 1969.

39. Lesse, S. Experimental studies on the relationship between anxiety, dreams and dream-like states. *Amer. J. Psychother.* 13:440–455, 1959.

40. Ibid. P. 451.

41. Breger, L. Function of dreams. *J. Abnor. Soc. Psychol.* 72:1–28, 1967.

42. Ephron, H. S., and Carrington, P. Ego Functioning in Rapid Eye Movement Sleep: Implications for Dream Theory. In Masserman, J. (Ed.), *Science and Psychoanalysis*. New York: Grune & Stratton, 1967. Vol. XI, pp. 75–102.

43. Hawkins, D. R. A review of psychoanalytic dream theory in the light of recent psychophysiological studies of sleep and dreaming. *Brit. J. Med. Psychol.* 39:85–104, 1966.

44. Meissner, W. Dreaming as process. *Int. J. Psychoanal.* 49:63–79, 1968.

45. Ephron, H. S., and Carrington, P. Ego Functioning in Rapid Eye Movement Sleep: Implications for Dream Theory. In Masserman, J. (Ed.), *Science and Psychoanalysis*. New York: Grune & Stratton, 1967. Vol. XI, p. 79.

46. Ibid. P. 89.

47. Ullman, M. Dreaming, altered states of consciousness and the problem of vigilance. *J. Nerv. Ment. Dis.* 133:529–535, 1961.

48. Snyder, F. Toward an evolutionary theory of dreaming. *Amer. J. Psychiat.* 123:121–142, 1966.

Index

Abandonment fear, nightmare and, 59–60, 217
Adaptation
  aggression and, 111
  effort and repeated nightmare, 220–221
  as function of nightmare, 138, 231–237
  sleep and, 184–185
Aggression
  anxiety and, 147–148
  behavioral view of, 112, 114
  clinical occurrence of nightmare and, 117–118
  conflict and, 111, 139–148, 221–224, 233–234
  defined, 111–112
  destructive, 111, 117, 118, 147–148; broader concept vs., 111–112
  developmental stage and, 113–115, 118, 134–139
  displacement of impulses, 124–125
  dreams and, 183, 188
  as drive, 116–117
  ego defenses and, 50, 124, 234
  environment and, 115–117
  as fundamental instinct, 113–115
  infantile
    expression in nightmare, 64

protection and, 50
intensity of latent, reality sense and, 178
internalized, operation in nightmare, 59
libidinization of, 118, 151
mastery, 188
  clinical study in two-year-old, 118–127
  nightmare and, 151–153, 188
  superego and, 139, 152–153
narcissism and, 113–114
in nightmare vs. psychosis, 112–113, 164, 167–168
oedipal period, nightmare associated with, 134–139
oral, in childhood nightmare, 26–27
outside, nightmare and, 148–149
parental, effects of, 117–118, 148–149, 175
phallic, in nightmare, 130–134
prohibition, effects of, 139
projection of impulses, 48–49, 124–125
as protection from psychosis, 151–152
psychoanalytic views of, 112, 113–115
psychosis as response to threat of, 172–173

245